HEARING ALLAH'S CALL

Hearing Allah's Call

Preaching and Performance
in Indonesian Islam

Julian Millie

Cornell University Press
Ithaca and London

First published 2017 by Cornell University Press

Printed in the United States of America

Library of Congress Cataloging-in-Publication Data

Names: Millie, Julian, 1967– author.
Title: Hearing Allah's call : preaching and performance in Indonesian Islam / Julian Millie.
Description: Ithaca : Cornell University Press, 2017. | Includes bibliographical references and index.
Identifiers: LCCN 2017003656 (print) | LCCN 2017006530 (ebook) | ISBN 9781501713118 (cloth : alk. paper) | ISBN 9781501713125 (pbk. : alk. paper) | ISBN 9781501712241 (epub/mobi) | ISBN 9781501709609 (pdf)
Subjects: LCSH: Islamic preaching—Indonesia—Bandung. | Islam and culture—Indonesia—Bandung. | Bandung (Indonesia)—Religious life and customs. | Ethnology—Indonesia—Bandung.
Classification: LCC BP184.25 .M55 2017 (print) | LCC BP184.25 (ebook) | DDC 297.3/709598—dc23
LC record available at https://lccn.loc.gov/2017003656

Cornell University Press strives to use environmentally responsible suppliers and materials to the fullest extent possible in the publishing of its books. Such materials include vegetable-based, low-VOC inks and acid-free papers that are recycled, totally chlorine-free, or partly composed of nonwood fibers. For further information, visit our website at www.cornellpress.cornell.edu.

This book is dedicated to all skillful speakers who have made
a difference in people's lives by materializing listeners' religion and
culture in meaningful and inspiring forms, but whose names and work
are scarcely remembered because they are not found in the written
record that determines knowledge of the past and present.

CONTENTS

Acknowledgments

I am above all indebted to a number of Bandung-based preachers who allowed me to accompany them as they fulfilled their invitations, and who were generous in sharing their experiences and perceptions about Islamic oratory with me. Jujun Junaedi and Miftah Faridl were outstanding among these people, and to both of them I am very grateful.

Dede Syarif was a wonderful companion throughout this research, and I acknowledge the value to this book of his critical insights on society and Islam in West Java. Asep Saepul Muhtadi was a stimulating and thought-provoking interlocutor throughout the latter stages of the research on which this book is based.

Several individuals gave advice and inspiration in the writing process. Two senior scholars must be mentioned in this regard. David Chandler read many drafts and never stopped encouraging me in the writing process. His great humor and big-heartedness sustained me through the preparation of the manuscript. Bill Watson generously read a number of drafts, helping me to present arguments with greater clarity and detail. The book is a better one thanks to his involvement. Apart from these two, I am indebted also to Matt Tomlinson, who gave time to provide critical feedback and pointed out to me certain academic directions, which I subsequently traversed and received great benefit from. None of these scholars are responsible for the book's faults; those are all my doing.

Apart from the two mentioned above, many other Bandung-based preachers generously assisted me by allowing me to attend their oratories and by sharing ideas with me, including Aceng Zakaria, Zainul Abidin, Daud Gunawan (alm), Agus Kusnadi, Atian 'Ali Da'i, Rahman Maas, Abdul Hamid, Irfan Royani, Tata Sukayat, and Abdul Mujib.

I benefited from conversations on preaching with other Bandung-based intellectuals including Dadang Kahmad, Acep Arifuddin, Atip Latipulhayat, Amin Aminuddin Aziz, Usep Romli, Dedi Mulyadi, Iwa Lukmana, Hawe Setiawan, Karman, Asep Salahuddin, Hedi Muhammad, and Hendar Riyadi. I received help in transcription from Ahmad Bukhori Muslim, Agus Ahmad Safei, Atep Kurnia, Ibnu Hijar Apandi, and other friends at the Centre for Sudanese Studies.

I am grateful to the support and collegiality of colleagues in the Monash School of Social Sciences, especially Penny Graham, Andrea Whittaker, Tommy Fung, Antje Missbach, Birgit Brauchler, Lejla Voloder, Max Richter, Narelle Warren, and Sara Niner, and to other Monash colleagues including Aline Scott-Maxwell, Hueimin Chen, Harry Aveling, and Howard Manns Jr. During the preparation of the book, I was privileged to work on related publication projects led by Emma Baulch, Greg Fealy, Sally White, Matt Tomlinson, Wendy Smith, Lenore Manderson, Alan Rumsey, Rupert Stasch, Lyn Parker, and Patrick Alcedo. Many thanks to you all!

I am indebted to the Zentrum Modern Orient (Berlin) for its hospitality during a writing fellowship in 2012, and especially to Ulrike Freitag, Kai Kresse, Silke Nagel, and Thomas Ripper. Indonesia's National Science Academy (LIPI) kindly granted a research permit for the original research. The welcome given to me by the Dakwah and Communications Faculty of UIN Sunan Gunung Djati, Bandung, and its deans, Syukriadi Sambas and Asep Muhyiddin, is much appreciated. I am grateful to Afif Muhammad for help with administrative matters in Bandung.

I acknowledge financial assistance for this project from the Australian Research Council, most notably through the Australian Post-Graduate Award

DP0773170, entitled Preaching Islam: Politics, Performers and Publics in Indonesia.

For their role in the discussion groups on which chapter 7 is based, I am thankful for the kind assistance of Abid Tarmidzi, Agus Safei, and women residents of Karang Tineung Indah (Cipadas/Sukajadi) and Mekarjati (Pasirbiru/Cibiru). Pak Kiki at the Bandung Water Board was helpful in sharing his perceptions of the Board's preaching program with me.

I am grateful to Wiley-Blackwell for publishing earlier versions of two chapters: a portion of chapter 4 was published as "The Languages of Preaching: Code Selection in Sundanese Islamic Oratory, West Java," *Australian Journal of Anthropology* 23, no. 3 (2012): 379–97, and a portion of chapter 6 as "Islamic Preaching and Women's Spectatorship in West Java," *Australian Journal of Anthropology* 22, no. 2 (2011): 151–69. SAGE Publications published an earlier version of chapter 8 as "The Situated Listener as Problem: 'Modern' and 'Traditional' Subjects in Muslim Indonesia," *International Journal of Cultural Studies* 16, no. 3 (2013): 271–88. I extend my thanks also to Peter Potter, Jim Lance, and the staff at Cornell, whose enthusiasm and professionalism have been outstanding.

I have been lucky to have wonderful students at Monash who have been generous sources of guidance on Islamic life in Indonesia and West Java, including Neneng Khozanatu Lahpan, Tisna Prabasmoro, Usep Abdul Matin, Edi Riyanto, and Ervan Nurtawab.

My most significant debt I acknowledge last: I am grateful to Ratih, Joseph, and Dewi for being such fun, loving, and engaging companions throughout the long trials leading to the publication of this book.

Note on Transcription

This book cites and reproduces writings and speech in Indonesian, Sundanese, Arabic, and English. In accordance with accepted Sundanese and Indonesian usage, I have marked the mid-front, unrounded vowel as *é* in Sundanese examples but have not differentiated the equivalent vowel in Indonesian examples.

Arabic is a scientific and sacred language for the communities in which the research on which this book is based was carried out. Where an Arabic term is in common usage in Indonesian and Sundanese, I have used Indonesian or Sundanese spelling (e.g., *dakwah* in place of *da'wah*). Aside from those examples, most of the Arabic found in the following pages appears in citations of Qur'an and hadith, and in the names of Islamic concepts known to Muslims throughout the world. The risk of misunderstanding or inaccuracy caused by insufficiently detailed transliteration of these examples is low, and for that reason, I have consistently applied a simple system for the transliteration of Arabic. Hamza and 'ayn are written, although hamza is written in initial position only when supported by a final vowel of the preceding word (*al-wasl*). No distinctions are made between similar consonants (*sad/sin, dad/dal, ta/ta*). Diacritics are not employed, and long vowels are not marked.

Hearing Allah's Call

Introduction

One afternoon in September 2009 I left Bandung, the capital city of Indonesia's West Java province, for a ninety-minute car journey to a village in the regional center of Sumedang, east of the city. There were three other men in the car, all of them lecturers in the Faculty of Dakwah [Predication] and Communication at Bandung's State Islamic University. One of them, Abdurrahman, was also a *muballigh*, a religious specialist whose particular skill was conveying Islam through the medium of speech. In other words, Abdurrahman was a preacher of Islam. He was to give a sermon in Sumedang, where a family was celebrating the circumcision of one of its sons. This was an everyday event, not much different from thousands of similar events that would have been held on that day among West Java's Muslim population.

The three men had been friends for a long time, so the conversation in the car was warm, humorous, and unrestricted by politeness. Abdurrahman, especially, was a great conversationalist. Like many *muballigh*, he moves easily between a number of languages, including Sundanese (the language of the ethnic group of the same name for which West Java is ancestral home),

Indonesian, Arabic, and a little English. Even in ordinary conversation, he cleverly replicates a range of language registers and manipulates words and their meanings for humorous effect. On the oratorical stage, he often calls on his skills as a baritone singer. During our journey Abdurrahman was the target of many affectionate jibes from Acep Hidayat, his colleague on the Faculty of Dakwah and Communication. It was Acep, a professor in the faculty, who had been invited to give the sermon. In the eyes of many Muslims in West Java, a professor at the State Islamic University is ideally qualified to speak at a circumcision. Acep, however, rejects these invitations whenever he can. Although he is a serious and productive writer, he lacks Abdurrahman's skills in language and performance and believes in any case that oratory offers little benefit to West Java's Muslims. For these reasons, he promised the family that he would attend the celebration with a "proper" *muballigh* and asked his friend Abdurrahman whether his busy preaching schedule would allow him to give the sermon in Sumedang.

As we drove, Acep did not hide his feelings about oratory. He said that Islam provided motivations and ethical frameworks for meaningful social and political change in West Java and Indonesia, but he added that this potential remained latent while the province's Muslims were enjoying themselves at pleasurable orations. "If these audiences aren't laughing, they're crying," he said, referring to a famous preacher from Jakarta whose trademark preaching strategy was to lead audiences in collective weeping. Acep's reduction of listeners to these caricatures was something I encountered frequently in West Java. Preaching styles that are popular with Bandung audiences provide perceptible forms that critics of oratory transform into emblematic images of oratory's affective, emotive, and nonserious aspects. He was not totally disapproving of preaching, but these caricatures strongly influenced his evaluations of the medium. Oratory's great weakness, Acep suggested, was that it could not lead people to think. This view is sui generis with Acep's deep concern for the quality of Indonesia's education system. In several academic writings (see chapter 5) he has emphasized the necessity for the Indonesian education system to produce graduates capable of independent thought and autonomous decision making. The problem with the oratorical styles popular among West Javanese Muslims, as he sees it, is that they will not help Muslims to become the capable, well-informed citizens required in Indonesia's fledgling democracy. Abdurrahman was not offended by his old friend's comments, which he had heard before. In fact, he agreed with many of Acep's remarks and made no effort to defend the activity on which his livelihood depended.

When we arrived at the village, the host welcomed us warmly, offering food and drink. At about 10:00 p.m. Abdurrahman mounted a portable stage and spoke through a microphone for over an hour to an audience of around a hundred women and forty men. The stage had not been erected solely for his sermon; it had been used the night before for a performance of *dangdut*—the infectiously rhythmic music that is common fare at circumcisions and weddings across Indonesia. Abdurrahman's sermon was the peak and conclusion of the circumcision celebration. I judged it to have been a success. The audience was clearly stimulated, amused, and disarmed by his eloquence, singing, and humor. At the same time, however, he mediated Islamic norms with sincere gravity in ways with which the audience members identified closely. In his sermon, Islam's teachings were not distant and unattainable; they were pleasantly and movingly mediated as shared norms that were relevant and efficacious in an everyday sense. When the sermon ended, the audience left quickly, carrying bags of food that their hosts had given them. The father of the boy just circumcised pressed an envelope containing money into Abdurrahman's hand while expressing gratitude for the sermon. We climbed back into the car and returned to Bandung.

This book is about the preaching that West Java's Muslims enjoy as they undertake the everyday routines of Islamic life in the province. It explores preaching styles that succeed because they enable preachers like Abdurrahman to captivate Muslims with Islamic mediations shaped for the diverse situations encountered in those routines. Based on the frequency of preaching events and their popular uptake, the book reveals preaching to be a successful public Islamic project; not a project pushed by a single actor, such as a government or activist organization, but one sustained by the informal cooperation of social, religious, and political actors that believe in the benefits of Islamic listening. The book also inquires into the social meanings of preaching beyond its performance by exploring the misgivings of elites like Acep as well as ordinary Muslims about its value. The styles that make preaching so popular with Bandung audiences conflict with progressive aspirations for Islamic communication as a tool for political and social advancement.

West Java is an ideal location for observing this tension, for its population gives strong support to the frequent reiteration of Islamic messages. About 97 percent of the province's population of 43 million (at the time of writing) self-identify as Muslims, and many of these are regular participants in routines of prayer, worship, study, and predication. Of these activities, preaching is among the most amenable. Attendance at a sermon does not usually require the listener to possess Islamic skills or knowledge, and preaching events are commonly held and easy to get to. The company of family and neighbors makes listening a social experience, which is especially important for women, who have less freedom than men to attend events without such company. Furthermore, the province is home to many virtuoso preachers who make successful careers from reaching out to listeners in linguistic forms that are appealing as well as pious. These preachers draw big audiences, and for good reason: in a society committed to the constant restatement of Islamic meanings, preaching's uptake is threatened by repetitiveness. The risk of repetitiveness vanishes when the restatements are performed by preachers who can mimic familiar television voices and the sounds of motor cars, sing like pop divas, recite the Qur'an in beautiful melodies, create humor with comedic routines, play musical instruments, and turn an ironic, playful lens on contemporary life. Through their virtuoso treatments of the everyday, these preachers lift religious observance above the often difficult conditions of everyday life.

Why Study Preaching Styles?

Some might question the value of this book's focus on preaching styles in the early twenty-first century, when anxiety about the futures of many Islamic communities is high. Why focus on the styles and routines of Islamic communication instead of analyzing the content of these communications? In other words, it can be argued that the more substantive task is to analyze the issues and points of debate that arise in sermons.[1] This task becomes even more pressing when we realize the range of problems confronting West Java's population at the present: poverty, lack of economic opportunity, exploitation of women and other vulnerable groups, depleted natural resources such as water, a concerning level of radicalization, corruption in governance, and so on. These issues are not all directly related to Islam, but they are important topics in contemporary Islamic discourse. It could be argued that formal aspects of preaching deserve less attention than the substantive positions Islamic elites express on these issues through the medium.

Without denying the importance of those substantive positions, two problems arise from such an argument. First, styles of mediation and Islamic communication are topics of dispute and deliberation within Muslim communities all over the Islamic world, not just in Indonesia. In these disputes some contributors cite Islamic norms, while in other contributions we can trace the standardizing effects of national publicness. These debates are windows into processes by which Islamic forms and practices are organized into ones that are acceptable publicly and others that are not. The process is not a mere abstraction, for it reveals tension between efforts by elites to transform Indonesia's Muslims in the shape of their idealization of Islamic subjects, on the one hand, and the preference of vast populations to enjoy forms appropriate within their specific contexts, on the other.

Moreover, if it is accepted that the issues raised in communication are so important that the specificities of individual mediating forms and practices are not worthy of attention, our capacity to understand social life in its full complexity is limited. Taking this position would involve an assumption that all media forms—print media, radio, oratory, theater genres, and so on—perform an essentially similar function of conveying messages about things outside the context of the communication itself.

The chapters that follow reveal the deficiencies of that assumption. First, joining a West Javanese listening audience is not something one does at one's convenience, like picking up a newspaper or journal, or switching on a television. In fact, listeners commit their bodies to the event alongside other listeners, and this commitment usually forms part of a routine relating to one's everyday undertakings. For many people, especially women, this embodied participation is a valued undertaking they experience frequently, in many cases daily, alongside their relatives and friends. The approach to preaching adopted here pays attention to the way preaching events are instantiated in embodied routines, revealing significances beyond the conveyance of information.

Furthermore, the sermons delivered by West Java's preaching virtuosos provide listeners with symbolic and representational experiences that they cannot enjoy in any other medium. A West Javanese sermon is not simply a replication of communicative processes we encounter in other genres. By means of preachers' performative capabilities, listeners behold impressions and representations of their lived realities in forms that they do not encounter elsewhere. The uniqueness of this experience enables us to understand why such vast numbers of Sundanese Muslims support the integration of preaching into their life routines. For these reasons, this book gives serious attention to the forms and styles of preaching.

An Embedded Medium

When expressing his views on our journey to Sumedang, Acep was not swimming against the current of public discourse in West Java. Such views about the potential of Islamic communication are held widely in contemporary Indonesia, especially among religious and cultural elites, and are a feature of Islamic publicness in many contemporary Islamic societies. Armando Salvatore (1998) has lucidly theorized the public meanings of communications styles in his writings on Islam and media in post-Nasser Egypt.[2] Like Egypt, Indonesia is a nation in which Islamic norms are integral to people's understanding of their national public spheres. Egyptians and Indonesians feel connected with their state and with other members of their national publics through communication that is explicitly Islamic or tinged by Islamic references. At the same time, Muslims in these countries recognize differing values in the communicative forms they experience. Not all forms are perceived as having equal worth as contributions to the common good. Citizenship shapes Muslims' awareness of which forms constitute "legitimate patterns of communication and etiquettes of discourse" (Salvatore 1998, 89), for it entails participation in a civilizing project in which elites play a leading role in formulating and expressing state agendas and priorities. And this awareness extends beyond the communications forms per se, embracing as well the kinds of human subjects that these forms stand for. Salvatore uses the term *competencies* to characterize the human attributes that people associate with various communicative forms. (In what follows, I mainly use the term *subjectivities*.) Acep's caricatures of listeners are representations of a subjectivity that he believes will not assist Indonesians and Indonesia to achieve the advancement that they require.

Preaching's embeddedness has much to do with the way its contributions to publicness are evaluated. Among the preaching activities I attended in West Java over a total of two years commencing in 2007, most were parts of other activities. These activities were frequently life-cycle events like the event in Sumedang described earlier. In this book I call these other activities "routines" in recognition of their repeated character. The routinized setting for preaching is a major cause for the low efficacy that elites like Acep attribute to it. First, the messages delivered in routine preaching defer to the activity in which they are embedded. They enable the event to be successful, for example, by making a celebration festive or by making a workplace sermon support the work ethic desired by the employer. These goals have priority over the empowerment programs that Acep sees as the key to Indonesia's future. Second, routine participation conflicts with an idealization of Muslims as subjects that are autonomous and empowered. Acep and other elites see education and media participation as processes that will liberate Muslims from their local hierarchies and traditional institutions and will enable them to weigh up alternatives in detachment from those constraints.[3] By contrast, audience members at Islamic orations in West Java are almost always connected in some way with the context in which the sermon takes place. They are family members, neighbors, employees, clients, members of study groups, or students, and their attendance takes place alongside all the obligations and responsibilities implied by these relationships. In their sermons, preachers are respectful and accepting of these connections, and thus, they endorse the status quos in which people work, celebrate, and live.

This does not mean that all oratorical mediations of Islam in West Java provide nothing but predictable and pleasing confirmations of status quos. Nor does it mean that all preaching is valued negatively against contemporary norms of publicness. From time to time preachers transcend routine contexts and emerge onto the national scene with preaching styles built from unanticipated combinations of new and old. This is not unique to Indonesia. Recent research about Islamic media and communications in diverse locations reveals the fascinating synergies being created between preaching traditions and contemporary culture industries (Bayat 2007; Salvatore 2001; Schulz 2011).

In the late 1990s, Bandung audiences witnessed the emergence of a preacher who was to capture the national imagination in ways that appeared to constitute a breakthrough moment, producing messages in forms so compellingly contemporary that his media persona transcended the conventional frames within which Indonesians understood preaching.[4] This man was Abdullah Gymnastiar (b. Bandung, 1962), popularly known as Aa Gym (Hoesterey 2008; Solahudin 2008; Watson 2005). By the early 2000s Aa Gym had become ubiquitous in Indonesia. His sermons, live and televised,

were enjoyed by a diverse national audience, and public admiration for him
was so great that politicians courted him and sought his opinion. He was
successful in commodifying Islamic concepts to the point where his profile
and resources enabled him to branch out into nonreligious business enter-
prises. Based on his preaching of tolerance and intergroup harmony, he took
on the role of national peacemaker, traveling to preach reconciliation in
conflict-ridden areas.

Aa Gym strikes an important contrast with the preachers featured in this
book because his success was extraordinary in its novelty. The early stages
of his career resembled those of many preachers in Bandung (see Solahudin
2008), and as C. W. Watson (2005) has pointed out, Aa Gym was careful to
selectively self-represent within the tradition of Islamic preaching. Yet his
success was achieved through careful impression management at a moment
in time—the transition to democratic rule—when the Indonesian public
was ready to accept Islamic mediations in forms other than the narrow range
of options prevailing during the Suharto period (1966–98). He managed his
self-image carefully through media representations and carefully scripted
sermonic performances, self-styling on some occasions as a male who enjoyed rugged, manly pursuits, and on other occasions as a loving and sensitive
husband. He objectified and packaged Islamic concepts in forms with
contemporary appeal, circulating them as commodities through media technologies. Through his business success and his appropriation of management-
speak, he exemplified success in business and marketing, creating an image
of broad appeal to Indonesians. These were not things the *muballigh* of
the past had done.

Aa Gym's career was drastically affected after he married a second wife
in 2007. Female followers deserted the preacher in the wake of this decision,
forcing him to rationalize his business activity and curtail his preaching
(Hoesterey 2008). He had succeeded because of his successful appropriation
of forms acceptable to the national public (Salvatore 1998), but fell when he
misjudged the conditions of that publicness. In retrospect, it is incorrect to
remember him primarily as a preacher. He was also a media and business
phenomenon based around a distinctive preaching style and persona. For
this reason, it would be a mistake to conflate the mediatized Islamic public
sphere, a cultural market that demands stars and celebrities for its success
(Salvatore 2001), with the pious routines that Muslims of Bandung respect
through their bodily attendance. It is not the case that these routines are in-

sulated from a figure like Aa Gym, for aspects of his style were emulated to varying degrees by all sorts of preachers. Yet he became an Islamic media product carefully calibrated for acceptance in the widest possible market (i.e., the national market), to meet the needs of a range of parties with interests in the national media sphere, including audiences, sponsors, business investors, and media owners as well as those of the preacher himself. As I show in the chapters to follow, the audiences of everyday preaching routines require their preachers to accommodate specific conditions of the context of the oration, conditions that differ greatly from those that determine the constructs that we call markets.

Aa Gym added to the richness of preaching activities that had developed to match the city's Islamic diversity. The Aa Gym media phenomenon did not, however, replace existing practices and routines. It enhanced rather than reshaped the myriad styles of Islamic speech that have developed around everyday Muslim life in Bandung. The contrasts between preaching styles appropriate to the media phenomenon and face-to-face routines are important in this book. When viewed alongside the products succeeding in the national media market, everyday preaching routines lack sheen and luster, but the preachers succeeding within them skillfully calibrate their performances to achieve good outcomes with listeners in specific segments of West Java's diverse Muslim population.

Routines of Islamic Listening

Islam arrived in West Java at the coastal settlements of Cirebon and Banten in the early sixteenth century (Guillot 1990; Kern 1898), and its following has subsequently grown to the point where the province is almost totally Islamic in its religious affiliation.[5] In 2007, when I began my research, West Java's population of 42,194,869 was the highest of any Indonesian province. The proportion of Muslims in its population is among the highest of the country's provinces; according to the 2000 census, 97.65 percent of West Java's population were Muslims, while the national average was 87.51 percent (Suryadinata et al. 2003, 108–11). At that time, the *kota* (municipality) of Bandung was home to 2,390,120 people, but the metropolitan spread of the city encompassed several abutting regencies and municipalities, bringing the population of greater Bandung to approximately 7.5 million.

West Java is also the most densely populated of Indonesia's provinces.[6] According to 2010 figures, the average number of people per square kilometer in Indonesia as a whole was 124, whereas in West Java province the comparable figure was 1,222. The municipality of Bandung is even more crowded, with one of its communities having a population density in 2007 of 14,080 people per square kilometer.

With its high population density and very high proportion of Muslims, it is unsurprising that Islamic symbols and doctrines have a ubiquitous presence in West Javanese public life. The region has been known as one where Muslims hold the religion's textual canon in high regard (Horikoshi 1976; Soemardjan 1964, 33–35; Steenbrink 2005; Williams 1990; Zimmer 2000). There are historical explanations for the high Qur'anic literacy encountered in West Java. The most commonly expressed of these explanations suggests that the spread of Islam in West Java did not have to contend with any rival, indigenous set of spiritual functionaries and concepts (Snouck Hurgronje 1970, 264). In Central and East Java, on the other hand, the spread of Islam had to accommodate ancient and deeply respected spiritual systems. The pre-Islamic spiritualities of West Java, such as they were, offered little resistance to the spread of Islam.[7]

This respect for Islam's textual resources goes some way to explaining how West Javanese Muslims place so much value in preaching. Qur'anic verses and hadith (accounts of the sayings and acts of the Prophet Muhammad and his companions) provide textual foundations for oratory's value and authenticity as an Islamic observance.[8] The core verses include, "The prophet has no other obligation than the communication [*al-balaghu*] [of Allah's message]" (Al-Qur'an 5:99). This Qur'anic obligation to communicate Allah's message underpins the convention by which preachers in Bandung are referred to as *muballigh* (or *muballighah* for women), a cognate term of *al-balaghu*, meaning *communicator*. Following popular usage in Bandung, I use the word *muballigh* for *preacher*.

In another widely known verse (Al-Qur'an 3:104), Muslims are obliged to support a group whose task is to "call [*yad'una*] to goodness" and "command right and forbid wrong." Through this verse, which forms a normative basis for the exercise of moral authority throughout the Islamic world, the preacher is empowered to act as a mediator of goodness and propriety to Muslims (Cook 2000, 13–31; Gaffney 1994, 198–203). Muslims in Bandung cite a key word of this verse, *yad'una* (to call, invite) when they refer to preachers as *dai*, the Indonesian version of *da'i* (caller, inviter), a cognate of *yad'una*. In Bandung usage, the *muballigh* is a preacher, while the *dai* is a person dedicated to Islamic propagation in a wider range of forms. This usage reflects the ethic and spirit of the historical moment referred to as the *dakwah* period (Arabic: *da'wah*, the call, challenge, or invitation to Islam, see chapter 1). Along with a number of other verses and hadith, these sources create legitimacy for public undertakings dedicated to communicating Islam's message and calling humans to the ways of Allah.

A more immediate and substantive explanation for the high participation by West Java's Muslims in preaching events is their pious submission to regimes of Islamic practice in everyday life. Preaching cannot occur without an audience, and the frequent formation of audiences is propelled by routines and cycles that lead Muslims out of their homes to join with others in worshiping, supplicating, listening, reciting, giving thanks, celebrating, learning, and so on. An oration is a major feature of many such gatherings, and even in events in which supplication or learning provides the substance of participation, skillful speech enhances the event in important ways. The pious submission of bodies to routines draws our attention to a distinctive characteristic of social life in the region and other highly Islamic parts of Indonesia. In these regions, religion's presence in daily life has not been attenuated by privatization of faith. In most West Javanese communities, everybody is a Muslim, so schedules of Islamic practice strongly influence the rhythms of everyday life.

For men, the schedule of practice includes a weekly obligation, the Friday collective prayer (in West Java, women do not attend the Friday prayer). Prophetic tradition requires a sermon to be delivered at this gathering.[9] Gatherings other than this are attended by Muslims of both sexes and include calendrical moments such as the feasts of the Prophet's ascension and birthday, the celebration marking the end of the fasting month, and the feast of sacrifice. The fasting month is busy with religious practice. In most West Javanese communities, every evening of this month is dedicated to activities involving collective listening. The departure of a person on pilgrimage to Mecca is frequently celebrated by a gathering to which family, neighbors, and clients are invited. This event usually involves a joint meal, sermon, and prayer. Life-cycle events such as circumcisions and weddings are frequently celebrated with preaching. The civil calendar also incorporates celebrations in which preachers are frequently involved, especially the annual celebration of Indonesian independence. These routines are performed not just in religious spaces such as mosques and Islamic schools but also in the bureaucratic and corporate spaces of contemporary West Java. Contemporary preaching routines cut across borders characterizing spaces as public and private, sacred and secular.

A Woman's Domain

Bandung's routines of preaching and learning display a striking imbalance: West Javanese women listen in greater numbers and more frequently than men. I observed this continually during my period of fieldwork in Bandung, where I often participated in pious routines established for women only. Counterpart routines directed to men were few and poorly attended by comparison. Even at events intended for both men and women, women attended in greater numbers than men. This discrepancy can be explained in large part by women's consciousness of their roles and responsibilities as mothers and educators, and by the characteristic patterns of group sociability and mobility enjoyed by women, which differ greatly from those enjoyed by men (chapter 6).

Even though West Java is a patriarchal society in which men's headship is rarely questioned, West Java's Muslim women are not all listeners—quite a few of them preach. This is notable when one considers that males generally dominate Islamic authority.[10] There is, for example, significant opposition on Islamic grounds to women playing leadership roles outside the domestic sphere. Women are not considered capable of leading ritual worship (Arabic, *salat*). Polygamy is common in some social contexts. Yet Indonesian women are able to develop successful preaching careers. An important legal statement on the matter was published by the nationally known scholar Haji Abdul Malik Karim Amrullah (1908–81) in 1937 (Amrullah 1937). His lengthy treatment of the issue acknowledged the value and influence of preaching by women and denied the legal opinion that it was prohibited for males to listen to the female preaching voice.[11] And although the preachers with the highest profiles in Bandung are men, many women have regular followings and relatively high profiles. At the time of writing, a Sundanese woman, Mamah Dedeh (b. 1951), enjoys massive national popularity through daily television broadcasts in which she provides Islamically framed responses to women's queries about everyday problems (Dedeh 2009). Her popularity is based on her ability to communicate sensitively with female listeners and confirms something well established in the ethnographic literature (e.g., Doorn-Harder 2006; Marcoes 1988): women's experiences of Islamic study are frequently enhanced by the intimacy and affinity arising from shared experience of womanhood between teacher and student.

The most common form of routine piety enjoyed by females involves regular attendance at *majlis taklim* (from Arabic: *majlis ta'lim*, a gathering for study). Members of these groups study the Qur'an and hadith, develop Islamic performance skills (supplication and praise songs), learn about Islamic obligation, and enjoy the company of other women. Women's demand for preaching and learning is met with a colorful range of styles and practices in Bandung. I once participated in a celebratory event in which a twelve-year-old boy dressed as an Arab sheikh urged Islamic norms on an adult audience, consisting mostly of women and children, who enjoyed his cuteness as much as his message.[12] On another occasion, I attended an oration by a hardworking preacher who tirelessly travels by foot and public transport across eastern Bandung to give sermons to groups assembling in poorer neighborhoods. His caricatures of unhappy housewives make him popular with female listeners, who respond enthusiastically to his dramatized imitations of complaining, overworked women. An entirely different take on oratory was described to me by a friend invited to preach by a women's study group in Cianjur, a municipality bordering Bandung. He was surprised to find that the group preferred to conduct the event without any visual contact between the preacher and his audience. A curtain obscured the speaker from the audience's vision, although the women were free to ask him questions from their side of the curtain. Other organizing committees enable close interaction between female audiences and male preachers, as at a mixed gender event I attended at a mosque in Garut, south of Bandung. The preacher's microphone was positioned directly in front of the women's section. There was no partition between him and the women, who responded to the preacher with lively comments throughout the event. The men of the audience were forced to sit behind the preacher, looking at his back for the duration of the oration.

This diversity is a natural product of the high demand from West Java's Muslim women for participation in Islamic learning and listening. It also leads us to core dilemmas arising in Indonesian debates about the value of this participation. On the one hand, women are well served by the range of options just mentioned. Through this variety, it is easy for most women to feel comfortable participating in pious routines. Women with no inclination toward formal learning, for example, comfortably participate in pious activities alongside their friends and family. On the other hand, there is a feminist critique similar to Acep's, described earlier, that questions the efficacy of the preaching routines now enjoyed by women (chapter 6). This critique relies upon a caricatured image of listening as an enjoyable experience lacking in critical engagement. Based on this caricature, women are evaluated as passive objects in the communication process and as participants in something that will impede rather than advance their welfare. The preaching they enjoy is devalued because it does not appear to foster the communicative reasoning upon which the common good is seen to depend.

Listening in the Global Narrative of Islamic Modernism

In considering the perceptions of preaching held by Acep and other academics and activists, it is impossible to avoid the dichotomy of traditional versus modern. In everyday discussions about oratory as well as academic discourse, Indonesians invoke these categories frequently and unreflectively. People self-identifying as modern often interpret the conventional frames for Islamic sermonizing and the styles that prevail within them as traditional and even anachronistic. And the people most enthusiastic in organizing and attending preaching routines frequently self-identify as traditional. In short, preaching and its styles are things that enable Indonesians to understand themselves and others according to their conceptions of traditional or modern subjects. The contrast between these subjects has been a significant element of Bandung's history. The city is a center of Islamic tradition where Islamic routines have for centuries been a part of everyday life, yet Bandung has also been a nodal point in the global narrative of Islamic modernism.

The modernist movement first emerged in the late nineteenth century, when Muslim activists in the Middle East and the subcontinent began to advocate—as Islamic projects—the imperatives of breaking free from colonialism and advancing Muslim populations.[13] In the Netherlands Indies, the early modernist movements grew out of urban populations. In the central

Javanese city of Surakarta, batik traders had united to form Sarekat Islam (the Islamic Union) in 1912. In the same year, a community of craftspeople and traders in Yogyakarta formed Indonesia's largest modernist Muslim movement, Muhammadiyah. By that time, Bandung had long been a center for commercial and institutional activities, and was a meeting place for individuals inspired to implement a forward-looking Islamic vision. These were the founders of the modernist organization named Persatuan Islam (Islamic Association), known widely by its acronym PERSIS. Originating in 1923 as an urban initiative supported by scholars and traders, PERSIS promoted an egalitarian, return-to-basics brand of reformism while urging Muslims to participate in Bandung's unfolding prosperity (Federspiel 2001). Their mission included an insistence that Muslims of the Indies abandon long-established vernacular Islamic conventions. Two Bandung modernists, famous critics of vernacular Islamic styles, appear often in this book, Ahmad Hassan (1887–1958) and Muhammad Natsir (1908–93).[14] Hassan was a Tamil born in Singapore, while Natsir was of the Minangkabau ethnicity. The fact that two outsiders to the Sundanese ethnicity could become leaders of PERSIS highlights the organization's translocal character. The group was not dependent on patronage or intellectual direction from within Sundanese society. It is largely to this organization that Bandung owes its reputation as a center for reformist initiatives.

PERSIS's Islamic reformism was not the only modernism to unfold in Bandung. The city was home also to a Western-oriented modernity that developed out of colonial society's liking for Bandung. The inland region of West Java was sparsely populated until the late 1800s, when the region's economic activity began to attract immigrants.[15] The regencies of West Java's elevated interior, together known as the Priangan, were sources of coffee, tea, and quinine, and in 1856 Bandung became the capital of these regencies. In 1884 the city became accessible from Batavia (now Jakarta) by rail. Its relatively cool climate and high level of commercial activity attracted service industries supporting leisure pursuits, recreation, and education. Visitors to early-twentieth-century Bandung enjoyed a racetrack, theaters, and scenic tours through the regions that surrounded the city. In 1920 the first tertiary education institute in Indonesia was opened in Bandung, the Technische Hogeschool (THS, Technical High School), which evolved into the Technical Faculty of Universitas Indonesia and then the Institut Teknologi Bandung (ITB, Bandung Institute of Technology).

The concentration of institutional activity in Bandung made it a stronghold of Western influence, but it also made the city attractive to intellectuals of diverse origins who would together form a multiethnic, forward-looking nationalist network. Indonesia's first president, Sukarno, one of the THS's most prominent graduates, once called the city his "passport to a white world" (Legge 2003, 87). A Europe-inspired vanguard continued to define the city in diverse ways after independence. Young artists studying at the THS, for example, enthusiastically appropriated Western modernism. After a celebrated exhibition in 1954, nationalist critics Trisno Sumardjo and Sitor Situmorang lashed out at these artists for their adaptations of Western styles, derisively describing Bandung as "the laboratory of the West" (Spanjaard 1990), a label that has stuck to the present day.

Indonesian independence in 1945 saw the end of colonial society. In contrast, rank-and-file support for Bandung's modernist Islamic elite strengthened, especially in the 1950s and 1960s, when large numbers of people fled to Bandung from Garut and Tasikmalaya to escape the conflict between the separatist movement known as Dar al-Islam (DI, Abode of Islam) and Republican troops (Dijk 1981). These immigrants expanded Bandung's materially underprivileged, scripturally literate Islamic population. The resulting social configuration has been important in defining the public sphere of contemporary Bandung, as the new arrivals came from communities where almost 100 percent of the population were Muslims and where respect for Islamic norms as guidelines for everyday life (*fiqh*) was very high. Many of the newcomers were attracted to the social conservatism propagated by Bandung's modernist Islamic movements.[16] To this day Bandung is a major source of support for PERSIS. I attended preaching events in the city's mosques and schools and had many long discussions with its members about oratory and Islam.

Hassan and Natsir were not artful communicators. They paid little attention to the packaging of their messages, and less attention still to the effects their message might create outside the ranks of their supporters. Commencing in 1929, Hassan published a series of short fatwa, initially appearing in the PERSIS journal *The Defender of Islam* and subsequently in book form. In these fatwa, Hassan urged Indonesian readers to revise their Islamic styles and beliefs, including their ritual, doctrine, clothing styles, pedagogical forms, language and theology (Hassan 2000).[17] These fatwa revealed the importance PERSIS attaches to a basic modernist principle—the correctness and value of Islamic observances and doctrines should be established by direct reference to the Qur'an and prophetic traditions. Hassan's indictments of Islamic vernaculars in Indonesia were so confronting that John Bowen (1997, 171) labeled them as "shrill blasts." Natsir came to West Java as a Sumatran accustomed to directness in speech (Luth 1999). He tried to lobby Javanese bureaucrats and politicians to accept his Islamist agenda but was never able to bridge the gap that separated him from that audience. The bureaucrats had been raised in environments where Javanese of different status were required to speak in ways that made their status obvious. Natsir never adjusted to this hierarchy (Luth 1999, 80–81, 135–36). But Hassan and Natsir did not need to be artful communicators, for their followers did not generally evaluate them according to their skill in communicating. They and their colleagues did not share the view that preachers who worked hard with skillful speech in order to be accepted by audiences might be doing something of value for Muslims and the religion. Instead, as shown in chapter 3, they produced ideological statements that problematized skillful preaching.

Their disregard for artifice in their communications makes sense against the background of the modernist ideology to which they subscribed. There have been many versions of Islamic modernism, but two general, overlapping features frequently recur. The first is discontinuity. As noted, modernist movements aspired to break free from those beliefs and practices that they viewed as innovations (Arabic, *bida'*) not sanctioned by the belief and practice of the Prophet and his companions. In the Indies, this put the movements in conflict with vernacular observances that had come to prevail among Muslims. Second, Islamic modernists emphasized transformations in Muslim selves. They framed this transformation as a religio-normative one, requiring believers to shape themselves anew according to the Qur'an and hadith. In her ethnographic study of veiling by Javanese women, for example, Susan Brenner (1996, 684) observes such a transformation to be a "rebirthing" occurring when a Muslim's awareness of "proper Islam" brings a reflexive awareness of an "altered subjectivity." As discussed in chapter 3, this concept of transformation does not repudiate the idealization of the educated, informed citizen-subject grounded in nationalist consciousness. In fact, it complements it: the ideal Muslim, modernists argue, is rational, autonomous, and capable of critical reflection on his or her environment, just like the ideal citizen (Atkinson 1983; Brenner 1996). This harmony between Islamic and nationalist models of transformative subjectivity explains why the caricatures of laughing listeners are so widely accepted in Indonesia today.

Preaching's Critics in the Present

The Bandung of today differs greatly from the city in which Hassan and Natsir were active. Public life is more Islamic than it was in their lifetimes. During the colonial period, Islamic modernity was subordinate to the Europe-inspired ideals of public life with which the city had become identified. The architects of the "Paris of Java," as Bandung was known, generally paid little attention to the religion of the province's inhabitants. Thus, the spacious grounds of the prestigious Bandung Institute of Technology (ITB) did not include a mosque until the Salman Mosque was opened in 1972. Imaduddin Abdulrahim, a student who came to ITB from a pious Sumatran background, told V. S. Naipaul that on his arrival in Bandung in 1953, he had been forced to walk three kilometers to a village mosque for Friday prayer and that he was amazed that some lecturers scheduled classes at the same time as the Friday congregational prayer (Naipaul 1981, 347–48).

The opening of the Salman Mosque occurred during a "reclaiming" of public space by Muslim initiatives. Islamic projects began to draw support from a wider range of influential segments of Bandung and West Javanese society, a development sometimes referred to with an old word given new meanings—*dakwah*.[18] A pertinent example of such projects is the West Java Centre for Islamic Dakwah. This multifunctional Islamic center was conceived by the provincial government in 1977–78 and completed at enormous expense in 1998. It occupies a large parcel of land in central Bandung and includes a mosque, a library, an exhibition space, a museum, and function rooms. It provides a mixed menu of activities, from routine worship to Islamic rock concerts, women's study groups, competitions, exhibitions, programs of instruction, and philanthropic activities (Yayasan 2009).

In this environment of increasing public piety, the modernist ethos of Hassan and Natsir has expanded to inform many ordinary Muslims' understanding of what constitutes valuable Islamic communication. Skepticism about the popular routines of oratory is expressed widely in everyday talk, often in catchy and easily remembered maxims. These popular expressions are evidence of how closely Islamic identity has synthesized with a progressive conception of citizenship. One of the most commonly expressed of these maxims is "[Preaching of that kind is] spectacle, not guidance" (Indonesian, *tontonan, bukan tuntunan*). This establishes a hierarchy in which guidance (*tuntunan*) is valued more highly than displays of communicative skill (*tontonan*). A kindred maxim is "Mastering the masses [is less valuable than] mastering the material" (Indonesian, *menguasai massa, menguasai materi*). The hierarchy established here places the orator's knowledge of Islam above his ability to command an audience's attention and feelings. The gaining of financial benefit from preaching also attracts attention in popular discourse about preaching practice. The relevant expression is "selling the verses [of the Qur'an]" (Indonesian, *menjualkan ayat*). This is used to condemn preachers who receive high fees for preaching. This list would be incomplete and misleading, however, without this telling example of folk reflexivity; "Although we criticize [this food], we nevertheless enjoy eating it" (Sundanese, *dipoyok dilebok*). When people use this to refer to preaching, they ironically acknowledge its powers of attraction.[19]

Critiques of preaching produced by Islamic figures with qualifications in social and political sciences caricature listening subjects as passive and irrational, and represent the medium as inefficacious. A notable critique of oratory was published by the Jakarta-based intellectual Yudi Latif (b. 1964), who holds a PhD in political science from the Australian National University. He has dismissively characterized Indonesian oratory as offering a "spiritual meal" that provides a satiating form of escapism for Indonesia's Muslims. He labels it as "triumphant shouting" in which audiences passively follow the words and actions of the preachers they idolize: "the preacher speaks, the audience listens; the preacher thinks, the audiences are thought for; the preacher decides, the audience accedes; the preacher organises, the audience obeys, and so on" (Latif 2000, 14). While doing this, he claims, they fail to work toward Islamically grounded resolutions to Indonesia's problems. Latif proposes a remedial trajectory for Indonesian Islamic communications involving a transition "from oral to written traditions, from a tradition of speechmaking to one of writing, and from one of listening to one of reading" (Latif 2000, 17).

The Bandung-based academic Agus Ahmad Safei (b. 1972), the holder of a PhD degree in media and communications from Bandung's elite Padjadjaran University, has characterized popular preaching as inefficacious, constructing an image of passive listeners who "come to sit, listen, laugh or cry. Once they go home, the messages are easily forgotten . . . the 'ritual' of conveying Islamic teaching is just a temporary stopping-place, something that comes in the right ear and out from the left" (Safei 2008, 129). Indonesia's most respected feminist, Siti Musdah Mulia (b. 1958), the first woman to be appointed as a research professor to the Indonesian Institute of Sciences, contrasts preaching's frivolity with her aspirations for its potential:

> Of more concern is the tendency to view dakwah merely as a form of entertainment for providing relief to the audience's hearts, for entertaining the listeners. Dakwah is provided in order to attract people to a celebration where they will be entertained by beautiful rhetoric, captivating poetry, funny illustrations, accompanied by music and smutty jokes, and so on. The success of dakwah is not to be measured by the level of the listeners' laughter or handclapping. In fact, dakwah's success should be evident in the impression it leaves in the listener's spirit, which is then reflected in their daily behaviour, in their individual behaviour as well as their social life in the community. (Mulia 2005, 503)

These caricatures convey skepticism about popular preferences for certain styles of preaching, and especially those enjoyed at celebratory events. They do not express misgivings about the value of speaking in public about Islam in toto. Some prominent critics of preaching styles frequently speak in public as Islamic authorities. It would be difficult for them to avoid this, for the fabric of Islamic sociability is largely woven from bodily attendance at gatherings. Yudi Latif, for example, is constantly speaking to forums in Jakarta and other Indonesian cities, where he has become a much-admired figure for his positive interpretations of the compatibility between Islam and Indonesia's inclusive state ideology, the Pancasila (Five Principles). In addition to writing books and articles, Siti Musdah Mulia regularly addresses listening audiences. Yet these figures are clear in their insistence that popular forms of Islamic oratory do not, to use Salvatore's words (1998, 89), constitute "legitimate patterns of communication and etiquettes of discourse."

The caricatures allow Muslim speakers to differentiate their Islamic speech from other kinds. Laughing, handclapping, forgetting, entertaining, crying, music, smut, and so on provide the emblems of difference. I witnessed this differentiation in an informal conversation I had with a lecturer at an Islamic university in Jakarta. This man, I had been told by friends, was a preacher affiliated with a progressive Islamic group. Early in our conversation, I referred to him as a preacher with the term most commonly used, *muballigh*. He corrected me, "I am not a muballigh." I asked in reply, "But do you not receive regular invitations to speak based on your authority on Islam?" He answered, "I regularly give talks of this kind, but so do many lecturers at this university. But we do not do what the *muballigh* do." He characterized the lecturers' work as being *rasional, akademis*, and free of *emosi* (emotions). This man had no deep objection to speaking about Islam to an audience but wished to disassociate himself from the routines and styles of Islamic communication that I had referenced with the word *muballigh*. In characterizing his own practice, he foregrounded an ethic of detached reason.

Processes of self-positioning and border-setting that use communications forms as symbolic resources are bigger than Islamic preaching. They appear wherever modernizing programs take issue with existing realities. As Richard Bauman and Charles Briggs (2003) have demonstrated, projects of modernization aspire to transparent, universal languages and communicative forms. They construct self-legitimizing, evolutionary narratives in which situated languages and communicative forms appear as prior episodes and as symptoms, or even causes, of unwanted realities. In characterizations of preaching that I encountered in Bandung, conceptual underpinning was frequently provided by the related concepts of democratic citizenship, civil society, and the public sphere (chapter 5).[20] These concepts are frequently referenced in Indonesian conversations about Islamic media and have a strong grip on the ways contemporary Indonesians view their political and social realities. For their supporters, these ideas presuppose communicative processes in which rational-critical subjects engage in deliberation—ideally mediated in written genres—in a detached manner. Caricatured images of listeners conflict with these ideals, for they depict subjects whom progressives believe to be redundant in the prosperous and democratic Indonesia that is constructed through idealizations of civil society and the public sphere.

NU: Standing up for Preaching

Does the modernist critique of preaching attract contrary expressions in support of the orators Bandung Muslims enjoy? Does the Islamic public sphere facilitate arguments in favor of the listening subject? Muslims of the world have reacted to the modernist movement in many ways. One important response emerged in Egypt, for example, where the Muslim Brotherhood was established in 1928 out of concern about what its supporters perceived as the modernists' secularizing trajectory. The main Indonesian response, Nahdlatul Ulama (The Rising of the Scholars, commonly referred to as NU), was founded in 1926 to protect the interests of the scholarly elite (*kyai*) based in Java's Islamic boarding schools as well as the Islamic outlook that was authoritative in that milieu (Fealy 1998; Marijan 1992; Noer 1973). The NU's founders were disturbed by the growing influence of modernism in the Indies and on the Arab Peninsula. They felt threatened by the modernists' revisionist perspective on Islamic observances and understandings because it devalued the legal schools (*madhab*) that had arisen after the passing of the Prophet's companions and his companions. The authority enjoyed by scholarly elites was based on their ability to mediate the normative literature of these schools. When modernists argued that being a Muslim required individual self-improvement rather than reliance on the authority of learned Muslims, they were directly challenging the authority of the traditional elites.

In their initial response to the modernist movement, the *kyai* who founded NU realized that their cause would gain definition and legitimacy if they framed it as "traditional." This framing remains acceptable to many Muslims in the present. In their everyday Islamic routines, millions of West Javanese Muslims continue to enjoy Islamic practices and styles—such as pilgrimage, grave visiting, and intercessory rituals—that had been critiqued by modernists like Hassan almost a century earlier. The NU provides Islamic advocacy and leadership for practices such as these.

Listening is prominent among these practices and styles. NU contexts are widely recognized as spaces where people enjoy listening to skilled Islamic orators (Muhtadi 2004; Muzadi 2002). While the modernists hold the celebration of feast days to be an innovation not supported by the Qur'an or practice of the Prophet, NU's largest gatherings occur on the dates of the Prophet's birthday or ascension. At these events, frequently labeled as "Great Preaching" (Tabligh Akbar), NU preachers address massive crowds. But in the face of the critiques of oratory cited in these pages, NU is not inclined to mount a persuasive defense of the efficacy of virtuoso preaching, at least not in the specific terms of the critiques. This is understandable because the basic principles of that critique, although initially produced out of modernist reflections on Islam and its relationship to social and political progress, have also served as fundamental principles underpinning the emergence of the modern Indonesian nation. The early-twentieth century modernists helped define the discursive agenda for the emergent nation, and NU people were compelled to a large degree to make this journey along with them. They could not directly deny the relevance of the new subjectivity that modernists were advocating, for this would amount to a denial of public rationalities situated at the core of the nation-building effort, such as universal education, equality for all, and democratic empowerment.

Nevertheless, NU stands firmly behind oratory. Chapter 8 analyses exactly how it does this. The organization literally creates spaces for listening in schools, mosques, parks, sports arenas, fields, and streetscapes. Less obviously, it also provides a conceptual buffer, constructed out of Islam's normative sources, against derogatory characterizations of listening. NU doctrines and practices legitimize the listening habits of Muslims by advocating an Islamic subjectivity that is not faulted for relying on the expert mediations of others (*taqlid*). This legitimization neutralizes the stigma of passivity encountered in the progressive critiques. In this way the modernist critique of oratory meets its ideological rival. NU's support for listening is a critical element of a public Islam that accommodates contrasting conceptions of Islamic subjectivity: it advocates listening as an acceptable mode of participation in Indonesia's Islamic public sphere.

Which Preaching?

A growing body of academic literature on Islamic preaching and listening reveals that the subject is too diverse to be analyzed as a singular object, and this book does not pretend to have application to all forms and settings for preaching and listening. It is therefore necessary to locate the preaching encountered in what follows in relation to that diversity. Three qualifications need to be stated. First, this book is not about the preaching that occurs as a ritual phase in the Friday congregational prayer, an activity that has received attention from scholars. Several ethnographic studies of Friday preaching have examined the interplay between the normative tradition defined by the Prophet's own practice and the conditions facing specific communities (Antoun 1989; Gaffney 1994). There are also valuable historical studies based on written genres associated with the science of rhetoric (Berkey 2001; Halldén

2005; Swartz 1999). Instead this book is concerned with preaching taking place in diverse civil and private spaces, held to correspond with a range of cycles and schedules wider than the Friday fixture alone.

The second qualification affecting this book is its regional focus. All preaching encountered in what follows took place in Bandung and its surrounds in West Java province. This regional focus is not significant for the ethnic contrast it implies (i.e., Sundanese versus Indonesian). The significant contrast is between communication styled to comply with norms of national publicness and communication that is successful in face-to-face encounters occurring within the routines of daily life. In the latter settings, preaching is not so constrained by the propriety Muslims sense to be a condition of their participation in the civilizing project of the Indonesian state. Aa Gym exemplifies this contrast. Aa Gym and others like him succeeded with preaching styles that were shaped by emerging modes of public correctness, and that simultaneously served the capital investment and industrial conditions that enable preaching to reach the national market (see Fealy 2008; Hoesterey 2008; Howell 2008; Kitley 2008; Rakhmani 2013; Watson 2005). In contrast, the preachers filling engagements within the routines of everyday Islamic life in Bandung do not address national media markets, but groups of people who come together as listening audiences in their workplaces, in domestic and neighborhood settings, or in study groups. The regional focus signals a distinction between two different listening subjects: a media consumer attuned to norms of national publicness and one engaged in daily undertakings of an embodied nature. Many Bandung Muslims feel comfortable embodying both subjectivities but are aware of the differences between them.

The third qualification is its focus on preachers who have succeeded in reaching audiences that broadly reflect social and political realities in the city. The preachers encountered in these pages have achieved a high level of public acceptability. This does not mean that all members of the Bandung public find them acceptable: Bandung's Islamic community includes preferences for many contrasting Islamic outlooks and styles, and no preacher is fully representative of all these styles. By allying themselves with various elements of West Javanese society (governments, mosque committees, political parties, employers, media organizations, educational institutions), the preachers discussed in this book have successfully negotiated audiences beyond the niches in which their preaching styles were first shaped, enabling them to emerge as widely accepted public figures.

Two such preachers, Shiddiq Amien (1955–2009) and Al-Jauhari (b. 1971), are directly compared in chapters 2 to 4. These men were chosen because they reveal the diversified public Islam that West Javanese Muslims have created through their investment in preaching as a publicly beneficial activity. Amien and Al-Jauhari have received public approval for their proficiency in performing the same task—preaching—but their styles point to contrasting and even opposing conceptions of Islamic subjectivity. Their styles display many similarities but embody opposing poles in this discourse on preaching's value as public communication.

Al-Jauhari specializes in preaching on the celebratory stages that are so frequently erected within Bandung Islamic routines. When preaching, he calls upon an extraordinary range of abilities in many cultural genres. A typical Al-Jauhari sermon is multivocal, full of surprises, and determined to engage with the cultural competencies of his listeners. This style has brought him great popularity but displays the features most disliked by the critics of oratory. Shiddiq Amien, on the other hand, was a respected and popular preacher who belonged to PERSIS. Amien's preaching style succeeded by avoiding the "excesses" the group identifies in Al-Jauhari's. The ideologues of PERSIS argue that the routines of Islamic life should be made bearable by the content of Islamic teachings and not by the communicative styles through which that content is conveyed.

These two preachers felt accountable to their membership of a broad, inclusive community of Muslims. That accountability distinguishes the specific focus of the book and determines its difference in comparison with other studies of preaching. Islamic counterpublics, for example, are important but tangential to the main narrative of the book.[21] Subjects within counterpublics, which Muslims in Bandung often refer to as *golongan tertentu* (specialized groups), are connected through communicative practices and discursive positions that set them in opposition to dominant publics (Hirschkind 2006). Examples in Bandung include groups dedicated to esoteric teachings or radical interpretations, revivalist movements, interfaith initiatives, and student movements.[22] In contrast to Al-Jauhari and Amien, who work positively with alliances with other social and political actors, these preachers and audiences frequently style in opposition to widely accepted norms of publicness.

Nonetheless, counterpublic outlooks on media and communication provide telling perspectives on the major themes of this book. Some specialized groups make distinctive analyses of public communication that open new ways of looking at preaching and the aspirations Muslims hold for it. Chapter 7 examines a specialized group that understands West Java as a mediated sphere in the shape of a "war of ideas" (Arabic, *ghazw ul-fikri*). This group, the Indonesian Council for Islamic Dakwah (DDII), is one of a number that advocate Islamically based programs of change. With oratory being such a popular medium in West Java, it is natural that such groups view it as a potentially useful tool; the preaching stage appears as a strategic position from which to promote projects of reform to large audiences. However, the group struggles to reach audiences through oratory because the high-profile preachers who might be sympathetic to its cause base their careers on preaching to audiences that are heterogeneous in their ideological orientation. A successful sermon before such audiences involves flattening out ideological content to avoid disagreement. A preacher failing to respect the internal character of a workplace, for example, will not be invited to return. Chapter 7 explores this distinction between idealizations of preaching as an instrument of reform and a publicly oriented pragmatism that frustrates this potential.

Affective Listening in Public

Successful preachers must work to ensure good outcomes. Of the Islamic messages that I encountered in Bandung, none was so compelling for its audience that it could be successfully mediated without the orator paying attention to its reception. Rather, all preachers mobilized oratorical skill to some degree to ensure a positive reception and regarded a successful sermon as one in which audience attention on the speaking was maintained throughout. For this reason, a preacher's success is grounded in his or her command of verbal artifice.[23] Many Bandung modernists would take issue with this observation. In their minds, Islamic mediations should not succeed through artifice. They point disapprovingly to orators whose verbal skills transfix an audience.[24] The reality is, however, that even those preachers who have ideological objections to displays of verbal skill rely on artful devices to ensure good reception. To be sure, their shows of skill are far less multivocal than those of unabashed virtuosos, but they demonstrate that no preacher can convey "content" without using language or behavior that defers to the communication situation, and this deference frequently appears in strategies that communicate affect.

Affect is a result of the listening process that occurs "in addition to the referential and social communicative functions of language," and consists of the "feelings, moods, dispositions, and attitudes" that orators and audiences co-create during their interaction (Besnier 1992, 162). Indonesian preachers create affect of varying kinds and communicate them with varying degrees of intensity. Refreshment strategies represent a minimal mobilization of affect; preachers restore a fatigued audience with doses of humor. Affective communication also assists in conveying material that might otherwise create the risk of audience disengagement, so preachers will often nest pedagogical content within affective structures that attract sustained audience attention and commitment to the interaction. Other preachers succeed by making affect the center of their practice. Some orators are known for putting their audiences into a state of sustained hilarity. In recent years, audiences have responded positively to preachers able to move listeners to tears (see the discussion in Rudnyckyj 2010).

The kinds of affect communicated to the audiences I joined in Bandung distinguish these audiences from those described in Hirschkind's major study. For the Muslim listeners who assisted Hirschkind with his research in Cairo, the affective properties of rhetorical speech have the capacity to shape them as ethical subjects. They are sensitive to "the poetic and performative dimensions of speech and its ethical resonances across multiple sensory registers" (Hirschkind 2006, 107). Their shared awareness and embodiment of these properties of oratory make them different from other Muslim audiences in Cairo. In contrast, the preachers featured here maintain listeners' engagement with oratory's ethical messages through their appropriations of ways of speaking and cultural forms with which listeners identify, and which make preaching an enjoyable and stimulating experience. Islamic oratory appears as a pious activity that is also enjoyable.

It is important to re-emphasize that the listeners in Hirschkind's study look at the world from a different Islamic space than the one in which I lodged myself. The Cairo counterpublic is distinguished by its commitment to ethical development of self and society. This commitment signals a unity of purpose in that audience. The preaching audiences discussed in these pages, on the other hand, were composed of listeners from multiple segments of Bandung society. Organizers of such events set out to create listening audiences combining segments that might otherwise be at a distance from each other. When organizing a village celebration, organizers consciously aim to provide a sermon acceptable to listeners from age categories who would not otherwise experience the same cultural genres. In planning a workplace event, the committee needs to be confident that a preacher will respect the workplace hierarchy and will not inflame differences between the Islamic orientations encountered within the workforce. In such situations, the preacher is constrained from accommodating the specificities of one group of listeners and responds by presenting a sermon that is broadly acceptable but must then work hard to avoid fatigue and boredom in an audience that will easily become disinterested. A number of types of affect will assist the preacher to do this, but the one most commonly called upon is humor. Thus, when studying heterogeneous preaching audiences in Bandung, what I observed was not so much an ethical soundscape, to reference the title of Hirschkind's book, as an ethical soundscape ringing with laughter and rippling with bodies moving in enjoyment. In what follows, I interpret this laughter and enjoyment as keys to the success of preaching as a participatory observance for West Javanese Muslims (chapter 7).

This book is structured in two parts. Chapters 1 to 4 convey the diversity of preaching styles enjoyed in Bandung. The first chapter of this part sketches diversity by looking back to document waves of novelty in preaching styles, plotting successive embraces by Bandung Muslims of new preaching forms that remain valid for contemporary audiences. Chapters 2 and 3 are a comparison of orations by two skilled preachers (summarized above), which provides contextual background to the evaluations of preaching explored in later chapters. Chapter 4 explores evaluations relating to these two preaching styles, pointing out the way in which public norms about appropriate communication inform negative judgments of one of them. My access to those norms is through language selection (Sundanese versus Indonesian), a variable that expresses listeners' recognition of a hierarchy of preaching styles.

The second part (chapters 5 to 8) refers to the ethnographic picture provided in the first part. These four chapters analyze the connections Indonesian Muslims make between preaching styles and subjectivities as well as the way norms of national publicness shape these connections. Concepts such as democratic citizenship, public sphere, and civil society are analyzed as idealizations against which certain oratorical routines appear inefficacious. Chapters 5 and 6 explore two progressive critiques of preaching routines. The first describes a competition in which contestants write about the Qur'an. This was specifically conceived by a Bandung activist concerned about the negative effects of listening on Indonesia's democratic future. Chapter 6 contrasts a feminist critique of women's routines of listening and learning with the appropriateness of these routines for women's spectatorship patterns. Bandung's women live under constraints affecting their social expectations and mobility. The chapter argues that they enjoy preaching in forms deliberately shaped by preachers to accommodate their situations. The resulting listening experience is not a disciplinary one but one that respects women's life conditions. Chapter 7 analyzes preaching as a medium for change, viewing it from the perspective of an activist group that contributes to public contest by circulating ideas through the province's media. The group is frustrated by the pragmatic tendencies of preachers who realize their careers depend on avoidance of contest. In the two closing chapters the question of the Islamic public sphere is revisited. Chapter 8 argues that its Indonesian manifestation is distinguished by the NU's advocacy of passivity as an acceptable Muslim position. Cutting across the logic of the progressive critique of preaching, this advocacy provides an ideological defense of the listening subject. In the conclusion, I reflect on the preceding chapters to characterize preaching's popular uptake as a successful project of public Islam, and I trace its contours and logics, referring to the preceding chapters.

A final note concerns the identities of those who helped me with this research, some of whom became the central subjects of individual chapters. The analysis in the following chapters is an academic one and might disappoint some Muslims in Bandung for whom preaching holds pious meanings, to which, they might consider, I have paid insufficient attention. To avoid implicating my helpers in such an evaluation, they appear in the book with altered names.

Chapter 1

Preaching Diversity in Bandung

My experience among Bandung's Muslims brought me into contact with several conceptions of oratory's function and practice. On some points, all these understandings meet, sharing certain general assumptions. For example, all West Javanese Muslims would support the general proposition that Islamic oratory's function is to communicate religious knowledge to Muslims (Arabic, *tabligh*), and to encourage them to implement these messages in their lives and the lives of their communities (Arabic, *da'wah*). But the divergences encountered beneath that generalization are significant. Some people conceived Islamic oratory as a medium for learning and personal empowerment. A related conception sees oratorical communication as something that should enable listeners to develop the qualities expected of Indonesian citizens. In some settings it is considered that oratory instills in listeners dedication to activities such as employment and study. Another understanding singles out the cultivation of personal piety as the crucial element—repeated exposure to Islamic messages inculcates moral virtues. Another conception sees preaching as an affective experience that has the special power of drawing large numbers of listeners into community mosques for celebration and commemoration.

These diverse functions relate to contrasting visions of what Islam has to offer for Indonesian individuals and collectives, and they point to disparate Islamic movements and outlooks. In this chapter, I connect distinct conceptions of preaching with these movements, visions, and outlooks that combine in the present to make Bandung and West Java a diverse environment for Islamic listening.

The chapter is structured around four tables. Each table presents a cluster of terms, distinguished as a group because they form a distinct lexicon for naming oratory and conceiving its meanings and functions. I derived these clusters from my discussions with Muslims in Bandung, from my observations at preaching events, from normative writings about oratory, from historical writings on Islam in West Java, and from programmatic statements of various groups that hold preaching events. Each cluster (other than the first) represents a moment of innovation or renewal, meaning a historically specific point of change at which this or that conception of oratory was foregrounded as superior to other conceptions. These moments of innovation should not be interpreted as forming a chronological sequence in which one conception succeeds the previous one, and neither do they designate four distinct currents of preaching activity. West Java is a complex, diversified society where audiences prefer a wide range of preaching styles, old and new. Furthermore, preachers tend to look sideways across borders between audiences, and the emergence of new styles often leads them to adapt and appropriate novel elements into their own style. To use a term from James Hoesterey (2012, 54), preachers "recalibrate" their styles in response to new possibilities. In this way, preaching novelties circulate beyond their originating contexts and blend into existing styles.

Most of the lexical items in the tables that follow are loanwords from Arabic. I present them here in their Indonesianized forms. If a term is not of Arabic origin, I indicate its linguistic origin in brackets.

Unlike the terms appearing in tables 2, 3 and 4, the terms in table 1 cannot be tied to any specific moment. Rather, they denote one of the many branches of the Islamic sciences to have emerged since the time of the Prophet (Halldén 2005; Swartz 1999). Their use is relatively stable and persistent, as they constitute the technical vocabulary used in the discipline's scientific literature, in its hierarchies of expertise, and in the institutions that provide

Table 1. Oratory amid the Islamic sciences

Term	Definition
khutbah	Sermon, and especially the Friday congregational sermon. *Khutbah* very often appears in the compound *khutbah jumat* (Friday sermon) and is rarely used to describe sermons outside of that context.
khatib	Person giving a sermon, orator.
'ilm al-khatabah	The science of sermonizing, public speech, or oratory. This term is the disciplinary designation used in Indonesian Islamic institutions. It consists of principles derived from accounts of the prophet Muhammad's own preaching and his conduct of the Friday prayer as well as theoretical treatments of topics such as rhetoric and philosophy of language (Halldén 2005; Swartz 1999). *'Ilm al-balaghah* is also used with similar meaning, although it points more strongly to rhetoric and eloquence than to the medium of oratory in particular. For the difference between *'ilm al-balaghah* and *'ilm al-khatabah*, see Halldén 2005.[a]
muballigh	Literally, messenger, bearer of news. This is one of the two terms used interchangeably by West Javanese Muslims to refer to preachers who deliver sermons outside the Friday prayer. The other is *dai*. Female preachers are referred to as *muballighah* or *daiyah*.
tabligh	Communication or transmission of a message. *Tabligh* often appears in the compound *tabligh akbar*, meaning great (in the sense of large scale) preaching. This is the preferred label for preaching events occurring in Islamic schools and mosques, which often feature a succession of preachers appearing on stage one after the other, commencing after the evening worship and concluding with the morning worship. Some Muslims in Bandung interpret the term negatively, under-standing it as a sign of the hierarchical ascendancy of the traditional clergy over their congregations.

[a] Charles Hirschkind (2006) notes that before the twentieth century, Arab writers in these fields did not evaluate oratory as a communicative resource. Muslim scholars were "relatively uncon-cerned with elaborating an art of sermon rhetoric or devising techniques to ensure the persuasive-ness of a preacher's discourse" (33). Rather, their focus was on the poetic and aesthetic qualities of the Qur'an.

courses in predication such as the Faculty of Dakwah and Communication and some of Indonesia's many Islamic schools.

The stipulations cultivated within this discipline are publicly visible in the formalities of the ritual order and conduct of oratory, especially in the Friday sermon, where they are understood as continuations of the Prophet's own practice.[1] In non-*khutbah* preaching, these formalities can be seen and heard at the opening of sermons. The opening utterances, which typically take approximately one minute to verbalize, include all or some of the following: a statement that all praise belongs to Allah (Arabic, *tahmid*); a statement of the Muslim creed (Arabic, *tashahhud*); and a request for Allah to bless the Prophet Muhammad, his family, and other notables (Arabic, *salawat*). Oratory's formalities are given heightened importance in competitions. The oratory component of Indonesia's Islamic competition, the Musabaqah Tilawat Al-Qur'an (MTQ: Competition in Qur'anic Recitation), is known as the Musabaqah Syarh Al-Qur'an (Competition in Qur'anic Declamation). Teams of three compete in this event. One team member recites a passage from the Qur'an, her colleague translates it poetically, and the third member, the *muballigh*, provides an oratorical interpretation. The contributions of all three are evaluated by judges. In the oratory phase, judges pay close attention to, among other things, the correct pronunciation of introductory invocations, blessings, and formulas.

The preachers encountered in the pages of this book, however, are career orators. A preaching career depends on repeat invitations, and these are not issued based on an orator's ability to reproduce the formal aspects of oratory. Bandung audiences expect much more of skillful preachers than that. Preachers succeed through their ability to mediate Islam with speech appropriate to context and to maintain audience attention to their speaking. Outside the Friday collective prayer, therefore, orations are more strongly shaped by embodied sociability than by formal norms. Nevertheless, Muslims in some segments of Bandung's Islamic society insist that oratory should reflect the stipulations found in *fiqh* (normative guidelines extracted from revelation and the Prophet's example). The guidelines constraining preaching are referred to as *adab al-da'wah* (Arabic, preaching etiquette). This code extends beyond the formal norms affecting ritual order and decorum, providing stipulations concerning the conduct and character of the preacher and evaluating the virtuousness of preachers' behavior on and off the preaching stage (see Hirschkind 2006, 130–37). In chapter 3, PERSIS's *fiqh*-based deliberations about Islamic communication are discussed. These problem-atize an excessive reliance on communicative skill and performance ability.

My final words on this group of terms concern competency. In some spaces of Islamic West Java there is a deeply held belief that a competent preacher should be an expert in the Islamic sciences. In other words, a per-son is qualified to preach if they belong to the learned class of Muslim lead-ers known as *kyai* in Java, *ajengan* in West Java, and *tuan guru* in Sumatra and Lombok.[2] In academic as well as popular representations, they are acknowledged as bearers of Islamic knowledge, who by necessity possess ver-bal communication skills in order to fulfill their roles as community leaders. Writing in the late 1950s, Clifford Geertz characterized this class as "cultural brokers" mediating both Islamic authority and postindependence modernity to Indonesia's Islamic communities. These men were "specialists in the communication of Islam to the mass of the peasantry" (Geertz 1960, 230). Although the archetype still bears enormous authority among listeners, especially in rural areas, contemporary preaching competencies suggest something different. Indonesians mostly enjoy preaching delivered by a class of Muslims who have received some training in the Islamic sciences and who generally self-represent in the form of *kyai* but whose basic capital lies in their skill in verbal performance.[3] Since Geertz presented his understanding, this class of specialists has flourished in forms and styles he could not have foreseen. He could not foresee, for example, the highly popular broadcasts of child preachers in reality television programs or the technologically sophis-ticated spirituality training popular in corporate environments (Rudnyckyj 2010). As I comment below in more detail, in contemporary Indonesia, *muballigh* rely on a broader range of skills in communication and performance than is encountered among the *kyai/ajengan*.[4]

Many Muslims prefer the terms in table 2 over those in table 1 as labels for describing preaching events. The preference for these terms has emerged as Indonesians have progressively come to value processes of individual learning more highly than "mere" listening. The value of Islamic education as an individual and social good became particularly apparent in two spe-cific moments of change. In the early twentieth century, Islamic groups with reformist or modernizing programs made the acquisition of Islamic knowl-edge a priority for individual Muslims, partly because of an egalitarian view of Islamic knowledge that took issue with the mediating role of the clerical elites. According to this view, Islam was a straightforward religion capable

Table 2. Self-improvement: Preaching as learning

Term	Definition
pengajian	(Indonesian) A gathering held to study Islam. A wide variety of events in which Muslims study and develop skills are labeled *pengajian*. It is frequently used as a label for preaching events with no explicit pedagogical or deliberative content.
(me)ngaji	(Indonesian) To study the Qur'an with a teacher.
kuliah	A university lecture, lesson. Although a loanword from Arabic, *kuliah* is commonly used in Indonesian to describe lectures and teaching taking place in nonreligious educational contexts. In contemporary Bandung, however, it is also used as a label for Islamic preaching/pedagogical events.
majlis taklim	Study gathering. This preaching/pedagogical context has shown rapid growth recently as a forum for participation by Indonesian women. It is not a new setting, having probably commenced in the circles of women members of genealogical elites early in the twentieth century (Doorn-Harder 2006; Alawiyah 1997). Since then, however, the *majlis taklim* has gained popularity across the social spectrum, especially with the more recent rise in public participation (see Marcoes 1988).
trening, studi, mentoring	These terms, borrowed from English, have been prestigious appellations for preaching events since the 1980s.

of being understood by all Muslims. Reformist groups such as PERSIS and Muhammadiyah promoted this principle and, in doing so, identified themselves as modern through their insistence that reflection and critical thinking were capabilities that all humans should attempt to cultivate.

The second moment was the epochal changes occurring after Indonesian independence. Mass education was among the highest priorities of the Sukarno governments (1945–66) as well as the New Order government that followed (1966–98). Dale Eickelman's (1992, 1998) account of coeval changes in the Arab world emphasizes the implications of these events for Islamic practice: widespread literacy increased Muslims' access to religious learning outside entrenched elites and stimulated the emergence of publications and media for new classes of readers. In conjunction with the uptake of mass communications technologies, literacy enabled the emergence of new styles of Islamic authority. These changes provide the background for the more recent phenomenon commonly described as the *kebangkitan Islam* (Islamic Resurgence). By the 1990s individualized projects of Qur'anic study and performance were so popular that anthropologist Anna Gade described them as "a new kind of educational movement that was sweeping Indonesia" (2004, 21). These movements idealized an individualized subjectivity that could be empowered through study; compared with this idealization, the collective implications of the earlier terms made them unattractive.

Bandung has been the location for projects that projected these novel understandings of Islamic learning (Rosyad 2006). The Salman/ITB movement, which caught national attention in the 1970s, was the most significant of these for its pioneering of new Islamic learning styles. Its intellectual leader was Imaduddin Abdulrahim (1931–2008), whose experience in the global Muslim student movement had given him knowledge of the Islamic education programs of organizations such as Egypt's Muslim Brotherhood. As a faculty member of the Bandung Institute of Technology (ITB), he oversaw the development of novel programs in the institute's mosque, known as Salman. Indonesian students were beginning to embrace an Islamic social identity and attended the programs in large numbers. The Salman movement's programs, in their appellations as well as substance, implied that Indonesian Muslims were individuals with potential to be developed for the benefit of the nation and that Islam provided the tools and motivations for this development. In accordance with this understanding, Salman followers were encouraged to engage positively with technology and science and to consider these as forming an integral part of Islamic revelation (Abdulrahim 2002, 70–104). Its programs, which spread throughout Indonesia through Salman's caderization program, were given English titles such as "mental training," "*dakwah* management," "mentoring," and "intensive study" (Rosyad 2006). This was not the audience for the traditional *kyai*, who relied on recognition of his scholarly authority as the bedrock of his competence. Salman/ITB programs resembled communications between equals rather than virtuoso displays by privileged mediators.

The Salman programs created waves even for Muslims not attracted to them because preaching events that did not have learning as their substantive aim were recalibrated as learning experiences. In some settings, the processes of relabeling are striking. The privately owned educational institution known as Siraman Iman (A Sprinkling of Faith), discussed in chapter 3, provides pay-for-entry Islamic instruction to wealthy residents of Bandung and is overwhelmingly patronized by women. Its premises are described as a "campus," and its programs are advertised with names such as intensive Islamic study (*kajian* Islam *intensif*), day classes (*kelas siang*), and training (*trening*). These events are thick with the trappings of contemporary pedagogical styles such as whiteboards, overhead projectors, and printed study materials. These trappings are clearly important tools that enable the institution to present itself as a center for serious study, but the success of the program I attended relied on the brilliant skills of the institute's orators. The presenter gave a compelling, energetic, and stimulating preaching performance to an audience for whom the word *pengajian* is more palatable than *tabligh*. This example not only signals the instability of the labels used for naming and promoting preaching events. It also demonstrates how oratory retains its value for Bandung Muslims. Siraman Iman packages oratorical skill in forms suitable to a specific niche of the Bandung community.

"*Dakwah*" is the label given to the pronounced surges of Islam into the public sphere occurring since the 1960s (table 3). The movement includes programs of Islamically informed change that implied differing meanings for contrasting Islamic segments.[5] For social scientists, *dakwah* was an umbrella theme for Islamically based projects of political and social development as well as a framework for dealing with social change that appeared to threaten the fabric of Indonesian society. For the government, it became a legitimizing tag for development goals. For politically oriented activists, it was a movement for bolstering Islam's presence in social life and the political sphere, ideally by working in partnership with a similarly committed government. For unspecialized *dakwah* audiences, the increasing volume and frequency of Islamic messages meant a broadening range of cultural forms for experiencing them.

The *dakwah* moment brought oratorical practice into the critical spotlight and gave rise to two incompatible trajectories. On the one hand, the forms for expressing and participating in Islam expanded in number and became more accessible; on the other, the conception of *dakwah* as a motivation for serious programs of reform and transformation gathered strength. These two trajectories, which I trace in the following pages, offer conflicting visions of how Islamic mediations should be performed and of the ends they should serve.

Table 3. Dakwah: The call to Islam

Term	Definition
dakwah	The call, invitation or challenge to Islam. This term came into broad usage in the early 1960s when reform movements, emulating Middle-Eastern models, introduced it as a label for predication and Islamisation programs. The term was widely known by Indonesian Muslims before then, for it appears in frequently cited Qur'anic verses on the topic of predication (Al-Nahl 125 and Al 'Imran 104). In the 1960s, however, its frequent use to describe Islamization projects was novel. M. Dawam Rahardjo identifies a dakwah workshop held by the Himpunan Mahasiswa Islam (HMI: Muslim Students' Association) in 1962 as the starting point (Rahardjo 1993, 158–67), whereas Anwar Harjono ([1996] 2000, xii) names Muhammad Natsir as the person who introduced the term into common use. Harjono ([1996] 2000) and B. J. Boland (1971, 193) suggest the term *dakwah* was introduced specifically as a replacement for *tabligh*, which was thought to be outmoded because its literal meaning, "conveyance," suggested predication forms that were too limited for the expanded possibilities aspired to at that time.
dai, pendakwah	A preacher (literally, one who invites). Some Bandung Muslims understand the *dai* to differ from the *muballigh* because the *dai*'s predication is not limited to verbal communication but is expressed in a wide range of forms, including acts of piety (*amal*) that might have no explicit communicative element.
siar (Indonesian)	Literally, "broadcast," but also "spreading" and "propaganda." This term emerged prominently in public forums involving government and Islamic leaders of the early New Order period (see Ali et al. 1971; Pusat Da'wah 1972). A key topic in these discussions was the extent and nature of the role of the state in a phase of history characterized by the sudden demise of the left (in 1966) and by the emergence of mass media, notably television, which was launched in Indonesia in 1963. The discussions reveal a strong willingness on the part of the government to contribute to the *penyiaran* (spreading) of Islam, and they also disclose a higher governmental priority— achievement of development goals.

Table 3. (continued)

Term	Definition
publisistik (Indonesian from Dutch)	In Dutch, *publicistiek* means mass media. Like *siar*, this term appealed to dakwah actors of the 1960s who envisaged that Islamic mediations would materialize in newly emerging forms of public communication. Hence, one of the first dakwah faculties to emerge in Indonesia's State Islamic University system (in Aceh) was named Fakultas Dakwah dan Publisistik. The word *publisistik* has been replaced in common usage by *media massa* and *komunikasi*.

An important background to the first trajectory is the low social cachet of Islam in the two decades following Indonesian independence in 1945. Aspirational classes in the larger cities were not attracted to Islam as a cultural affiliation. Politics had much to do with this, for Islamic political parties of the time dealt in Islamic symbols and ideas that appealed to heartland communities rather than to the sensibilities of contemporary, forward-looking Indonesians (Madjid 1987). In the segments of society where preaching events were regular occurrences, the preaching stage was a site for political campaigning. In West Java, where support for Islamic movements and political parties had been high throughout the twentieth century, politician-preachers were prominent on preaching stages. The best known of these were the Minangkabau M. Isa Anshary (1916–69) and the Sundanese E. Z. Muttaqien (1925–85).

Developments in Indonesian politics killed the preaching stage as a site for party-political contest, especially in 1973, when the Suharto government prohibited all Islamically motivated political initiatives except for those of one party, the United Development Party (PPP). Government largesse for Islamic education was channeled to institutions supporting Golkar, the pro-regime party that achieved dominance through an electoral system rigged to minimize opposition. West Javanese religious leaders supporting the PPP instead of Golkar ran the risk of isolating their communities from development programs, depriving them of important economic and infrastructure development opportunities (Hadad 1998).[6]

As a result, the preaching stage's value as a political platform diminished, but this does not mean that preaching events declined in frequency or scale.

Many key orators acquiesced to Golkar's political hegemony. Rural communities were enjoying increasing prosperity at this time as a result of agricultural
innovations and were thus able to divert more of their resources to life-cycle
and calendrical celebrations. According to the preacher described in the
opening pages of this book, Abdurrahman, the combination of increased
prosperity and depoliticization brought important changes to the nature of
oratorical mediations of Islam, enabling an expanding range of possibilities.
Abdurrahman, who has a pleasant baritone voice, first experimented with
bringing music into his *dakwah* during the 1980s; he told me he may have
been the first orator to bring a guitar on stage. Radio broadcasts of Islamic
orations by the government-owned broadcaster spread the unique styles of
individual orators to mass audiences. A competitive preaching environment
in which skill and artifice were valued commodities was taking shape.[7]

This turn to diversity in religious communication was a national phenomenon. In the 1970s and 1980s, public displays of Islamic piety began to
appear in segments of society that had previously worn their Islamic identities lightly, notably students and the bureaucracy. The New Order government encouraged public piety in its efforts to channel Muslim support to its
development programs. Displays of Islamic piety were no longer restricted
to the *santri* (scholarly devotees) (Frederick 1982; Muzakki 2008; *Tempo* 1978;
Tempo 1992). As institutions and individuals responded to this expansion of
public piety, the range of preaching situations multiplied. In the words of
Charles Hirschkind (2006, 55), "The revival . . . had the effect of dispersing
the loci of religious authority across a variety of new locations, media, and
associational forms." Performers with established reputations as actors, puppeteers, musicians, and comedians were being accepted by audiences as
muballigh. The poet and dramatist Rendra, for example, began to give
Islamic orations in the early 1990s to small, well-heeled crowds in expensive
hotels, as did his former wife, Sitoresmi Prabuningrat (Millie 2010; *Tempo*
1992, 14). In Bandung, performers crossed genre boundaries to become
muballigh. Kang Ibing, already established as a comedian in the highly
successful group De Kabayans, commenced a new career giving sermons at
weddings and circumcisions and found success with his *dakwah*-themed
radio broadcasting. High profile stars of *wayang golék* (rod-puppet theater)
gave performances at life-cycle celebrations not only as puppeteers with
their puppets and musical ensembles but also as solo orators on religious
topics (*Cupumanik* 2009).

The second trajectory emerging in the *dakwah* period, however, problematized Muslims' enthusiasm for competency diversification. For some *dakwah* organizations, activists, scholars, and commentators, the extremely popular, accessible oratorical mediations were a sign that something was going wrong. They argued that if Islam were to achieve a wider and more substantive relevance in Indonesian society, the concept of *dakwah* should indeed be broadened, but not in the direction of a pluralization of oratorical competencies. Rather, *dakwah* should materialize in practical good works and programs of social development, and the exploitation of new media forms should support these activities. *Dakwah* called for practical action, not just clever speaking. Writings of the time—for example, those of Natsir—commonly emphasize that oratory, or *da'wah bi al-lisan* (Arabic: *dakwah* with the tongue) is merely one outlet for *dakwah*. He points to other *dakwah* forms such as *da'wah bi al-hal* (through action) and *da'wah bi al-qalam* (through the pen) (Natsir [1996] 2000). In effect, while oratorical mediations were diversifying and attracting broader audiences, some activists were arguing that oratory should be removed from its central position in popular understandings of *dakwah* (see also Achmad 1983; Omar 1967).

Yet the advocates of the idea that *dakwah* should go beyond talking could do nothing about one key aspect of the *dakwah* story, and that is the increasing audience heterogeneity developing during the period. As the increase in public support for Islamic messages increased, the audiences for them became more heterogeneous. This trend is evident across the Muslim world (for Egypt, see Bayat 2007; for Mali, see Schulz 2011). Many of the audiences I joined in Bandung were made up of Muslims holding to a wide range of potentially conflicting Islamic positions. Successful interaction with such an audience requires the preacher to work with Islamic materials that are broadly acceptable. This imperative is a reality of much contemporary Bandung preaching and was made emphatically clear by one preacher who told me that mosque committees, concerned that their event should appeal to all audience members, frequently specified in advance the themes they would prefer him to deal with. The most commonly requested theme, he told me, was *akhlaq* (moral qualities of the human character). No listener would object to a sermon on how desirable Islamic characteristics could be developed in people. For his part, if this flattening out of subject matter were to be a condition for a successful oration, he was more than happy to comply with it.

Audience heterogeneity has also increase the value of novelty in Islamic communication, for heterogeneous audiences respond to sermons expressed in forms that are contemporary and appealing. The workplace spirituality program implemented in 2004 in Krakatau Steel is illustrative (Rudnyckyj 2010, 74–93). The program involves workers in a sequence of activities including a highly affective, two-hour multimedia representation of the experience of death. This spirituality training was taken up enthusiastically by corporations because they perceived it to have potential in shaping Islamic subjects who would understand performance of work duties as a form of *ibadah* (Islamic worship). At the same time, the highly contemporary forms of the program clearly were a key to its success. Bandung's preaching celebrity, Aa Gym, introduced earlier, was a pioneer of this kind of mediation, succeeding through his skillful communication of broadly acceptable Islamic messages in forms registering positively against contemporary cultural dispositions.

The uneasy contrast between these two trajectories expresses the fundamental dilemma explored in what follows. More people than ever are participating in the circulation of Islamic messages, signaling the broad support for *dakwah* as a popular Islamic project. Yet this high participation has emerged while Islamic communications have more and more come to resemble nonreligious communication styles and to deliver Islamic outlooks that, while acceptable to all, lack the program-oriented commitment to which the change-oriented *dakwah* trajectory aspires.

One of the major political reforms implemented in Indonesia after the fall of Suharto in 1998 was the regional autonomy program (table 4). During the Suharto era, appointments to positions of authority in the regions were made by the central government. Since 2004 Indonesians have elected leaders at provincial and municipal/regency levels, which has meant an increase in the accountability of regional officials to those who elected them. Yet Indonesians remain critical and cynical about the quality and commitment of their elected representatives and public servants largely because of the prevalence of corruption among them. Against that background, governments in provinces with high Muslim populations such as West Java consider religious programs not only as important tools for increasing the quality of their service and reducing corruption; they also function as statements to voters about the government's Islamically motivated commitment to these goals. To some degree, the orations provided for state employees in workplaces and in state-owned

Table 4. Governmental visions

Term	Definition
pencerahan	(Indonesian) Enlightenment, illumination.
pembinaan	(Indonesian) Cultivation, pastoral care. The term implies that listeners can be shaped as ethical subjects through exposure to Islamic mediations. The Bandung municipal government's recent program for creation of a "religious Bandung" (see Millie and Safei 2010) includes the following activity: "Routine religious cultivation [*pembinaan*] for all civil servants" (Walikota et al. 2009, 110). In this program, municipal employees are required to attend sermons in their workplaces and in the mosques owned by the municipal government.
peningkatan	(Indonesian) Raising, increase. In the fasting month of 2009, provincial-level civil servants in West Java participated in a program of religious activities that included sermons. The head of human resources for the province explained the program to the West Javanese newspaper, *Pikiran Rakyat*; "These sermons are not just a spiritual watering [*siraman rohani*], but are also a form of cultivation [*pembinaan*] directed at civil servants to increase [*meningkatkan*] their discipline and mental quality" (*Pikiran Rakyat*, August 27, 2009).
pembekalan	(Indonesian) Provisioning, equipping. A recent publication of the provincial government's measures for improving work performance by civil servants mentioned two programs in which well-known Bandung *muballigh* participate: the *pembekalan wawasan keagamaan* (equipping with religious insight) and *pembekalan kecerdasan sosial* (equipping with social intelligence) (Supratman 2008).

mosques are symbolic performances in which Islam, in Gregory Starrett's words (1998), is "put to work" for the sake of managing public perceptions. At the same time, they are also indications of emerging conceptions of Islam's public value. As Indonesians' understanding of their dependence on global economic conditions for their livelihoods grows, quality performance of work obligations is being represented and interpreted as an Islamic obligation (see Rudnyckyj 2010).

All the nouns in table 4 are nominal forms of transitive verbs. They presuppose Islamic oratory and other observances as processes of improvement or enhancement acting upon listening subjects, a paradigm that resonates strongly with the ethical sedimentation experienced by members of Cairo's *dakwah* counterpublics after repeated oratorical listening (Hirschkind 2006, 67–104). From the government's perspective, this paradigm is attractive because of the positive effects it promises. Gains in service and honesty are sought by challenging workers to act in accordance with their shared Islamic ethical aspirations.

The workplace programs also demonstrate an important quality of Bandung's career preachers—their adaptability. Some of the government programs are pastoral measures aimed at specific vulnerabilities and needs in the workplace and require mediation by professionals with knowledge of those vulnerabilities and needs. Capable *muballigh* can provide this specialized mediation. I once attended a two-day event intended to prepare retiring civil servants for life after leaving government service. The speaker was Abdurrahman, the preacher featured in the opening paragraphs of this book. Although his career had been built on preaching success in more conventional religious settings, it was no problem for him to assume the role of personal development advisor. He convincingly imparted advice in the manner of a life coach, delivering a motivating presentation that succeeded by representing Islamic norms and concepts as empowering tools for visualizing opportunities lying ahead in the next phase of the lives of his audience of retirees. His success in this illustrates preachers' abilities to absorb recent developments in Islam's social meanings and to adapt them to the specific needs of situation.

Many Bandung Muslims are skeptical about the sincerity of governmental preaching programs. From one perspective, the programs support regimes of observance that are standard fare for West Javanese Islamic life. It seems natural and proper that governments should support pious routines through direct funding of preaching and other programs such as the grants made available for religious celebrations and—more controversially—grants to Islamic civil society organizations. Yet on several occasions I was told that preaching programs and grants for Islamic organizations were tools for candidates and incumbents to channel funds to Islamic leaders from whom they hoped to obtain political support. Where the program was delivered by an incumbent, the funds quite often came from social development budgets that should be free from political interests. The mayor of Bandung between 2003 and 2013, Dada Rosada, was famously sentenced in

2014 to ten years in jail for a bribe paid to a judge hearing a case against his subordinates concerning misuse of social assistance funds. Rosada had spent large sums on a consultative program involving religious groups in Bandung (Millie and Safei 2010, 2016). Friends and colleagues in Bandung did not oppose government support for Islamic observance but were disappointed by the waste of large sums on Rosada's attempts to secure his political future.

Chapter 2

THE UNIQUE VOICE . . . AND ITS TRAVAILS

My fieldwork in Bandung consisted, for the most part, of accompanying preachers as they fulfilled their engagements. I frequently accompanied Kyai Haji Al-Jauhari, who was at the time of my fieldwork (and is still at the time of writing) the most popular preacher among West Javanese village audiences. Most of the invitations he received were for celebratory situations, especially life-cycle festivities and the feast days of the Islamic calendar. His popularity has made him the first choice for mosque committees desiring a good attendance from the communities they represent. When word spreads that Al-Jauhari will mount the stage, crowds of five thousand or more are common. His popularity has created a widespread demand for cassettes and videos of his sermons, and he also appears frequently on regional and sometimes on national television. His style has also generated a negative discourse; on several occasions people warned me that I should not make a case study of his style because it was not a proper reflection of Islamic preaching. I explore the reasons for this in what follows.

At the same time as I was accompanying Al-Jauhari, I routinely attended a preaching event held every Sunday morning by PERSIS at the Viaduct Mosque in central Bandung. The Sunday Study, as I call it here, is well attended by crowds ranging from three thousand to more than six thousand, depending on the orator rostered to appear. PERSIS owns other mosques and religious schools in West Java at which similar events are held. The organization has quite a large public presence in Bandung and West Java, and some of its preachers are frequent contributors to public discourse. The PERSIS preacher whose oration is analyzed here, Shiddiq Amien, had achieved a level of public recognition that extended wider than the PERSIS constituency alone. His opinions and comments, along with those of other PERSIS figures living and dead, circulate through the province's electronic and print media.

Muslims in Bandung refer to Al-Jauhari and Amien by the same terms— *muballigh* or *dai*—but their oratorical mediations of Islam differ greatly. From their position on the celebratory stage, Al-Jauhari and other preachers like him create sermons out of a wide range of cultural materials and references within the knowledge of their audiences. They communicate affect by mobilizing many voices, languages, and registers, and by calling upon many genres of verbal performance, not all of them religious. Some of them can recite and sing Al-Qur'an with skill and emotion. Others are captivating storytellers, frequently narrating in Sundanese, a language that opens the sermon up to the everyday realities of village life. Some can sing in secular genres and perform popular songs as well as religious melodies. They replay voices that the audience members recognize instantly from their own knowledge of local and national media and culture. Others bring physical theater and mimicry into their performances. Some specialize in risqué double entendre. Audiences welcome the bravura, color, boldness, and moving capacities of these performances, which frequently create that quality of *ramai* (busy festivity) appreciated widely in Indonesian social life. In short, preachers like Al-Jauhari clearly *perform* for their listeners, and many of them have developed reputations based on specific performance skills by which audiences distinguish them among the range of preachers in West Java.

In contrast, PERSIS preachers display a limited range of communication skills. Beside the heteroglossia of the performances I observed on the celebratory stage, PERSIS orations are restrained and orderly. I did not hear an

orator sing at the Viaduct events, nor did I observe a PERSIS preacher singing verses of the Qur'an, although all are comfortable reciting them without
melody. They seldom invoke nonreligious genres. They frequently preach in
Indonesian, a language more suggestive of officialdom and civic life than
Sundanese. Body movements by preacher and audience are minimal, and a
general lack of animation is considered proper. PERSIS audiences do not
expect dynamic performances from their preachers and they consider a measured and subdued sermon to be appropriate. They do not evaluate their
orators for their virtuosity as speakers and performers.

Considered together, Al-Jauhari and Amien provide a comparative
template for the examination in this chapter and the two that follow. It is
emphasized throughout that Al-Jauhari and Amien have much in common
as preachers, for they rely on preaching abilities displayed by all career
preachers in West Java. But, at the same time, their styles signal contrasting
agreements between orators and audiences about what is acceptable preaching practice. The comparison to follow enables an exploration of the relations between distinctiveness in preaching voices and public conceptions of
propriety.

It was humor that first alerted me to the simultaneous resemblance and
difference exemplified by Al-Jauhari and Amien. All preachers in Bandung
create some level of humor among their audiences, almost always by reproducing voices familiar to their audiences from their experiences outside Islamic contexts. Some preachers told me they do this as part of their ongoing
surveillance of the audience for signs of attention fatigue. They monitor
back-channel cues from the audience, especially listeners' body language and
posture, and use humor as a refreshing strategy when they notice that audience attention is flagging.[1]

This strategy raises questions relating to whether and to what extent it
should be constrained: What limits should be imposed on refreshing strategies? How prominent should they be? What sort of genres may be mobilized as refreshing strategies, and which should not? If a refreshing strategy
in the form of a joke is successful, should the preacher continue with another,
or should he or she restore seriousness to the performance? Is audience
laughter a good outcome? Should the preacher diligently protect his image
as a learned Muslim, or should he invite evaluation from the audiences as a
comedic performer? And, most crucially for the comparison explored here,

is it really a problem if audience attention is flagging? Must flagging attention be addressed with recuperative strategies?

Al-Jauhari and Amien are distinguished here by the contrasting ways in which they respond to questions of this kind. West Javanese audiences also recognize these distinctions and act on them. They issue repeat invitations to preachers because of their prior knowledge of their styles, which means that the inviting committee and the invited preacher are in prior agreement about the level of respect to be shown to norms that constrain preaching performance. Audiences know Al-Jauhari as a preacher with a unique style characterized by his virtuosity in a wide variety of performance genres.

An analyst could map diverse preaching styles against the situations in which they find favor. Al-Jauhari could be considered as a preacher for festive contexts, for example. Amien appealed to a number of audiences but was perhaps most closely associated with Bandung's Islamist demographic. But a simple account of correspondences between style and situation would give a far from adequate understanding of how normative constraints affect preaching in West Java. After an extended period of attendance at Al-Jauhari's preaching events, I saw that his sermons included negotiations and mediation around concepts of oratorical propriety (Bauman and Briggs 1990, 66–72). Al-Jauhari defends himself against negative conclusions that are implied by these norms, something which PERSIS preachers never did. They did not seem to be worried by whatever it was that compelled Al-Jauhari to plead his case. PERSIS preachers do not obviously attempt to manage audience impressions, but they are also not known as distinctive preaching voices.

In this chapter and in chapter 3, two differing conceptions of appropriate performance are described and contextualized, referring to two representative sermons by Al-Jauhari and Amien. The same methodological path is followed in both chapters—the comparison of three features of the oratorical styles of both men. The first of these features is generic variation, meaning the intertextuality and polyphony generated by orators' use of languages, dialects, registers, speech act types, performance genres, ways of speaking, existing texts, and discursive structures.[2] The second feature is the preachers' skillful deployment of affective strategies, with particular attention to their communication of affect in their translations and mediations of Qur'anic and hadith materials. Both preachers rely on affect to maintain audience support while doing these things, but the difference between their approaches illustrates the gulf between their understandings of successful oratory. The third feature is the reflexivity that enables preachers to establish sympathetic dialogue with their listeners. Both preachers put effort into maintaining an ongoing conversation with their listeners, speaking to them directly and calling for expressions of commitment from them. By doing this, they establish and affirm a shared position *about* the ongoing interaction. Once again, however, the contrasting positions established in this metacommentary reveal much about the diversity of preaching styles accepted in West Java.

The analysis does not merely point out differences under these three heads; it connects the differences to Al-Jauhari's defensiveness and Amien's comfort about their respective preaching styles. These contrasting dispositions are a product of an Islamic public sphere that attributes different levels of social power to their oratorical styles.

A West Javanese Favorite

The community-based committees appointed to organize celebrations of Islamic feasts in contemporary Bandung are generally worried about the low rate of mosque-attendance among younger members of their communities. Because their mosques were constructed by the effort and sacrifice of ancestors, it is understandable that the level of patronage of the mosques is a major community preoccupation. Al-Jauhari offers a solution to this problem through his ability to attract capacity audiences to preaching events. The public's recognition and enjoyment of Al-Jauhari's unique style translates into high attendances, which are, of course, good outcomes for their organizational efforts.

He is also a favored choice for weddings and circumcisions, events that frequently extend over two or three days. At these events a sermon by Al-Jauhari is often the high point of a program that typically includes a *dangdut* concert and, if hosts are willing to spend very large sums, a *wayang golék* performance. In many cases, the host of such an event is bringing him back to a village where he has already appeared; he estimates that it is normal for him to receive up to twelve repeat invitations before a village turns to another preacher. Al-Jauhari is also a favored preacher for the West Java branch of Golkar, a major nationalist-oriented political party, and often preaches and leads prayer at the party's meetings. Mindful of his popularity with village audiences, a candidate of the party invited him in 2007 to join his *tim sukses* (campaign team), booking him in blocks of one month, during which campaign speeches were held on every night in the villages of the electorate. On some nights, the *tim sukses* also included a *dangdut* singer and band. These events consisted of performances by Al-Jauhari and the *dangdut* singer followed by an address by the candidate.[3]

Al-Jauhari's name is widely recognized in West Java. When using public transport, I often chatted with people about my project and found that most of them would name Al-Jauhari as their favorite preacher. Taxi drivers expressed very high levels of approval. Communications technologies have had a role in spreading his name. For a long time he has had contractual agreements for the manufacture and sale of sound recordings of his sermons. While these products are authorized, others are not. In the bus terminals and busy thoroughfares of Bandung, many DVD-sellers sell unauthorized video recordings of his performances alongside unauthorized videos of performances by popular *wayang golék* groups. Al-Jauhari welcomes the benefit his reputation receives from the circulation of the recordings of his sermons.

Al-Jauhari's reputation as a unique voice among preachers has allowed him to attain a privileged position in the economy within which high-profile preachers operate. It is common for him to fulfill three engagements a day, each of which last about seventy minutes. For each engagement he receives a large sum of money, which does not all come from villagers' pockets, as committees raise money from sponsorship and receive subsidies from a division of the municipal government that offers grants for religious activities.[4] Committees also circulate a donation box through the audience and—because Al-Jauhari's audiences are typically large, often including visitors from neighboring villages—the accumulated donations can add up to a large amount.

A typical Al-Jauhari event takes place in a broad, open space such as a football stadium, streetscape, or mosque yard. The committee erects a stage about one meter high and hires a powerful sound system. Some seating is provided for selected guests, but most of the audience sits on the ground, often bringing a mat or newspaper to sit on. Events are well publicized in advance with banners and notices that generate a sense of anticipation not just in the village where the celebration is to be held but also in surrounding villages. In this way, the events provide opportunities to meet and socialize, and the host or committee adds to the festive ambience by encouraging a spirited, busy atmosphere. People are prepared to make sacrifices to experience an Al-Jauhari event. It was not uncommon for people to walk more than five kilometers from neighboring villages to attend and then to walk home again the same night.

Al-Jauhari's Generic Variation

Appendix A presents an excerpt from a typical Al-Jauhari performance, given at a wedding celebration in Sumedang, a town about one hour's drive to the east of Bandung. This was a large-scale celebration, and Al-Jauhari, whose performance lasted for seventy minutes, was the third of three *muballigh* to take the stage. Sermons delivered at wedding celebrations are generally referred to as *tawsiyah* (Arabic, advice), and are expected to contain education and encouragement on the topic of marriage. Al-Jauhari's sermon on this night was no exception and was rich in admonishments, Qur'anic referencing and instructions on that theme.

Yet his performance also succeeded, as usual, through its amazing generic variety and multivocality. He usually uses Sundanese as the dominant language, but he frequently uses Arabic (for referencing Qur'an and hadith) and Indonesian. The sermon also switches at times to the Jakarta-centered youth language, *bahasa gaul* (language of sociability), and occasional snippets of English appear. He summons registers and styles associated with social spaces familiar for his listeners, such as the voice-over styles of advertising, the characteristic tones of Islamic admonitions, mechanical sounds, the romantic dialogue of television drama, the enfeebled voices of old people, the question-and-answer forms of pedagogy, and even "texting language." Many of these styles are introduced through the reported speech of men (and women) in his replays of (imagined) conversational exchanges. He uses these voices to introduce outlandish and hilarious scenarios. These imagined dialogues are rich in mimicry, caricature, and parodic stylizing of male and female voices.

The most striking example of his use of multivocality is his summoning of performance genres. His performances of songs in contemporary and traditional styles—Sundanese, Arabic, and Indonesian—have become his trademark. They amaze audiences because of the studio-like quality he gives to them. Listeners also find his singing of Qur'anic verses highly moving. Genres of Sundanese talk such as *kirata* (folk etymologies), *pelesetan* (wordplay), contrived acronyms, and proverbs also fill his sermons. Al-Jauhari moves between all these materials with rapid speed, compelling listeners to focus their attention intensely on the performance. Listeners arrive early, climb trees, and crane their necks to establish and maintain visual contact with the stage.

He carefully manages his intertextuality to match the range of cultural competencies present in the audience, but not everyone can be catered for all the time, however, and he works hard to mitigate the risk that segments of his audience will lose their commitment to his oratory. The ways in which he does this highlight an important element of his style: Al-Jauhari does not merely communicate messages; he also strives to maintain a relationship of close and ongoing mutual attention, something that requires continuous effort on his part. This comes out clearly in the metacommentary that buffers his performance of profane songs. Al-Jauhari's sermons always include songs from the popular charts. In doing so he invites a high level of audience identification with the content of his sermons, but his use of such contemporary material puts him at risk of alienating older people who form a substantial segment of his audience. Al-Jauhari reflects on this risk in performance and employs tricks to mitigate it. After singing a song that heavily references national youth culture (see appendix A, segment 22), he points to a section of his audience and says: "That grandma looks confused. 'What song is that?' she asks." A short while later (see appendix A, segment 44), after another Indonesian song, he says, "That grandma looks confused again! She doesn't know the song! That song is 'Dealova,' ladies; the singer is Once."

Listeners find these comments very funny. His acknowledgment of generational difference and its gentle mockery delight the entire audience. The metacommentary affectionately points out the older generation's disconnection from contemporary Indonesian culture but, at the same time, is a very inclusive move in their direction. They feel acknowledged while being gently teased for the amusement of all. His strategies pay dividends in the establishment of a close and satisfying interaction between himself and his audience. He works hard to establish and maintain an interactive frame within which he and his audience will together enjoy the generic variation that defines his performance style.

Mediating the Qur'an with Affect

Al-Jauhari's entextualizations of the Qur'an account in large part for his popularity, for they are among the most affective parts of his sermon. Entextualization takes place when a stretch of language is lifted out of an interactional setting and recontextualized in another (Bauman and Briggs 1990, 72–78). When West Javanese *muballigh* entextualize the Qur'an and hadith in their orations, audiences accept this as a sign of their competency as Islamic authorities. They frequently nest their entextualizations within attractive structures to maintain audience commitment. Al-Jauhari is outstanding in this regard; his quotations of Arabic texts are densely multivocal passages in which his performance skills take center stage. I focus on two of the skills he uses in the following paragraphs—melodic performance and the communication of affect through reported speech.

Appendix A is a narrative retelling based on the Qur'an. In keeping with the theme of the situation, the event narrated is the first ever marriage—namely, that between Adam and Hawa (Eve), which Al-Jauhari embellishes with all sorts of apocryphal touches.[5] The Qur'anic verses that relate the story are entextualized within the narrative retelling (appendix A, segments 34, 35, 51, and 55). Reduced to a basic narrative sequence, Al-Jauhari's retelling is as follows: Allah grants the Prophet Adam and Hawa a place in heaven. Allah informs Adam that he may remain in heaven as long as he refrains from going near the Tree of Eternity. Iblis (the devil) introduces himself to Adam and tries to entice him to eat the fruit of the tree. He refuses, so Iblis corrupts Hawa, who then uses her feminine wiles to convince Adam to climb the tree and pick the fruit. He does so, and they eat it. Allah expels them from heaven and separates the couple. Adam repents over a period of two hundred years and is then reunited with Hawa.

This narrative is a lesson in Islamic *shariah* relating to marriage, which Al-Jauhari uses as a template for admonitions about the moral values associated with marriage. The passage is, therefore, highly didactic. At the same time, however, the retelling is thick with performances that draw on Al-Jauhari's verbal artistry. Expertly executed Qur'anic vocalizations are prominent in this performance. The sermon opens with such a recitation, where he performs several verses from the Qur'anic Adam-Hawa narrative (appendix A, segment 6). He does not hurry through this performance but takes his time, demonstrating the range of expression that skillful performers develop over years of training. The audience responds in the conventional way by uttering the response "Al-lah" (the second syllable is elongated) during the pauses between phrases. With these recitations, he successfully imports a revered performance genre into the frame of oratory.

This crossing of borders is notable because of the skills required to achieve it successfully. In West Java, the class of expert Qur'anic singers, known as *qori*, is separate from the *muballigh* class. In celebrations of the kind at which Al-Jauhari speaks, the Qur'anic recitation is usually performed by a specialist who utters no words other than the sacred text before leaving the stage. The separate specialist performance of the recitation reflects West Javanese Muslims' highly tuned sensibilities for evaluating *qori*. The Qur'an and its performance are studied throughout the childhood of many Sundanese, and many adults continue their study as an act of piety and a means of personal improvement (see, generally, Gade 2004). Only accomplished reciters perform before audiences as big as those that Al-Jauhari appears before. He is rare among preachers in that he is accepted as *qori* as well as *muballigh*, and his blend of the competencies of both distinguishes him as a unique voice and allows him to provide his audience with a moving and striking opening.

The melodic Qur'anic performances are received with solemn appreciation by the audience, but a wholly different affect is created through his three replays of conversational dialogue (appendix A, segments 35, 36–38, 42–48), which bring on an atmosphere of excited levity. Quotations of Qur'anic verses nest inside, or lie directly adjacent to, these dialogues, and for this reason, the audience remains aware that the passages are intended as a *shariah* lesson at the same time as they are shocked and delighted by the three striking and rapid relocations of the narrating voice.[6] They are performed in specific speech registers and interlocutory relationships with which the audience intimately identifies. Iblis's attempt to seduce Adam, for example, is introduced in the language conventional for the introductions that occur when newcomers come into a neighborhood and when students meet in a dormitory. Such communications would frequently unfold in the national language, Indonesian, because of the necessity for interethnic communication implicit in such encounters. The following translation (see appendix A, segments 36–37) involves three languages. Underlined text indicates the use of Indonesian in the sermon. The Arabic Qur'anic fragments are untranslated and rendered in italics. The regular font indicates Sundanese, the dominant language of the sermon:

The Prophet Adam went right on enjoying his life together with Eve. That's the meaning of *uskun anta. Uskun* means living a peaceful life, we can also call it *sakinah*. While the prophet Adam was enjoying paradise, along comes Satan. If we tell this as a story it could go like this:

"Hi, what's your name?"

"Adam."

"And you?"

"Eve."

"I'm Satan." [audience: laughter] "You are new residents here, aren't you?"

"Yes."

"I'm your senior," Satan said. "What are you doing here, Dam?" "I am free to do whatever I want. One thing is not allowed; approaching that tree."

In this exchange, Al-Jauhari mimics the polite casualness that would dictate the tone of such an encounter. It is a skillful translation of the Qur'an into an identifiable conversational register, conveying its emotive-affective aspects through his full attention to the timbre and intonation of those recognizable voices. And his ability to move across voices knows no boundaries of gender, as Al-Jauhari shows in the following example. This is a dialogue in which Hawa seduces Adam into picking the fruit. It is performed in the voices of prime-time Indonesian romantic drama, and specifically its breathy romantic exchanges. Al-Jauhari's mimicry of these is a highly stylized one, being more breathy, more coy, more feminine, more alluring than the actual television dramas, and this infiltrates the caricatures with ironic intent. The parodies tap into shared emotional dispositions, for they express the shallowness and general fallibility people recognize in the roles and characters of romantic drama. Hawa is caricatured as vain, and Adam as weakened by infatuation.[7] The reports succeed by confronting listeners with colorful images at once recognizable and humorous—the failings of humans affected by romantic love. Al-Jauhari's Hawa speaks with exaggerated femininity and feigned helplessness to a lover ready to forget propriety to satisfy his beloved:

After Eva was tempted, then Satan started to persuade Adam. If I tell it as a story, it could go like this:

"Adam, come here!"

"What's up, Honey?"

"Do you still love me?"

"Of course, I do, Eve. I love no woman but you."

Of course there weren't any other women then, just one [audience: laughter].

"If you really love me, <u>how do I appear to you?</u>"

If the Prophet Adam acted like a youngster of today, he might have sung it [like this]: [Indonesian pop song]

> <u>You are like a song in my heart</u>
> <u>That summons my longing for you, ooh . . .</u>
> <u>Like the air I inhale, you are always there, Ha . . . ha . . .</u>

That grandma looks confused again. She doesn't know the song! [audience: laughter]. That song is "Dealova," Grandma, the singer is Once.

Do you know everything, Al-Jauhari? <u>Hang out, man!</u> [Gaul, man!] <u>So what, that's how it is . . . !</u> [audience: laughter]

"If you really love me, prove your love for me!"

"How can I show my love to you? Do you want my life? Or can I give you the life of a duck?" [audience: laughter]

"No. I only want that fruit," said Eve. "I want you to pick that fruit for me."

"Don't ask me to pick that fruit. You know Allah has forbidden it. Ask for something else."

"No . . . I only want that. If you don't pick it for me, I will commit suicide. I will kill myself with a lost knife." [audience: laughter]

Of course, she won't die, will she? The thing is, if we tell it as a story, it's got to be like that, however it might unfold. Finally, the Prophet Adam gave up. (appendix A, segments 41–48)

This passage forms part of the shariah lesson, and the normative content is familiar for most listeners. But the didacticism of this passage has no banality for his audience, for listeners are treated to a succession of appropriations of other voices, each of which centers the narrating again into a recognizable situation that registers affectively with shared emotional dispositions. The succession of reported speeches holds listeners in suspense about the identity of the next voice or everyday situation they will encounter in the retelling. This is Al-Jauhari's skill: the narrative and lesson might be repetitions, but they are transformed into a gripping exercise in multivocality.

All West Javanese *muballigh* entextualize the Qur'an into their sermons, but few add value to their referencing by convincingly mobilizing so many other genres and cultural resources. This is what makes his preaching style unique. With his singing of Qur'anic verses, he invokes the deep and finely developed responsiveness of his audiences toward that mode of performance.

With his enactments of reported speech, he confronts the audience with recognizable but differing scenarios in quick succession, making the *shariah* lesson attractive and surprising.

An Audience in Thrall

Al-Jauhari cannot be confident of achieving success simply by reproducing his performance skills on stage. He also relies on careful management of the interaction as it unfolds. This was illustrated during a sermon delivered at a 2007 meeting of the executive of a political party. On that day, the sermon was to take place at the end of a day-long meeting of delegates from all over the province. This presented a difficult task, for it was the fasting month, during which sermons are frequently scheduled in the time leading up to the breaking of the daily fast. Hungry delegates, already tired from the meeting, were to sit and listen to a sermon of about forty-five minutes' duration. Nevertheless, by the time Al-Jauhari took up the microphone, the atmosphere was light and boisterous. The business part of the day was over, and the delegates were enjoying meeting up again with old friends and colleagues.

This audience, consisting of business people, public servants, military figures, and politicians, along with their spouses, was very receptive to Al-Jauhari's busy, multivoiced preaching style. As the sermon progressed, however, it was obvious that the attention of some audience members was moving away from the lectern. Quite a number had formed small groups within which they were chatting. A number were sending or reading text messages. Others were sitting in very relaxed body positions that suggested fatigue and lack of engagement with the sermon. I observed Al-Jauhari noticing these developments and detected anxiety in his demeanor. After sensing the direction in which the event was heading, Al-Jauhari began to sing a well-known Sundanese children's song about a frog in a rice paddy. Singing with strong rhythm, he left out key words and phrases, inviting the audience to sing these in his place. He pointed the microphone to the audience in the spaces created by his omissions. Attracted by the familiar melody and heavy rhythm, many of those who were chatting turned from their conversations and joined in the singing. With this move, the attention of the audience was once again centered on the preacher. After the conclusion of the performance, I confirmed my observations with Al-Jauhari; the drop in the audience's attention levels was a cue to which he had responded. He performed the song as a way of refreshing the audience and bringing the attention of its members back to him.

From Al-Jauhari's perspective, losing the attention of the audience is a failure that requires the implementation of strategies to regain it. In a successful performance, audience attention is totally focused on him, which gives another level of meaning to the displays of skill discussed earlier. They enable him to create a relationship of thralldom, summarized nicely in Bauman's classic article on performance: "It is part of the essence of performance that it offers to the participants a special enhancement of experience, bringing with it a heightened intensity of communicative interaction which binds the audience to the performer in a way that is specific to performance as a mode of communication. Through his performance, the performer elicits the participative attention and energy of his audience, and to the extent that they value his performance, they will allow themselves to be caught up in it" (Bauman 1977, 43).

But as the remedial strategy of singing the frog song indicates, the audience's total submission to the performance is not a given but is something that requires work. Situations will arise that require strategies for maintaining audience attention and commitment. Al-Jauhari's sermon is full of such strategies. His mediation of his performances of profane song has already been mentioned. Another example is something common in many pedagogical genres, especially those involving rote learning—the use of rhythm and rising intonation (indicated by the symbol ◄ in the passage below) to encourage audience members to complete phrases, a move that gives the audience a role in the event (italics indicate Arabic):

> I am sure you know the Prophet Adam's prayer for repentance, don't you? *Our Lord! We have wronged our* [audience: *selves*]. *If Thou do not forgive* ◄ [audience: *us*] *and have no mercy on* ◄ [audience: *us*] *surely* ◄ [audience: *we*] *are among the* ◄ [audience: *lost*]. (appendix A, segment 55; see also segments 9, 30 and 33)

Direct questions to the audience and requests to confirm the veracity of his statements are numerous. Humorous tricks are sometimes employed, one of his most successful being his conspicuous checking of his wristwatch, always after approximately thirty minutes on stage. When the audience, and especially its female members, observe this, they assume he is contemplating the end of the sermon and respond by shouting "No! Keep going!" His reply would inevitably be, "What? You say that because you are not tired. But I am tired, for I am the one up here on top!" motioning to the stage on which he sits. "Have you ever tried it on top ladies? Try it, you will see how tiring it is." Great mirth ensues. Humorous exchanges such as this one, contrived over a threat to the continuation of the performance, enable Al-Jauhari to maintain an intensely interactive relationship for the duration of his sermon.

Al-Jauhari sustains the metaconversation with his audience throughout his sermon, rarely missing an opportunity to enliven the sermon. We might well ask: what is it about? Or, in other words, what is the subject of this metadialogue? To what does it draw attention? The answer is that much of the metapositioning he performs with his audience refers to his own performance skills. The comments to the old ladies and the wristwatch gag, for example, are dialogues *about* his exercise of his skill as a performer. These devices establish his performance as the central spectacle. This positioning is a critical element of Al-Jauhari's oratory, one that distinguishes him clearly from the orator discussed in the next chapter. So, as much as participants understand this to be a *shariah* lesson, all are very aware that they are engaged in the mutual enjoyment of Al-Jauhari's virtuosity. His conversational metacommentary confirms the centrality of his skills to the ongoing interaction.

The Unique Voice Pleads Its Case

Not surprisingly, an ambience of excitement prevails at an Al-Jauhari event. The audience, many of whom will have attended an oration by him previously or watched DVDs of his sermons, are excited by the prospect of experiencing a live performance. For these reasons, one might reasonably think that, at a performance by him, there could be no dispute or ambivalence arising from normative conceptions of proper preaching. All would seem to be in harmony. However, this is not the case. In his interaction with his audiences, Al-Jauhari makes serious attempts at managing his image, pleading his case against the effects of preaching norms, even though those norms are not problematized within specific preaching situations. In the remainder of this chapter and in chapter 4, I analyze the background to the case he pleads, and I interpret his pleas not as responses to the audience before him but as responses to an Islamic public sphere in which preaching styles are not granted equal value as contributions to the public good, especially by elites.

This analysis requires some reflection on the position to which unique preaching voices are assigned within the constellation of religious authority in Bandung. He is not the only preacher to exploit his virtuosity on the preaching stage, nor is he the most open in asserting and protecting his uniqueness. The comedian-turned-*muballigh* Kang Ibing (d. 2010) told the *Pikiran Rakyat* newspaper that he openly forbade any recording of his sermons by audience members because he was concerned that other preachers would copy his material (*Pikiran Rakyat*, October 14, 2009). From Ibing's perspective, such copying would reduce his capacity to exploit his own unique voice. Uniqueness appears here as a form of capital that Kang Ibing perceived as requiring protection.

Kang Ibing, however, was not perturbed by the exclusions to which Al-Jauhari is sensitive. Both men succeeded through exploiting their unique abilities, but important differences can be seen in the ways in which they styled themselves. Kang Ibing openly identified himself as a comedian-turned-*muballigh* and nothing more.[8] He did not reveal any aspiration to be acknowledged in any of the Islamic leadership roles recognized and supported in West Java, such as the *ajengan* (leader of religious school), *ulama* (scholar), or *cendekiawan* (intellectual). By taking this position, he minimized the implications of normative judgments about his preaching style; negative appraisals of his unique style could not be held as inconsistent with behavior expected of other roles to which he aspired.

Al-Jauhari is different in that, in addition to his activities as *muballigh*, he embodies two other Islamic roles. The first is that of the traditional *ajengan/kyai*. He dresses in the distinctive white tunic, black or white cap, and scarf that are characteristic of this class. His preaching is rich with the Arabic-language referencing of the Qur'an and hadith that signals traditional Islamic learning. He heads and finances a *pesantren* (Islamic school) in Garut. The other role he takes on is that of *dosen* (lecturer), and he holds a lecturing post in the Faculty of Dakwah and Communication at the State Islamic

University. His tenure of this position implies that he contributes to civil and public life in commentary, participation in public debate, and teaching. It is not unusual for these roles to be combined in Indonesia, as the roles of preacher, *ajengan*, and university scholar are not mutually exclusive. Al-Jauhari's aspiration to be recognized in these roles, however, causes a problem for him that did not affect Kang Ibing. For some segments of Bandung's Islamic society, his preaching style works against the social value they see as inherent in these roles. In particular, for those who charge Islamic leadership with responsibility for progress in projects of transformation and renewal, his preaching style registers as obstructive and anachronistic.

I expand at length on this background in the chapters that follow; what is important at this point are the representations he makes on his own behalf to audiences through his orations and the reasons for which he does this. I do not believe that normative critiques are directly voiced to him as he goes about fulfilling engagements. Audience members do not bring them up in his presence and critiques that target him personally do not often arise in print media, for members of Bandung's religious elites encounter each other constantly and generally refrain from publishing negative judgments of each other that might threaten relations. Nevertheless, unfavorable judgments of Al-Jauhari's style circulate in conversation. Al-Jauhari's biographer acknowledged these judgments in a chapter entitled "Replies to Accusations" (Safei 2002, 109–26). No specific accusers are mentioned or cited in the chapter, but reference is made to generalized opinions circulating within society, without reference to the agents of their circulation. The criticisms are introduced through general phrases such as "*Muncullah anggapan . . .*" (An opinion emerged that . . .) and "*Muncullah pertanyaan dari masyarakat . . .*" (A query emerged from society as to . . .). Two criticisms are raised by the biographer: that Al-Jauhari improperly seeks high fees for his performances, and that his true skill is verbal performance, especially singing, rather than the verbalization of Islamic knowledge.

Defenses to these charges appear prominently in his oratorical interactions with audiences. In the remainder of this chapter, I highlight two claims he makes to audiences on his own behalf. In the first, he uses the Indonesian concept of *gaul* (language of sociability) to advocate the propriety of multivocal preaching. The second claim takes shape as a defense of his financial circumstances.

Gaul, Man!

The performance captured in appendix A includes examples of *gaul* language as well as advocacy for the *gaul* concept. This word describes the Jakarta-centered youth prestige language (*basa gaul*) (Smith-Hefner 2007). Al-Jauhari uses catchy *gaul* phrases such as *cewek matre* (material girl), which is also a popular song; *emang gue pikirin?* (I should care?); and *So what? Gitu loh!* (So what? That's how it is!), also the title of a 2005 hit by hip-hop artist Saykoji. There is some incongruity in Al-Jauhari's invocation of *gaul*, for *gaul* culture projects a metropolitan hipness against which regional cultures inevitably appear provincial. The social environments in which Al-Jauhari regularly preaches are very far from the urban centers that are the typical locus of *gaul* society. Furthermore, *gaul* is at odds with Islamic conservatism. It implies, for example, socializing between unmarried men and women, which transgresses highly valued prohibitions on socializing before marriage. For Al-Jauhari's audiences, *gaul* is a source of unease because it signals the decline in moral standards rural West Javanese associate with metropolitan centers. There is a specific class of preachers known as *gaul* preachers, but these are chic, young urbanites mediated through national media networks (see Abdurrahman 2008). Al-Jauhari's natural home is within the conservative and pious middle- to lower-class communities of Islamic West Java.

    Gaul is, therefore, by no means a language or ethic shared between Al-Jauhari and his audience. It has specific value for Al-Jauhari because the concept works against the widely held discourses that problematize his preaching style. He mobilizes the *gaul* concept as a defense against those who would denigrate his style on the grounds of preaching propriety. *Gaul* language and culture provide informal counterpoints to conventional notions of social propriety, for they project a sociability less constrained by hierarchies. *Gaul* and a number of synonymous terms (for example, *banding-banding*, to make comparisons) are a practically beneficial form of self-identification for Al-Jauhari because they work in opposition to singularity. In the following excerpt from the same Al-Jauhari performance quoted above, I translate *gaul* as "hang out." The example illustrates the appeal the concept holds for Al-Jauhari: it stands for multiple possibilities and militates against homogeneity: "And when you are learning, don't rely on one teacher only. Look for others!

So you don't think like a *square*. *Hang out* [gaul]! Make comparisons! Don't just choose one and hup! That's it! That means problems. . . . Try to *hang out* a bit. Even I have many teachers. Even I compare them. That's normal."[9]

For Al-Jauhari, *gaul* stands for a refusal to dogmatically recognize one possibility as innately superior to others. It stands for tolerance of difference, and Al-Jauhari mobilizes it to defend his generic variation, as he demonstrated when he used it to defend himself against potential criticism from older people after his beautiful rendition of "Dealova," quoted earlier. In this example and others, he is not invoking *gaul* to appear urbane but as a response to the argument that preaching styles such as his are cultural hybrids. He borrows a core constituent of *gaul*, its embrace of heterogeneity, to argue that preaching in which a broad range of communicative possibilities are mobilized is proper.

The Roving Moneybox

Organizing committees accept the financial commitment involved in engaging Al-Jauhari.[10] Some of the committee members I spoke with expressed surprise and concern that a preacher should be rewarded so generously. At the same time, the economic framework within which preachers of high repute operate is not new in West Java, so committee members accept that the expense is necessary. Al-Jauhari provides them with something that other preachers cannot guarantee—the very high participation in the event of members of the community—so they accept the financial undertaking as essential to achieve the high participation.

In these communities, normative disapproval of "selling the verses" does not determine decisions about preaching events. Nevertheless, Al-Jauhari finds it necessary to negotiate this norm with his audience during preaching performances and uses several strategies to do so. One involves being upfront about it (for examples, see appendix A, segments 17, 28–29), a strategy that is entirely consistent with the general bravura of his style.[11] The performance translated in part in appendix A included a substantial attempt to resolve this normative problem, which I have not included in the appendix. The scene lasted for about five and a half minutes, during which the preacher made representations that cast his financial situation in a favorable light. It forms a discrete block in the middle of the sermon, commencing with a short pause, after which he says, "Before I go on, I wish to ask for your prayers and blessings [*doa restu*]." This request tells the audience that he is temporarily suspending the exciting performance mode of the oration. He then asks the audience whether they have heard gossip describing him as an *ajengan mahal* (expensive *ajengan*). That gossip, he says with typical boldness, is true! He then describes the financial burden of the upkeep and management of his Islamic boarding school in rural West Java, telling the audience about the school and its activities, and about the costs involved in its management. He informs the audience that he is responsible for paying monthly salaries to seven Qur'an teachers and two champion reciters. He then uses the image of the *kéncléng* (Sundanese, moneybox) to illustrate his role. When visitors come to the school, they are not asked for money. Nor does he seek government largesse to cover the costs of the school. The school is funded by Al-Jauhari's preaching and he is its *kéncléng nguriling* (Sundanese, roving moneybox). He also incorporates a description of a typical week from his grueling schedule, emphasizing the exhausting effort required to meet his obligations.[12]

Throughout the scene, the level of generic variation is extremely low in comparison to the main body of the sermon. Songs are absent, and jokes are rare and subdued in scope and execution. The audience is addressed in plain, conversational language, creating a five-and-a-half-minute lull in what is otherwise a frenetic and brilliant performance. Although Al-Jauhari receives significant donations from audience members for the upkeep of his school, it would be incorrect to interpret the scene merely as a plea for financial contributions. Rather, it is intended to make an impact on the audience members' sense of fairness. The passage is a direct, plain-language appeal to the rationality and goodwill of his audiences, whom I observed to be highly interested in this passage, despite its low-key mode. Al-Jauhari's audiences respect the task of managing and financing a boarding school as a laudable undertaking and the appeal is interpreted sympathetically.

But why should Al-Jauhari make these representations? As noted, negative evaluations based on the norm concerning financial rewards are not a problem in the immediate context. The audience is in his thrall; he is the preacher of choice for the organizing committee; he is not being confronted by any normative judgments about his preaching. Why is it necessary for him to allow the issue of preaching norms to materialize in his oratory in such an intrusive way?

The complete resolution of this question involves extending the gaze beyond the situations in which Al-Jauhari preaches, which is undertaken in the two chapters that follow. It involves considering Al-Jauhari's style against contrasting oratorical projects and styles in Bandung as well as the ways in which these are variously evaluated in public discourse. His defenses make sense in the light of those evaluations, for they have the effect of denying his preaching the social efficacy with which Islam is charged in contemporary West Java. They make it hard for a virtuoso dakwah performer to be accepted as an Islamic authority in the categories of intellectual and *ajengan*. Influential actors in West Java attribute serious efficacy to these roles, which they claim are impeded by a preaching style that treats its audiences as subjects able to be captivated through oratorical virtuosity. In short, his defenses are responses to the limitations placed by others on his aspirations. Although his unique voice achieves successful outcomes on the preaching stage, he pays a price off the stage for that success.

Chapter 3

Preaching "without Performing"

During the time that I was traveling with Al-Jauhari in 2007 and 2009, I regularly attended a routine preaching event called Ji-had: Pengajian Ahad (The Struggle: Sunday Study). This event, held every Sunday morning at seven o'clock, is organized by PERSIS. The preachers addressing the crowds at this gathering are all PERSIS leaders, and their appearances are managed on a rotating roster prepared by the organization's administration. The event is held at the Viaduct Mosque, one of many mosques owned or run by PERSIS in West Java. The mosque is a well-known landmark because of its central location, almost underneath a colonial-era railway bridge a few hundred meters east of Bandung's central station.

The Sunday Study routinely draws between 3,000 and 6,000 people. The mosque can only accommodate a crowd of no more than 1,500 (my estimate), so thousands of people sit on the road outside the mosque, listening to the event through loudspeakers without being able to see the orator. By arrangement between PERSIS and the Bandung police, the road is closed to traffic for the duration of the event so that people can sit on mats spread on the road. The mosque has separate areas for males and females, and only males occupy the room from which the orator delivers the sermon. The orator's performance is filmed by a video camera positioned about three meters in front of him. PERSIS produces videodiscs from this recording, which are reproduced for sale and distribution throughout the PERSIS network. (The text in appendix B is a translation and transcription of one of these reproductions.)

The theme of each Sunday Study is planned in advance. The speaker prepares a worksheet, which is photocopied and distributed through the audience on the day of the sermon. These give the Qur'anic and hadith citations, in Arabic with Indonesian translations, to which the speaker will refer. On some Sundays, the sheet gives Arabic terms with definitions in both Arabic and Indonesian. The sheet is simple and its text unelaborated; none of the sheets I encountered had any text that gave advice, exhortation or extended interpretation.

The *muballigh* speaks for at least forty-five minutes, referring at times to the photocopied sheet. At the end of the sermon, he answers questions from the audience. This question-and-answer procedure is regarded by PERSIS people as a tradition of the organization (Saefuddin 2014, 67). Some of these questions are written on pieces of paper and submitted by members of the audience; others are relayed by text message to the event's master of ceremonies, who stands or sits beside the pulpit. (The number for sending of questions by text message is given on the photocopied sheet.) The master of ceremonies selects which questions are to be answered by the speaker, who gives an impromptu response. The questions are mostly about PERSIS's main institutional preoccupation: formal aspects of worship practice. A smaller number of questions raise issues of other kinds, seeking guidance and directions about current religiopolitical issues.

Following is an analysis of a preaching performance delivered by a PERSIS preacher of note at the Sunday Study. The analysis explores the same three foci that were studied in Al-Jauhari's text in chapter 2—generic variation, affect, reflexive dialogue. My goal is to explore a conception of oratorical appropriateness that is widely accepted in Bandung but that is in opposition to the one emerging from Al-Jauhari's example. This exploration includes consideration of the specific Islamic worldview of PERSIS, which crystallizes for its followers as a project of self and social transformation.

Figure 1. Listeners at the Sunday Study are too many to be accommodated inside the Viaduct Mosque, located at the left of the image. Police routinely close off the road in front of the mosque to enable listeners to enjoy a broadcast of the sermon while seated on mats on the road. Photo by author.

About PERSIS

Although PERSIS is represented in many locations in Indonesia, Bandung is its home. It was established in this city on September 12, 1923, by a small group of Muslim traders, none of them of Sundanese origin (Noer 1973, 84; Pijper 1977, 121). Their initial goal was to establish a forum for religious study, but this developed into a broader social modernization program inspired by a particular reformist religious vision (Federspiel 2001). Today PERSIS owns religious schools and mosques across Indonesia but enjoys an especially high level of acceptance and support in Bandung. As a result of endowments from supporters both wealthy and poor, its infrastructure in central Bandung is outstanding.

One PERSIS official informed me in 2009 that although the organization has about ten thousand formal members, the number of Muslims who affiliate with the organization and support its programs, a class he called *simpatisan* (sympathizers), was more than one million in West Java. It is therefore a sizable group, although it has far fewer sympathizers than the two largest Islamic organizations, Muhammadiyah and Nahdlatul Ulama.

Scholars have described the PERSIS socioreligious program with a number of epithets. It is commonly labeled "modernist" (Federspiel 2001, 53–61; Noer 1973, 83–91; Pijper 1977), a term that acknowledges the period during which PERSIS was established. Like other early-twentieth-century modernist movements, PERSIS identified two challenges as motivations for action. One was the subjugated and undeveloped state of the Muslim peoples of the Netherlands Indies and other colonized lands. The second was what it viewed as the degraded state of their Islamic knowledge and practice, which PERSIS and other modernists attributed partly to Muslims' reliance on *kyai* (scholastic elites). These two themes were, for modernist groups, essentially interrelated, although in different ways. In the case of PERSIS, emphasis has fallen on the second of these themes. While Muhammadiyah pursued its mission of modernizing social life and creating civil institutions and while Nahdlatul Ulama prosecuted the interests of the *ulama* and their traditionalist constituency, PERSIS has focused its primary endeavors on achieving correctness in Islamic personal conduct and on propagandizing this program (Federspiel 2001, 87–88).

Other scholars have called them "puritans," focusing on PERSIS's determination to practice and proselytize an understanding of Islamic practice and doctrine that is rigorously insulated from what it regards as accretions appearing since the first generations of Muslims (Federspiel 2001, 139; Pijper 1977, 130). The group's insistence on purity has led scholars to identify the group in the tradition of backward-looking Islamic purification movements. Hasan (2006, 33) has located them as bearers of the *salafi* legacy.[1] Yet another epithet is "fundamentalist." Herb Feith (1962, 136–37) called the group's foremost ideologues "radical fundamentalists" because of their uncompromising demand for an Islamic state during the 1950s. Although PERSIS has not held that political position for a long time, the epithet still resonates today because of popular perceptions of its strong focus on correctness on worship practice.

An ethos of transformation is ubiquitous in PERSIS's project. There are two poles to this ethos. In PERSIS thinking, Allah has revealed guidelines for human behavior, inscribed in the Qur'an and Traditions, which humans are bound to implement. This obligation leads some PERSIS followers to adopt a textual literalism in which the Qur'an and hadith serve as exclusive frameworks for daily life. This literalism is prominent within the organization's method for deliberating over Islamic issues (Abbas 2013), and some PERSIS followers in Bandung map textual norms quite literally onto daily life, recalling the Christian fundamentalist epistemologies described by Vincent Crapanzano (2000). PERSIS followers are motivated to make their own lives as Qur'anic as possible, "to obliterate the gap between the ideal, literally described and commanded by Scripture, and the real" (Crapanzano 2000, 16). I know PERSIS members who consciously evaluate their own actions with reference to categories established in Islamic law. By doing this, the group often supports context-independent understandings of proper Islamic practice and doctrine.[2]

While its literalism puts the group at a distance from mainstream Islamic society, the second pole of transformation points to its closeness to the center of Indonesian society. The group has a "this-worldly" orientation, seeking to transform contemporary Indonesian realities through engagement. Its founders were traders, and contemporary PERSIS leaders likewise do not seek to create a community at a distance from the rest of society. PERSIS members have played prominent roles in Indonesian and West Javanese public life, and continue to do so (Federspiel 2001, 182; Kahin 2012). They do not model their clothing and appearance on that of the Prophet and the three generations of his followers, as other salafists in contemporary Indonesia have come to do, and the group's theological statements, which it publicizes energetically, do not differ in significant ways from Islamic doctrines that are accepted by Indonesia's Sunni majority. The group certainly expresses much antagonism toward the world outside of their own group, especially toward the West and Judaism, and toward aspects of contemporary Indonesian society, but they do not withdraw from the world. Contemporary PERSIS understands its role as a modernizing one to be played within a democratic Indonesia.

Nevertheless, the group's insistence on literal application of Islamic norms and their vocal criticisms of difference distance many Indonesians from the group. It is frequently labeled as *keras* (harsh) or *sombong* (arrogant). Indeed, conflicts with PERSIS members have sometimes been pursued to the point of open confrontation. As Deliar Noer (1973, 94) put it, "PERSIS seemed to create antagonism if not enemies, everywhere." One mosque official of a traditional congregation in a Bandung village told me that he had once challenged a PERSIS follower to a wrestling match! The PERSIS follower had challenged the correctness of the ritual conduct followed in the community's mosque, thereby presenting a major threat to the official's authority and position. Such stories are not uncommon.

Mediating Hadith with Affect

The transcription and translation contained in appendix B is excerpted from an oration delivered in the Sunday series on May 9, 2009, by Shiddiq Amien, who died later in that same year. The sermon presented the Qur'anic and hadith sources on the creation of humans from the time of conception and gave instruction on female ritual obligation.

At the time of my attendance at Sunday Study, Amien was serving as national head of PERSIS. Before his sudden death, he was the most popular of all the orators affiliated with the organization. This popularity enabled him to be accepted by audiences outside of the organization to an extent achieved by few PERSIS orators of recent times. The preacher's willingness to reach out to audiences is expressed by his biographer as followers: "While before him there was an agreement [within PERSIS] that it was okay for the organisation to have few followers, as long as they were of high quality, Shiddiq Amien thought that it was preferable for the organisation to have many members, as long as they were of good quality" (Saefuddin 2014, 134).

His monthly oration drew the biggest crowds to Sunday Study. Unlike Al-Jauhari, his popularity cannot be explained by overt displays of oratorical virtuosity. While Al-Jauhari exploits a unique voice to achieve successful outcomes, Amien gave the appearance of avoiding uniqueness or stylistic distinction of any kind. In comparison with Al-Jauhari's preaching, his seemed dour and minimalist. He verbalized Qur'anic verses in everyday speech, not in melody, and did not sing songs of any kind. When reporting the speech of others, imitation of the sonic qualities of those voices was minimal. Mechanical sounds were absent, as are the elaborate, preplanned frame manipulations for generating humor. Writing in *Pikiran Rakyat*, a Sundanese reporter described Amien's oratorical style as "*kagok*" (awkward) (*Pikiran Rakyat*, August 21, 2007). Yet a friend active in PERSIS told me he was the "best preacher in Bandung," a claim also made by his biographer (Saefuddin 2014, 26). I had heard taxi drivers and others in Bandung give the same ranking to Al-Jauhari. This is why the two are matched together in this analysis; both are considered as exemplars of oratorical style, but their exemplariness connects to contrasting notions of appropriateness.

The excerpts drawn upon here illustrate his verbalization and translation of hadith. I focus on his treatment of hadith because, for one thing, much of Amien's preaching was dedicated to this. More than that, his work with hadith points to a challenge facing PERSIS orators. For PERSIS followers, textual norms are central to the process of shaping self and society. When they attend Sunday Study, PERSIS followers expect guidance in this process. Hadith are transmitted in unchanging textual forms, in a language not well understood by all listeners (Arabic). The danger is that mediations of hadith might become arid and uninviting. A *muballigh*'s injunctions toward implementation of textual norms can, without adequate attention to reception, be received as dry, studied monologue. Even more so in the case studied below, for the content of this sermon analyzed here is potentially oppressive toward female listeners, and a less skilled preacher might preach these messages in a way that treats the female listener as a passive subject with no volition other than to fulfill Qur'anic norms.[3] Amien was skilled at softening the reception of these messages, and as much as Amien's admirers might hear his sermons as awkward or unstudied, in fact he relied upon considerable skill to create positive listening experiences for his listeners. Like Al-Jauhari, Amien mediated Islamic norms in narratives rich with reported speech, creating a polyphony that attracted through its dynamic and arresting play of voices.

Two narrative sequences can be read in appendix B (segments 2–5 and 7–21), both constructed around entextualizations of hadith. In their textual forms, the source hadith are in fact narratives that convey brief meetings and exchanges between the Prophet and the person who subsequently became the source of the hadith (e.g., "Aishah asked the Prophet. . . . He answered . . .").[4] Like Al-Jauhari, Amien's method is to fragment the Arabic texts of hadith (which in this sermon concern women's obligations) into small pieces, which he immediately translates into Indonesian. The following example is significant because it reveals Amien's enhancement of the simple narrative of the hadith texts. He fleshes out the encounters and conversational exchanges between the Prophet Muhammad and his interlocutors.

The languages used below are the same as those used by Al-Jauhari (Sundanese, Indonesian and Arabic), with one critical difference. Amien used Indonesian as the dominant code, not Sundanese (for reasons explored in the following chapter). In the transcript that follows, I have left Amien's Arabic entextualizations in Arabic for almost all of them are immediately translated into Indonesian. The nonitalicized English text is translated from Indonesian, the dominant code in this sermon. The symbol ◄ indicates rising intonation intended to draw an affirmation from listeners:

> . . . *'an 'aishah taqulu* Siti Aishah said, *kharajna* we went out, *la nara illa al-hajj* with no intention other than to do pilgrimage. Siti Aishah left Medina in the direction of [inaudible] to perform her pilgrimage. *Fa lamma kunna bi sarib hidtu* when we arrived at Sarib, this is the name of a place, "*Hidtu*," said Siti Aishah, "I
> 5   was menstruating. *Fa dakhala 'alayya rasulu 'llah* and the Messenger of Allah came, into my tent, *wa ana abki* and I was crying."
> *Qala al-nabi* the Prophet asked, "*Ma laki* why are you crying? *Anafasti* Are you *giving birth* [*nifas*]?" But he meant menstruation here, not *giving-birth*.
> *Qultu* Siti Aisah said, "*Na'm* [yes]."
> 10   *Qala* then the Prophet explained, "You should not cry because of menstruation, *inna hadha* for indeed this, this menstruation, *amrun* is something, *katabahu 'llah* that Allah has decreed, *'ala banati adam* for all women. *Fa aqdi* [go ahead and do the pilgrimage]!"
> Perhaps Aishah was crying because she had come so far from Madinah to perform
> 15   pilgrimage, but when near to Mecca, she began menstruating.
> Siti Aishah imagined, "That means I cannot do my pilgrimage" probably.
> So the Prophet made it clear, "*Fa aqdi* carry it out! *Ma* whatever, *ya'malu al-hajju* the pilgrims do, *ghaira* except, *'ala tatufa bi al-bait* you may not walk around the House of Allah." This means that all the procedures and journeys of the pilgrimage
> 20   may be performed by a menstruating woman except for circumambulation. When will she perform circumambulation? Later when she is ◄ . . . [audience: ritually clean] . . . ritually clean. [That is the] second [forbidden thing] (appendix B, segments 2–5).

The statement "You should not cry because of menstruation" (line 10); the speculation about Aishah's pious emotions and thoughts (line 14–16); and the Prophet's responsiveness to those emotions (line 17): these are extrinsic to the hadith in its written form. They enhance Amien's telling of the encounter by giving emotive texture to the bare sequence of the Arabic. More importantly, they enable Amien to replay these exchanges as interactions between people whose reactions and concerns replicate those of his audience. In their questions to the Prophet, Aishah and the women of Medina (appendix B, segments 11 and 17) express the very same concerns that Amien knows his female listeners hold, and the Prophet's answers anticipate those concerns. Their affective value is enhanced by the personas invoked, for the speakers (Aishah and the Prophet Muhammad) are not ordinary people; they are figures understood by Amien's audiences as paragons of selfless love and compassion.

Significant contrasts to Al-Jauhari emerge when we consider the reflections on the interaction that Amien shares with his listeners. As noted, when Al-Jauhari reflects with his audience on the unfolding sermon, he refers to his own performance. Their shared enjoyment of his skills is the object of reflection. Amien reflected on something different. In his metacommentary, he established a pedagogically oriented conversation with his audience *about* the hadith and the process of learning. So, although he plays the role of authoritative mediator of Islamic knowledge for his audience, he also positions himself as a coparticipant in a conversational circle in which all are dedicated to learning. He creates the illusion that he too is engaged in the learning process with his listeners. In the example to follow, a less sensitive speaker might have simply pointed out the error from his position of authority, but Amien's sympathy for the learning efforts of his listeners is clear through his self-positioning as a colearner, seen in the use of the inclusive pronoun "we":

> *'An abi sa'id bin khudri qala* [According to Abu Said bin Hudri, the Prophet said], *kharaja rasulu 'llah* the Messenger of Allah left his house, *fi adha au fitrin*, probably forgetting whether it was the festival of adha or fitri, but it was certainly a feast day, *ila al-musalla* and went to the *musalla* [place of prayer]. We often translate this among ourselves as 'went to the mosque', but in fact *musalla*, in this context, is the name of a field in the eastern part of Medinah. (appendix B, segment 7)

As he conveys gendered principles that create the possibility of a negative response from women listeners, he anticipates their responses to his words and softens the reception of the message: "In reality, don't be shocked, ladies! For we need to pay attention to the first sentence, *tasaddaqna* [give alms], only that one" (appendix B, segment 10). He seeks affirmations of his interpretations: "Based on the verses in the chapter of Al-Nisa, verse 43, *ya ayyuha alladhina amanu* Oh people of faith! *La taqrabu al-salat* you may not approach the place of ritual prayer, *wa antum sukara* while in a state of drunkenness, *hatta ta'lamu ma taqulun* until you, *ta'lamu* are aware of what you are saying. For if a person is drunk, he doesn't know his own words and deeds, does he?" (Appendix B, segment 23). In these reflections and others, he declares solidarity with his listeners' dedication to the PERSIS project of self-shaping: "We are all learning together."

These moments of shared metareflection are high in affect, which is enabled significantly by his switches to Sundanese, as appendix B, segment 25 illustrates (the underlined text is translated from Sundanese): "You are not allowed to be close to the *salat* when you are ritually impure, *illa* except for *'abiri sabil*. *'Abiri sabil* means a passerby, *hatta taghtasilu* until you have bathed. Someone may ask, are we not allowed to go close to prayer except in passing? What's this about? We are not allowed to perform our ritual prayer except in passing? *Salat* here means mosque, *salat* in the second meaning." Once more, this passage objectifies the learning process as something being confronted by himself as well as his listeners. Although the dominant language of this sermon was Indonesian, the question "What's this about?" was uttered in Sundanese (*Kumaha ieu téh?*). As I argue in more detail in the following chapter, the Sundanese language allows him to establish a more intimate and less formal rapport with his audience than Indonesian does. By uttering this question in Sundanese, Amien locates himself empathetically as a seeker of knowledge experiencing the same difficulty and confusion as his listeners. The effect is disarming, as this question reduces the distance between him and his audience.

These strategies address the risk that the textual orientation of the interaction might result in a sermon that is too severe. The content of the sermon excerpted in appendix B could be alienating for women listeners. Amien's sensitively pitched multivocality and his creation of an inclusive conversation with female listeners about the textual content soften the messages and provide reassuring interpretations. This enables him to recognize the humanity and concerns of his listeners and thereby cushion the disciplinary potential of the norms being discussed. His metacommunication sympathetically creates a circle of listeners in which he is included as an equal.

But Amien's multivocality is minimalist and ascetic beside Al-Jauhari's. I have already noted Amien's avoidance of performance genres outside of conversational registers, but there are more distinctions than that. When Amien reports the speech of others, for example, he does not mimic. When he speaks "as a woman," as he does frequently in segments 2 to 21, the listener heard the timbre and intonation of Amien's voice, not an imitation of the timbre and intonation of a woman's voice. In contrast, Al-Jauhari draws attention to recognizable ways of speaking by creating parodic stylizations of them. There is irony in Amien's reproductions of others' voices (see segments 11 to 14), but the uniformness of his delivery is nothing like the rapid shifts between generic caricatures that keep Al-Jauhari's listeners enthralled. When Amien invests effort in affirming his communicative relationship with his audience, he maintains and nurtures a welcoming circle of interested listeners. In fact, Amien's ordinariness was underpinned by an ideological problematization of unique oratorical voices, to which I now turn. This ideology suggests that it would almost certainly have pleased Amien to have a reputation as an "awkward" speaker.

Competency

Amien could not fail *as a performer*. His style did not expose him to such a risk, and his listeners did not expect from him those competencies on which Al-Jauhari's reputation was made. If Amien's jokes did not work, or if audience members' attention lagged, his name would not be struck off the list of invitable preachers. He was not obliged to refocus listener attention. PERSIS followers are, at least ideally, struggling with the challenge of fashioning pious selves. The Sunday Study sessions are routine events at which they meet and receive guidance in that struggle (Arabic: jihad), and such guidance can only be obtained from a person with sufficient knowledge to provide it, such as Shiddiq Amien. Listener and speaker expect that the sermon will assist listeners in applying Islamic norms in daily life, and this expectation is a distinguishing trait of the PERSIS project.[5]

This expectation, and the competency that it implies, emerges clearly during the question-and-answer phase of the Sunday Study sessions. As noted earlier, after the sermon, the master of ceremonies reads out questions from the audience, which are answered by the orator, who has no notice of them. I heard questions including: What are my prayer obligations while traveling overseas? How are we to know when the fasting month ends? Is it permissible to carry a copy of the Qur'an into the toilet?[6] These questions subject the orator to an ordeal that points to PERSIS understandings of oratorical competency. Although Shiddiq Amien could not fail as a performer before the Viaduct audience, the questions and answers imply a possibility of failure in the form of a wrong answer or a display of uncertainty. In reality, such a failure is not likely to occur at a Sunday Study session, for its orators are experienced members of the PERSIS hierarchy who have, in all likelihood, previously encountered all the questions they would likely receive at the event. But the question-and-answer session is an ordeal that implies a life-long process of study and testing from which only a few emerge as leaders. A PERSIS leader is a person whose sound knowledge and reliable judgment have been validated over a period of years leading up to his appointment to a leadership role. In the PERSIS view, this validation signals oratorical competency.

A PERSIS orator, then, is competent to mount the stage as a speaker when he has survived ordeals experienced offstage. The group expects their preachers to give value in offstage as well as onstage settings. And this offstage competency includes the role of supporting the PERSIS project in public discourse. This is especially the case in the moments of crisis that regularly appear on the PERSIS radar. By crises I mean clashes between PERSIS ideology and the realities of political and social life in Indonesia. PERSIS is a group that attempts to change Indonesian realities and frequently reacts to unfolding issues, usually in the wake of their broadcast through the mass media. Some such issues require resolution in the methodology of *fiqh*, the deliberation over Islamic legal sources that are required to produce normative statement on specific issues. The resolutions are provided in forums such as the Sunday Study and through the organization's extensive publicity network (Federspiel 2001, 92–106).

The organization's Bandung-produced journal, *Risalah*, of which Amien was the leading editor, gave attention to several issues that required fatwa during the period of my fieldwork, including: What is the status for Indonesians of the fatwa of Saudi sheikhs who state that jihad in Lebanon and Palestine is not obligatory because the Muslims engaged in those conflicts were Shia? (*Risalah* 2006); is it permissible for Muslims to take part in the new Islamic movements that emerge from time to time within Indonesia, such as the Jaringan Islam Liberal (JIL, Liberal Islam Network), or the many local-based movements created around charismatic individuals that frequently appear in West Java? (*Risalah* 2007); what is the legal status of multilevel marketing? (*Risalah* 2009); and, considering that pork enzymes might be involved in the manufacture of the meningitis vaccination made obligatory for pilgrimage travelers by the Saudi government, is it permissible for Muslims to receive it? (*Risalah* 2009).[7] Because PERSIS followers place such emphasis on a literal implementation of Islamic norms in their lives, they need to have authoritative interpretations on these issues, and they expect to hear them from the orators who appear at the Sunday Study sessions.

Nothing of the practice described earlier actually excludes virtuoso display of communication skills, so it would still appear possible that an orator competent to produce fatwa could also be a brilliant performer on the stage. In reality, however, this is not possible, or it is at most extremely unlikely. PERSIS' religious program excludes virtuoso displays of generic variation. Clear constraints on such displays emerge in statements of key thinkers within the movement.

PERSIS Ideology of Mediation

Influential PERSIS ideologues have published statements about proper ways to communicate Islam, allowing us to construct a distinct ideology of mediation. By ideology of mediation, I mean a complex of notions of what constitutes a "proper" mediation and the deliberative background that supports those notions. The statements of Ahmad Hassan and Muhammad Natsir quoted below reveal two overarching values. The first is the primacy of intelligibility. In the PERSIS view, the Islamic faith can be reduced to accessible statements. This value entails a particular view of human agency: Muslims are capable of deploying *akal* (from Arabic, rational faculties) in comprehending the religion's intelligible meanings. These meanings are constantly presented to the PERSIS follower in the form of translations and entextualizations of Qur'anic verses and hadith, such as those discussed above. In PERSIS ideology, a rational, thinking Muslim will not fail to heed these intelligible signs and messages.

The second value emerges from constant injunctions to evaluate Islamic acts and utterances according to their *nilai 'ibadah* (worth as worship). PERSIS followers need to know the value and correctness of their acts and utterances when assessed against the Qur'an and the practice of the Prophet and his companions. Much PERSIS discourse is dedicated to rigorous surveillance of this value, which results in a strict drawing of borders between acts and utterances with Islamic value, on the one hand, and practices with no such value, on the other.

Taken together, these values downgrade those aspects of mediation and communication that are shaped by the context in which the mediation or communication takes place. Artful and affective communication drawing on shared knowledge and experience is not necessary because PERSIS followers adhere to a rationalized conviction of the value of the Qur'an and hadith. Local conventions in Islamic ritual and performance are not only redundant but also denied religious value for they were not the practice of the Prophet and his companions. The practical effect of these positions is to remove religious communication from the communications styles specific to West Java. Instead, it is projected as a task that takes similar forms universally. Oratorical mediations need not be tailored to the specific competencies of Sundanese cultural subjects.

These values are expressed clearly by PERSIS ideologues in debates in which mediation and communication are at issue. The group has argued against culturally situated mediations in favor of clarity, brevity, and easily understandable linguistic forms (Federspiel 2001, 110, 183–84). A good example is the contest over the language to be used in the Friday sermon. It was—and still is, in some areas of West Java—common practice for the *khutbah* (sermon) delivered after the Friday prayer to be uttered in Arabic. Often it was read verbatim in Arabic from a compilation of sermons. In Ahmad Hassan's view, this way of conducting the sermon was a sign of a repugnant traditionalism. His fatwa on the issue was first published in a PERSIS journal between 1931 and 1934 and republished in a 1968 compilation that has been in print ever since (Hassan 2000, 203–5).[8] Hassan argued that the Qur'an commands people to think. He made this the basis for a further assertion that runs directly against deeply rooted conventions of performing and studying the Qur'an in Indonesia: the only way to read the Qur'an is to do so while engaging with its referential meanings (Hassan 2000, 203). It follows that people must be able to understand the content of the Friday sermon, for it contains advice, admonitions, and teachings based on the Qur'an. It will have no meaning if it is delivered in a language not understood by those listening and, furthermore, there is no religious norm decreeing that it must be uttered in Arabic. For Hassan, the referential meaning of the sermon was everything, and its social and affective meanings bore no weight in comparison.[9]

A similar tension emerged in contest over *mawlid*, the ritual reading of the Prophet Muhammad's life, which is a widely practiced commemoration and supplication in West Java and Indonesia generally (Kaptein 1993; Pijper 1934). The *mawlid* performances take place in settings prepared according to local convention, and participants frequently celebrate through vernacular performance genres. Hassan took issue with these rituals. Even though he resided in Bandung, where such performances have been highly popular, he expressed his position without disguising his lack of sympathy for the conventions of Sundanese piety:

> It is good and proper to read the story of the Prophet, for by doing this we can learn of the circumstances and difficulties faced by the Prophet, peace and blessings of Allah be upon him, in spreading the religion. . . . But this is not what happens nowadays. People just gather together in a festive atmosphere, then take turns in reading the book of [the *mawlid* author] Barzanji, using vocal melodies and shouting while yelling and screaming with all their heart, sometimes accompanied by drums. After that, they eat. It is not their stupidity that we find amazing, for Dutch Christians who don't know English confess their sins before English priests who don't know Dutch, and this is even more stupid. What we find strange is that they think reading the *mawlid* without knowing its contents is a meritorious act, and will give them a benefit in the hereafter . . . there is neither religious nor logical explanation that states a person will obtain a benefit from reading something he or she does not understand. (Hassan 2000, 372)

The final sentence neatly expresses PERSIS ideology of mediation: rational thinking and textual justifications set limits on the range of communicative possibilities.[10] It follows that PERSIS followers need not bring their cultural selves to the Sunday Study sessions, for they should not expect their orators to reflect on their cultural competencies in oratorical performance. But the practical reality is different, as my analysis of Amien's oratory in this chapter and the one to follow indicate; Amien's oratory, though sober and dour in comparison with Al-Jauhari's, is nevertheless carefully crafted and relies heavily on its engagement with Sundanese competencies. His work suggests that the PERSIS ideology of mediation is an ideal unlikely to be achieved in practice and that its architect, Ahmad Hassan, was insufficiently aware of how preaching communications, no matter how clear and plain they might appear, are inevitably shaped to some degree according to situation.

Even so, the "work of purification" is like a beacon signaling the contrasting conceptions of appropriateness in Al-Jauhari's and Amien's oratory.

While PERSIS mediations ideally avoid those aspects of communication that are grounded in the social interaction between preacher and audience, an Al-Jauhari performance relies on those aspects for the achievement of a good outcome.

Proscribing the Unique Oratorical Voice

PERSIS ideology also identifies and proscribes connections between the unique oratorical voice and the ego of the preacher. These connections were instrumental in a recent parting of ways between PERSIS and an up-and-coming *muballigh* named Ustad Rahmat Hidayat (b. 1965). This man studied Islam for six years at a PERSIS *pesantren* in Bandung before continuing his Islamic education in Pakistan. On his return, he maintained his connection with PERSIS while studying public relations at an Islamic University in Bandung, then enrolled in a doctorate program in communications studies at another of the city's best-known universities. While he was studying, he worked as a radio announcer and hosted an early morning program on Islamic themes called *Siraman Iman* (A Sprinkling of Faith). The program was highly successful with younger listeners, which enabled him in 1999 to establish a routine study event at a large mosque in northern Bandung.

This regular event provided him with a stage for him to use speaking abilities. His audience subsequently grew to the extent that Rahmat is now the head of a large organization, also called Siraman Iman, briefly described in chapter 1, which offers a number of services and products for the Muslims of Bandung and West Java, including educational programs promoted with labels such as *kajian* Islam *intensif* (intensive Islamic study), *tafsir intensif* (intensive Qur'anic interpretation), and *cara memelihara semangat ibadah* (ways to nurture the will to worship). Rahmat leads many of the sessions, while others are led by capable *muballigh* he has engaged for that purpose. Participation is not cheap; a fee of 60,000 rupiah (about US$6) was paid by each participant in the session I attended in 2009. This was a large sum in Bandung at that time, and, indeed, the participants—mostly women—appeared to be economically privileged and drawn from what my research assistant described as Bandung's "leisure class." I counted about thirty female participants and only one male participant other than myself.

Rahmat is a brilliant performer with a charming and attractive bearing. His deep knowledge of Qur'an and hadith was very evident in the many references to them, and his origins in PERSIS were evident in his careful attention to translation. Nevertheless, his classes include much humor, storytelling, and energetic and expressive body movements. His strategies directed specifically at his female audience were highly successful. Sundanese language was used in a highly affective way to create intimacy and identification. His ability to use media and to manage his image in ways that appeal to contemporary, urban sensibilities has also brought success to him and his organization. Several people described him to me as the successor to Aa Gym, the preaching superstar of Indonesia during the 1990s and early 2000s.

To my knowledge, there was never a moment of separation between Rahmat and PERSIS. Simply put, Rahmat was a promising young orator who chose to continue his career outside of the organization. The parting of ways has not resulted in bad feeling between Rahmat and the group. From Rahmat's point of view, the development of his own voice outside the PERSIS fold would clearly offer financial rewards, but it seems financial considerations had no role in the amicable split. A telling interpretation of this was provided to me by a PERSIS insider, who explained to me in 2010 that Rahmat's congregation had become focused on him as an individual and valued his orations more highly because they were delivered by him. His mediations had become *terpersonalisasi* (personalized). Underpinning this interpretation is a conviction that the cultivation of a unique preaching voice and the exploitation of its power to attract attention and prestige to its owner were not acceptable to PERSIS. Skill in mediation should not be used as a criterion in evaluating one *muballigh* positively over another.

This is basic PERSIS doctrine. Muhammad Natsir composed a detailed critique of the exploitation of unique oratorical voices, which appeared in an oratory manual entitled *Fiqhud Da'wah* (The Islamic Precepts concerning Dakwah). Regarded as a classic work within the broader movement for which Natsir served as a figurehead (see Luth 1999, 64–66), the book has been reprinted frequently since its initial publication in 1966. Such is its status within PERSIS that the testimonial volume published to mark the passing of Shiddiq Amien, the successor of Natsir and Ahmad Hassan, was also called *Fiqhud Da'wah* (Saefuddin 2014).

Natsir's systemization of *dakwah* was built on his conviction that a community's participation in *dakwah* was a fundamental step in progress toward the creation of a just and pious society. In his vision, Islam obliged individual Muslims not only to implement the call to religion using their own talents and abilities but also to support *korps para ahli* (a corps of specialists) for carrying out this task (Natsir [1996] 2000, 116–19). Natsir makes rigorous demands upon this specialist class, membership of which requires the obliteration of self-interest. A *muballigh* answers the call of Islam because he or she has accepted the truth of that call, not because he or she hopes to receive any personal gain from doing so. By accepting the call, a *muballigh* assumes a certain status that needs to be protected from compromise, and any financial dependence upon his audience erodes that status. For this reason, a preacher should not *menjualkan ayat-ayat* (sell the Qur'an's verses) (Natsir [1996] 2000, 145). He should live in the "world of aspirations," not in the *kancah kebendaan* (abyss of materialism) (Natsir [1996] 2000, 268).

Financial and material gains are not the only risks. In fact, Natsir identifies a risk precisely in the performance abilities that we observe so clearly in Al-Jauhari. According to Natsir, these abilities are risky because of their connection with the ego. A *muballigh* who satisfies an audience, or is tempted to mesmerize it through his performance and later receive praise for doing so, is in fact accepting a recognition that is just as improper as a financial one. Such recognition is felt within the preacher's *hawa ananiyah* (Arabic, desiring ego) (Natsir [1996] 2000, 140–45, 233). Based on this, a *muballigh* must be ready to accept not only material poverty but also a lack of public recognition.[11] All this does not mean, however, that the *muballigh* should hope for nothing from his audience. His reward is a meaningful emotional connection between speaker and audience, which is expressed in the Qur'anic term *al-mawaddah fi al-qurba* (loving kindness among kinsfolk).[12] This connection is founded on the *muballigh*'s love and compassion for his audience and was instrumental in allowing the Prophet Muhammad to establish his following. This "loving kindness among kinsfolk" creates a "bridge of feeling, a radiance from the heart that penetrated the divide between the leader [Muhammad] and the nation [*umat*] that followed him: and does so now between the *muballigh* and the nation that he is nurturing by means of dakwah" (Natsir [1996] 2000, 234). In Natsir's vision, this is the preacher's supreme reward.

There is a radical idealism in this systemization that is of one spirit with the textual literalism of PERSIS ideology. Natsir expunges worldly realities from the activity of preaching, just as PERSIS ideology imagines Muslims

not as social subjects but in the shape of textual norms. Natsir's vision problematizes the achievements and oratorical practice of Al-Jauhari and Rahmat Hidayat: material gain is proscribed; the use of strategies to control the
undivided attention of an audience is depicted as a personal failing; recognition and adulation are signs of the desiring self; the development of a
unique voice through performance abilities is a harmful vanity. In effect, the
PERSIS position on mediation conceptualizes oratory as an expression of
pious aspirations. Rahmat's movement away from PERSIS appears as a
movement away from the aspirational world of the Islamic ideal, where
communications are insulated from social realities, into a world tarnished
by unrestrained egotism, financial rewards, and the situated realities of
human communication.

Chapter 4

The Languages of Preaching
in the Islamic Public Sphere

In the two preceding chapters, I flagged two issues that remain unre-
solved. The first concerns language selection. When Al-Jauhari preaches
at celebrations held by Sundanese communities, he generally speaks in
Sundanese. In the Sunday sessions, Shiddiq Amien chose Indonesian as the
dominant language, even though his audience was almost all Sundanese.
How, then, do we account for the contrasting language selections, and what
do these choices tell us about Islamic oratory in West Java? The second issue
relates to questions partially resolved in the conclusion of chapter 2: If
Al-Jauhari's preaching style finds such strong approval among his audiences, why do his sermons include defenses against negative judgments
arising from the application of norms about preaching? Why does Al-Jauhari
feel compelled to defend himself and his preaching style?

These questions are answered here in one move that sets in place a frame
for the chapters to follow. Indonesian Muslims often distinguish between
styles of Islamic communication according to the extent to which they appear to contribute to the national public good.[1] These processes of distinc-

tion have different consequences for Amien and Al-Jauhari. Not many In-donesians would be aware of or sympathetic to the Islamic deliberations informing Hassan and Natsir's ideologies of mediation, yet it is clear that the styles of mediation validated by those ideologies harmonize far more closely with national norms of public Islam than Al-Jauhari's. Hassan and Natsir advocate a literate, rational subject. By contrast, Al-Jauhari's listeners are acknowledged in public commentary through caricatures that characterize them as emotional and inefficacious. As answers to the question of how Islam should play a role in Indonesian public life, the conceptions of preaching appropriateness of Amien and Al-Jauhari point in differing directions. In this chapter, I show how language selection is a variable in that difference.

Preaching's Outcomes

A few months into my time in Bandung, after I had attended many preach-ing events in diverse situations, I developed an intuition about which lan-guage would be preferred in which situation. At festive events, like those at which Al-Jauhari was the orator, Sundanese would generally be used. By contrast, at any event I attended within the ambit of the institutions and roles associated with the state, Indonesian was used. Events taking place within self-consciously modernist programs, such as the Sunday Study sessions, were also frequently conducted in Indonesian.

I did not notice any normative prescriptions about how the choice be-tween Indonesian and Sundanese should be resolved. The question of lan-guage choice arises very rarely in preaching manuals, and the selection of one or the other appeared to be accepted and supported without reflection by preachers and audiences.[2] Remarkably, they all appear to share the same sense for the correct choice of language. When I asked preachers about the issue, they usually gave me answers that suggested there were relationships between languages and specific social segments: "Village people are con-fused by Indonesian"; "Sundanese has more feeling, so villagers like it"; or "Civil servants are more modern than villagers, so they prefer Indonesian." There is some value in these intuitive responses, but they tended to essentialize correspondences between social segments and linguistic form. In reality, I soon realized these correspondences did not materialize neatly. I often noticed, for example, that many listeners reacted positively to Sundanese orations by

Al-Jauhari as well as Indonesian orations by Amien, but did so in different situations. It was not the case that certain social types preferred this or that preaching style.

It *was* the case, however, that West Javanese Muslims did not view these two preachers as doing the same thing. The caricatures of emotional listeners are widely circulating expressions of that differentiation. West Javanese Muslims recognize that Al-Jauhari works for success registering within the spatial and temporal boundaries of the performance and that the bodies moving with enjoyment are signs of that success. They recognize that Amien's preaching succeeds by supporting the ongoing PERSIS project, a project that has transformation as its basic ethos.

These contrasting outcomes (in situ affect and transformation) merge into the broader contexts of social and political life in different ways. The PERSIS transformation project, which is essentially very similar to that of Muhammadiyah and other modernist groups, resembles the national transformation project that is such a core component of national awareness and public commemoration in Indonesia. This correspondence has been a reality of Indonesia's recent past; the narratives of Islamic reform and national transformation dovetail and overlap.

At every turn, we can observe points of overlap and correspondence. In their early stages, both the nationalist and Islamic reform movements acknowledged the social, religious, and political forms of earlier Indonesian societies as restrictions from which Indonesians should break free. The father of the secular indigenous press, Tirto Adhi Soerjo (1880–1918), for example, wrote passionately about the negative aspects of the customs and traditions (Indonesian from Arabic, *adat*) that were so influential within Indonesian societies. The wedding celebrations that were so important to the Javanese, he wrote in 1909, were wasteful exercises in social vanity that should be "thrown away" (Soerjo 2008, 400–401). This sentiment manifested in conflict during the Indonesian revolution, which was waged not only against external colonizers; it also broke, sometimes violently, with longstanding hierarchies of the societies of the Indies (see, e.g., Reid 1979). Muslim modernists wished for a similar break with the past. An example is the Gayo modernists of North Sumatra described by John Bowen, who "aimed at shaking up ideas taken for granted about the world, at interrupting the normal social fabric and etiquette, so that it could be replaced by something else" (Bowen 1997, 171; see also Williams 1990).

Those changes were to affect social and political life, but the national and Islamic modernist projects also advocated the self as a site for change. They have both privileged a conception of human subjectivity that is autonomous and reflective as well as capable of critical reflection on its environment (Baso 2002). Aspirations to such transformation have been expressed since the emergence of Islamic modernism, with Ahmad Hassan's idealization of Muslims as rational subjects being a prime example. In holding this position, he was stating—in religious terms—a project highly similar to that being advocated by modernizing nationalist elites.

Against this background, Islamic and national modernities are hard to disentangle, and their merger has provided a defining backdrop for many contemporary Indonesian lives. Many Indonesians grew up and were educated in environments in which the modernity of the Republic of Indonesia was at the same time an Islamic modernity. They have "learned about the ideas of Indonesia and modernity in contexts of religious education, and they learned to be part of a public, multiethnic sphere largely under religious auspices" (Bowen 1993, 327). Successive Indonesian governments have contributed to this by positioning monotheism as an essential characteristic of citizenship (Kipp and Rodgers 1987). Thus, for contemporary Indonesians, the category of religion implies "notions of progress, modernization, and adherence to nationalist goals" (Atkinson 1983, 688; see also Brenner 1996; Hefner 1987). No wonder that it was Amien, not Al-Jauhari, who appeared to listeners to be working toward the transformation widely aspired to by Indonesian Muslims. I argue below that language selection in preaching is determined by this evaluation.

The Linguistic Background

Like members of other Indonesian ethnicities, Sundanese are generally bilingual, speaking a regional language (Sundanese) as well as Indonesian. Both Amien and Al-Jauhari were native speakers of Sundanese and Indonesian. The contemporary Sundanese language developed from the ancient languages of the peoples of West Java's interior, whereas Indonesian, a variant of Malay that is the national standard for the Republic of Indonesia, arrived in West Java more recently.[3] Intensive contact between speakers of Sundanese and Malay commenced when the West Java interior was opened to commercial activity by the colonial government in the latter part of the eighteenth century. The Dutch had promoted Malay as the colony's administrative language and lingua franca. In 1928, by which time the nationalist movement was gathering momentum across the archipelago, activists from a number of ethnic groups of the Netherlands East Indies announced that Indonesian, a variant of Malay, was to be the language of the united peoples of Indonesia (Foulcher 2000). After independence was declared in 1945 and then secured in an anticolonial struggle, use of the national language increased rapidly as national media increased in relevance for Indonesian citizens and as participation in the developing national education system increased. Today there are still Sundanese with low Indonesian competency who may not have attended an Indonesian educational institution and may not have experienced a pressing need to learn the national standard. Nevertheless, most contemporary Sundanese have mother-tongue competency in both languages and are competent to interpret oratory in either language.

The coexistence of these languages in contemporary West Java is remarkably free of tension. Indonesian is the national standard, deriving authority from Indonesia's relatively recent national project. Sundanese is an ancient language of a subnational language group. In many parts of the world, linguistic plurality such as this transforms languages into signs within conflictual identity politics, but for the most part this does not occur in West Java. The national standard does not signify a history of foreign encroachment, economic disadvantage, or status inequality for Sundanese.[4] In fact, Sundanese do not regard any group as being more authentically Indonesian than themselves, and they do not have to deal with any group that makes such a claim. In other words, they do not behold a "native-speaking Indonesian 'they'" (Errington 1998, 157).[5]

This does not mean the languages are not perceived as signs of ethnic difference. When Sundanese elites express concern about what they perceive as cultural decline, they inevitably reflect on the decline in Sundanese competency among younger people (e.g., Rosidi 2004). And the symbolic value of language differentiation has increased in the postauthoritarian period ensuing after Suharto stepped down in 1998, when constraints concerning public discourse on ethnicity were weakened (Moriyama 2012). In the early 2000s, when Indonesians began to vote for the members of their local parliaments, candidates for election began to promote Sundanese language and tradition as signs of authenticity. These promotions of Sundanese are not, however, antagonistic toward Indonesian; they do not promote the national language as the inauthentic or illegitimate other of Sundanese. Overall, Sundanese feel themselves to be authentic owners of both languages.

The Choice for Sundanese: Preaching's Affect

Al-Jauhari's emphasis on in situ affect necessarily requires him to pay close attention to the cultural competency and particularities of his audience, and to mobilize these skillfully. The Sundanese language is a highly productive resource in this process. An engaging, affective oration is more effectively delivered in Sundanese because it is the language of shared experience in the informal, domestic, and intimate areas of life: Sundanese understand kinship relations and obligations in Sundanese structures; their earliest experiences in the family environment are mediated in that language; daily experiences such as eating and socializing are represented through a Sundanese lexicon far richer than its Indonesian equivalent; the characteristics of the human personality are affectionately represented in a rich Sundanese lexicon; ethical values are circulated in an extensive repertoire of figurative constructions, proverbs, and maxims; and so on. The affective qualities of Sundanese give it a special potency in oratory.

Sundanese orators are highly aware of the affective value of Sundanese, and in conversation make frequent claims for it, often in comparisons they draw between Sundanese and Indonesian. A number of them described the language to me as *basa rasa* (Sundanese, language of feeling).[6] Writers make similar comparisons. One writer with a vast literary output in both Sundanese and Indonesian, Ajip Rosidi (b. 1938), has identified various deficiencies in Indonesian as a literary medium. When writing in Indonesian, he claimed, he inserts Sundanese terms when that term expresses a *rasa* (Indonesian and Sundanese, feeling) for which there is no equivalent in the national standard (Rosidi 1983, 209–12; see also Anderson 1966, 105–9).

Such characterizations do not, however, directly motivate Al-Jauhari's selection of Sundanese. His preference for Sundanese is a functional imperative created out of his desire to produce an oration that is high in affect. The language code is only one of the resources that enable him to do that. As chapter 2 has indicated, his performances traverse a wide variety of possibilities. The use of Sundanese, then, is part of a mobilization of performance genres and cultural competencies shared by the speaker and audience. To put it another way, Al-Jauhari's oratorical style reveals a pattern of co-occurrence between the use of Sundanese, the communication of affect, and high levels of generic variation.

The Choice for Indonesian: Preaching Transformations

Given the functional value of Sundanese relative to Indonesian, it might seem strange that orators would choose Indonesian when addressing Sundanese audiences. Why would an orator not choose the language that provided the best option for affective communication? But Sundanese preachers frequently choose to speak in Indonesian even where the numerical superiority of Sundanese in the listening audience would suggest otherwise.[7] While I was attending the PERSIS Sunday Study sessions in 2007 and 2009, I also attended regularly the preaching program held at the Bandung Municipal Water Board, a state-owned utility that requires its employees to assemble once a month to listen to a sermon from a visiting preacher. The audience included many Sundanese, yet the Sundanese preachers invited to preach in that setting invariably preferred to use Indonesian as the dominant code. The preachers of the Sunday sessions usually showed the same preference. The majority of its listeners are from Sundanese communities, yet Indonesian is frequently used.

The reason behind preachers' preference for Indonesian lies in the indexical meanings that Sundanese (and other Indonesians) identify in the national standard—Indonesian points to an aspirational transformation that is central to civic awareness.[8] Indonesian has been both medium for and symbol of momentous transformations in which all Indonesians are involved (Errington 2000, 209). Ben Anderson (1966) has described these transformative meanings: Indonesian was a suitable language for the new republic because it enabled a breaking away from the hierarchical modes of its ethnic societies; it was an "enterprise" that offered solutions to the problems involved in shaping a unified nation that had to be self-consciously "modern"; and it formed the cross-cultural code of communication during the independence struggle, providing a "means of communication for the aspirations of the Republic" in its "wager on the future."

These meanings were later consolidated by governments, especially Suharto's, in support of development programs. For the New Order government, the cultivation of a single national language served the logic by which a standardized language appeared as a prerequisite for Indonesia's ethnic heterogeneity (Errington 2000, 209–11; see also Foulcher 2000; Heryanto 1995). Indonesia's standard language was monologically asserted as the standard language of a singular national identity. As a result of these developments, Indonesians have developed a feeling for Indonesian as the right language for many situations, even when their first language might be another.[9] Furthermore, the national standard has attracted very strong participation and support from Indonesians, who have identified the republic's modernizing and development aspirations with their own goals. Kathryn Woolard (1998, 21) labeled Indonesia's standardization project as "the wonder child of language planning."

The associations Indonesians sense between language and the national aspiration for transformation are instrumental in the decisions preachers make about language selection. Where a preaching situation is underpinned by a program dedicated to transformation, or when it takes place in a setting where respect for that transformation is demanded, the national standard's indexical meanings in this direction are unavoidable. The listeners at the Sunday Study sessions orient themselves appropriately for an oratory that resonates with their shared commitment to self and societal transformation, and Indonesian is the language that signals that commitment.

This aspiration for transformation means different things to different people. Many PERSIS followers are actively engaged in self-imposed projects of transformation, but transformation does not always demand active steps of that kind. For other Indonesians, transformation is something far less demanding, being a social value to which deference must be shown. The preaching program of the water board is illustrative of this. Some of the audience at these preaching events might be committed to personal projects of transformation, but, for most, their awareness of transformation is triggered by an environment that symbolically restates national aspirations: the Indonesian flag flies in the yard; photographic portraits of the president and vice president are prominent in a number of rooms of the complex; large reproductions of the Garuda bird, the national symbol whose feathers numerically signify the date of independence, are present. The water board's employees

are very conscious of their roles within the project of the independent republic and an ethic of transformation is fundamental to their self-awareness.
When the preacher arrives, his choice to speak in Indonesian expresses a
shared appreciation for the value of transformation.

It is not the case that Sundanese per se is uncongenial in such a setting.
Sundanese might not index in the same direction as Indonesian, but it does
not index in the opposite direction. Rather, it is the multivocal preaching of
in situ affect that is uncongenial. The national standard points to the idealization of Islamic subjects as critical, reflective ones whose Islamicness is to
be dedicated to national development. A preacher who works with shared
cultural realities in order to please an audience in situ does not show respect
for this idealization, nor does he respect the critical and reflective capacities
of his audience. In modernist thinking, the ideal Muslim subject, committed to religious and national transformation, is not captivated by the affective strategies of oratory.

Ward Keeler's (1998) analysis of audience evaluations of oratorical language illustrates the national standard's instrumental value in performing
transformation. His research was carried out within the Javanese ethnic
group, which occupies the provinces of Java to the east of West Java Province.
During a lengthy stay in a Javanese village, he compared festive, multivocal
preaching drawing on regional cultural resources with formally consistent,
stylistically nondescript preaching in a combination of Indonesian and the
formal variant of Javanese. Male audience members mostly gave negative
critiques of festive, multivocal preaching, even when such performances stimulated them. They approved of preaching delivered in a "constricted style"
characterized by a "single, serious tone, constant use of either refined Javanese
or the national language, Indonesian, or perhaps a mixture of the two, plus
a great deal of Arabic, and the exclusion of song and narrative" (Keeler
1998, 166). It is important to note precisely what was excluded when the
Javanese villagers described their preferred preaching style. They did not
exclude the use of the expressive registers of Javanese, but they gave
secondary ranking to a preaching style that was rich in multivocality and
generic variation ("songs and narrative"). The exclusion of multivocality and
generic variation, however, effects the exclusion of the regional language,
for as I have argued above, in preaching to regional audiences, a satisfying
multivocality can best materialize in the expressive modes of the regional
language rather than Indonesian.

Keeler found this preference to be motivated by the status aspirations of listeners.[10] They associated the formal, monotonous style with the lives and aspirations of modern, urban elites and perceived it as an expression of the power of the modern state, and for that reason "the serious, monological tone of official speech strikes [Javanese villagers] as more persuasive than a more entertaining tone" (Keeler 1998, 175). For these listeners, a positive evaluation of the "ponderous, weighty Indonesian style" was a foundation for claiming personal status. The same metadiscursive understanding underpins language selection by Sundanese orators: they sense, along with their listeners, when the situation demands recognition of the aspirations of the national project.[11]

Code-Switching and Refreshment

The choice for Indonesian connects oratory with widely held conceptions about the role Islam should play in public life and how Muslims should engage with it. By contrast, the choice of Sundanese appears as a functional one made in response to the pragmatics of the situation. Orators often exploit these distinctions by using both languages within the same oration. In fact, although I found preachers unable to accurately describe the reasons behind their choice of one language over the other in a given sermon, the switches preachers make between the two languages in sermons reveal their intuitive awareness of the situational implications of language selection. The excerpt below is an example from Shiddiq Amien that illustrates something I observed constantly when listening to Sundanese preachers who preached in Indonesian: even though they preferred Indonesian because it indexes the national transformation, they frequently mobilized Sundanese in refreshing strategies that created, if only temporarily, the affective connection that the regional language enables.

This observation suggests a lack of resemblance between the PERSIS ideology of mediation and the actual practice of PERSIS preachers. I have argued that this ideology devalues those aspects of mediation that are distinctive traits of the cultural context in which it takes place. Natsir and Ahmad Hassan idealized mediation that is free of the realities of social interaction: preachers are not to be influenced by financial interests; they should not seek to use verbal artistry or tricks to impress other Muslims; they should overcome the constraints posed by situated conventions for performing observances. However, the realities of oratorical mediation must be distinguished from their idealizations. In reality, Amien, the heir to these two renowned PERSIS ideologues, was an orator who understood the value of affective strategies in oratorical practice and who exploited them in his preaching. His prestige as an orator cannot be attributed solely to his role as leader in the program of self- and society-shaping that he shares with PERSIS members. Amien was in fact a skillful orator whose mediations were open, to a degree, to the communicative resources that created the sociability he shared with his fellow Sundanese.

The example of Amien's language switching given here is from his Sunday Study oration (Amien 2009). In the hour-long Sunday sermon, Amien switched to Sundanese on twenty-three occasions. Many of the switches were just single words, while the longest consisted of a couple of sentences. In the following translated excerpt, words and phrases that were delivered in Sundanese are underlined. Because Amien translates his Arabic as he speaks, I have left the Qur'anic references untranslated:

> So the first bodily organ to be created, the first of the sensory ones, apart from the nose, was of course the hearing. Now, with this hearing, when a family tries to speak with their newborn baby, the baby smiles not because she can see but because her hearing is already at work. The ears and hearing are first. In the same way, when a person is old, the first things to go to ruin are the ears. *Summun, bukmun, umyun. Summun* means deaf. When someone is getting old they have difficulty hearing even when we shout at them [subdued audience laughter]. You have to nudge them to make them look around [subdued audience laughter]. *Bukmun* means dumb, meaning there are no teeth left, not even one, toothless, so when they speak it becomes . . . [audience: stammering!]. That's right, stammering. When they speak they go "offside" [subdued audience laughter]. Then when the eyes go, one must wear glasses. (Amien 2009)

The example reveals skillful oratorical exploitation of the affective value of Sundanese. Throughout almost every moment of the hour-long sermon, Amien's dour delivery in Indonesian drew minimal responses from audience members. Although many focused intently on his words, their bodily positions indicated relaxation. Many never lifted their heads and some chatted quietly with the person sitting beside them. People were massaging each other. But this example and others like it caused changes to the audience's demeanor. In this case, the switch to Sundanese was a humorous reference to a recognizable stereotype of village life—the toothless, old person who has difficulty hearing and speaking. Amien represented this person's vulnerability in a way that was humorous but affectionate, and many audience members responded to Amien's switch by calling back in the regional language. Remarkably, their interjection of the Sundanese word *réro* (stammering) was delivered to a prompt Amien had supplied in Indonesian. This interaction strengthened the connection between preacher and audience. Amien, whose general demeanor almost always showed a detached concentration bordering on melancholy, smiled during the switching.

I observed moments such as these in almost every Indonesian-language sermon I attended in Bandung. Their effects are like ripples through the previously immobile audience: bodies rock gently, people turn to the side, the audience is refreshed. The switches enable Amien to reach into the shared cultural context in a playful voice and to establish a more intimate and less formal rapport than the one achieved through use of the national standard, which remains faithful to the strict letter of the PERSIS program.[12] Because laughter and play are so strictly controlled throughout the sermon, the switches appear as striking variations in the interaction between preacher and audience. They provide momentary glimpses of the preaching outcome that Al-Jauhari's audiences expect of him. Nevertheless, he is spare and disciplined with these switches. The playful voice is restrained, and the audience members do not sense any notable verbal or performing skill on his part. Too much affective gratification would be harmful to the shared commitment to transformation.

The Unique Voice Constrained

The overlaps between PERSIS's ideology of mediation and nationally authoritative idealizations of self and society provide a fuller context for understanding the defensiveness that materializes in Al-Jauhari's oratory. At the conclusion of chapter 2, I noted that even though Al-Jauhari's oratorical style receives high approval from the audiences to which he preaches, his sermons include pleas on his own behalf. He defends his personal integrity from the slur of selling the verses, and he mobilizes the concept of *gaul* (youth sociability) in defense of his preaching. His reasons for giving these defenses are not immediately obvious, for his audiences do not critique his style. They receive his orations warmly and with enthusiasm, and his career is a successful one.

Amien was held in a public regard that will always be out of Al-Jauhari's reach. This was caused by the different ways in which their preaching styles were treated as contributions to the public good. First, the Islamic public sphere does not facilitate positive recognition of those features that make Al-Jauhari so popular in those communities that invite him. There is no doubting his wild success, as Al-Jauhari is so successful that he cannot fulfill all the invitations extended to him. Event organizers love him because only he and a few other preachers like him can ensure that their mosques and football fields are full for the celebrations they hold as important. He appeals to young and old, and he brings families together in religious activities in a way that few preachers can. Nevertheless, there is no public category for acknowledging or recognizing those skills. Affective orators are not commemorated as contributors to the public good. As Keeler (1998, 175) puts it, "A speaker who chooses to entertain his listeners through contrasting voices, song, and stories, attracts and maintains his listeners' attention. Speakers who enjoy a responsive audience will opt for this mode and win public appreciation in the form of laughter and attentiveness. What they will not win is the esteem that is accorded people who are seen to be in possession of or linked to power. They will be appreciated as entertainers rather than as authorities."

In contrast, Amien was recognized publicly as an authority on Islam, a recognition seen most clearly in the way governments treated him. Although the province's governments aspire to treat all religious currents equally and are not generally more sympathetic to PERSIS than to other groups, Shiddiq Amien was considered a more suitable reference point in state and civil contexts than Al-Jauhari. Amien was a regular participant in state-sponsored preaching programs and consultative projects. His opinion and counsel on questions of social policy and religion were often sought by government. So when the mayor of Bandung attempted to legislate a public morality program, Shiddiq Amien was a member of the consultative board. He was invited on to *shariah* advisory boards in banking and other fields (Saefuddin 2014). He achieved the status of public intellectual and was accepted by government and media as a spokesperson for a segment of Bandung's Muslims.

Al-Jauhari is not involved in consultative processes relating to the public good. He has been involved in politics, but the nature of this involvement is telling, for it is based on recognition of his masterful capabilities in the conveyance of affect. As described in chapter 2, Al-Jauhari has engaged in political activity as member of a "success team" assembled for the electoral campaign of a candidate for the nationalist political party known as Golkar. The team was booked to give performances over a period of one month, during which he traveled with the candidate and a popular singer, appearing on stages erected in villages and public spaces throughout the electorate.[13] The events had earlier been publicized by campaign workers as Tabligh Akbar (Great Preaching) and drew audiences numbering in the thousands. His value as a success team preacher is due to the highly affective impact of his preaching on Sundanese audiences, and his reputation for this drew villagers out of their homes to attend the events. Yet this reputation would not provide the basis for recognition as a public authority on Islam. By contrast, Amien's preaching reputation would draw very few villagers out of their homes, but governments of West Java treated him as a valued contributor to the public sphere.

If Al-Jauhari's aspirations were limited to the preaching stage, these limitations would not be a problem. However, he takes his roles as Islamic leader and contributor to public discourse seriously. As described in chapter 2, he would like to have influence in the Islamic public sphere beyond the preaching stage. For this reason, even though reservations about his style are not expressed in the settings in which he preaches, it is surely difficult for him to ignore the limitations imposed on his aspirations, and this explains his frequent mentions of the concept of *gaul* (chapter 2). This idea does not have importance for him on the level of self-representation, for he does not style as an urbane and trendy figure. It is a resource for contesting the limitations placed by the public on his range of competencies. It works in two ways. First, the concept is a positive representation of his own style, which has the character of *gaul* not because of its urbanity or hipness but because it moves freely over the cultural knowledge and understandings of his listeners. An oration by Al-Jauhari moves into his audience's sphere of recognition, ignoring the discursive borders and restraints set in place by the PERSIS ideology of mediation. Second, it asserts a subversive position about the relation between authority and forms of communication and mediation. *Gaul* militates against the idea that ways of speaking and communicating can be ranked hierarchically. It opposes the tendency to characterize utterances that cross over ideologically determined borders as hybrids, recognizing transformation as only one of many possible values to be referenced through preaching. And it enables Al-Jauhari to advocate for the value of his unique preaching voice on behalf of the multitudes for whom it provides an attractive and powerful religious experience.

Chapter 5

The Listening Audience Laughs and Cries, the Writing Public Thinks

In the preceding chapters I have used the term *audience* to refer to the people gathering to hear the sermons of Al-Jauhari and Shiddiq Amien. I have used the word in the common sense of an assemblage of people listening to orations. In the broader contexts into which this discussion is being directed, however, the term has potential meanings that cannot be easily ignored. Alongside other terms for describing media and their reception, *audience* is far from neutral in its implications. In particular, it takes on specific connotations alongside the concepts of "the public" or "publics" (see Butsch 2008; Livingstone 2005). And in the critical literature about Islamic oratory produced in contemporary Indonesia—some of which I explore in this chapter—the distinction between public and audience is unavoidable.

The concept of "the public" has its origins in social and political life in the city-states of classical times. Urban centers typically included a space at which members of the public could gather within sight of each other (in Greek, *agora*; in Roman, *forum*). "It was here that free citizens argued, legislated and adjudicated, both in their own interests and on behalf of others who were not free—slaves, women, foreigners, children" (Hartley 2002, 189). Populations of urban centers have grown since then, and the public, in the sense of a mutually visible group, has mutated into an abstract group unified by common interest and responsiveness toward specific forms of publicity. In Jürgen Habermas's (1989) conception of the "bourgeois public sphere," "publics" are granted a prime role in the workings of the democratic polity. The public sphere was the place in which people emerged from their privacy to engage in criticism of public authority through rational exchange and informed debate.

The concepts of the public and the public sphere have influenced thinking about how modern democracies bridge the gaps between private life, public action, and state authority. Yet scholars have found it very difficult to specify precisely what constitutes the public or a public. Michael Warner's (2002) frequently cited analysis makes the circulation of media—especially written media—the primary reference point for understanding the ways in which liberal democracies have imagined their publics and public spheres. Written media have features that create the impression of circulation. This circulation signals relations between people with similar interest and concerns, and it enables people who are in fact strangers to each other to be imagined as a cohesive group called "a public." According to this definition, a public is imagined in the shape of the impressions texts create about their own circulation. There is not one public but as many as there are shared interests that sustain the impression of relations among strangers (the hunting and fishing public, the queer public, etc.). But as Warner (2002, 81–84) has pointed out, one model of stranger-relations has become broadly accepted as "the public" or the "general public," and that is the one in which the relationship among strangers is styled as a conversation among private readers engaged in rational-critical discussion. This is the kind of exchange that is associated with the development and expression of public opinion; thus, this public is regarded as approximating and superintending the state in its coverage of and attention to shared interests. After all, in the democratic imaginary, public opinion plays a role in shaping the exercise of state power.

In my introduction to this book I have quoted Indonesian critiques of oratory that reflect a consensus that oratory in its popular forms is outside the range of media through which a legitimate publicness is shaped. They caricature listeners as subjects unsuited to processes through which public opinion is formed. Rather, some of them argue, that process is to be found in the reflections, deliberations, and contributions of well-informed people reading in private. Critics of oratory relegate the listener to the periphery of the public sphere. The audiences for orators are held to be inferior to the public that is emblematized by the figure of "the private reader, whose stillness and solitude became privileged icons of a distinct kind of critical reasoning within the imaginary of the bourgeois public" (Hirschkind 2006, 107).

Agency is another idealization that is held negatively against oratory. Oratory's critics fault it because its audience members appear to lack this quality. As part of the same historical process by which rational-critical dialogue has been privileged as the model of exchange for stranger-relations, the narrative of modernity has privileged a version of human agency characterized by autonomy and freedom from custom and tradition (Mahmood 2005, 1–39; Keane 2007). Modern agency implies subjects breaking free from the constraints of conventional social structures; for several reasons, oratory's critics do not see this emancipation as achievable through participation in preaching events. First, as noted earlier, their idealizations of public subjectivity are based on writing and reading, not speaking and listening. Second, the Indonesian critiques of oratory reflect the Enlightenment's mistrust of the sensorium. Its key thinkers doubted the rationality, judgment, and reliability of listening subjects (Hirschkind 2006, 13–18). Third, the routines and conventions of oratory imply collective obligations and group behaviors that are interpreted as constraints and limitations on human agency. They suggest models for social behavior that, ideally, Indonesian Muslims should have left behind. As a result, the subjects who make up oratorical audiences are located by oratory's critics at the wrong end of what Webb Keane (2007) has called "the moral narrative of modernity." Listening audiences appear to belong to the past because they do not display the "human self-emancipation and self-mastery" identified as requisites for contemporary subjectivity (Keane 2007, 6–7).

These conceptualizations of democratic citizenship, publics, agency, and media efficacy shape dispositions toward oratory in contemporary Bandung and form the subject of this chapter and the next. In chapter 6 I explore the frustration Islamic feminists feel at the apparent lack of autonomy displayed by female listening subjects. In this chapter I describe a radical critique of oratorical practice that takes shape in a program designed to foster writing as an Islamic medium for the exchange of ideas and opinion. This program, which emerged in Bandung and has rapidly gained support nationally, locates oratory as a retardant in the development of a creative, prosperous, and competitive Islamic *peradaban* (civilization) and aims to transform *dakwah* audiences into rational and informed publics. It emanates from an academic environment, namely the Faculty of Dakwah and Communication at Bandung's State Islamic University.

Faculty of Dakwah and Communication

Although Bandung's State Islamic University was established in Bandung in 1968, a separate *dakwah* faculty was not opened until 1993. As was the case with other universities of the UIN/IAIN system, the study of the science of *dakwah* (Indonesian, from Arabic, *ilmu dakwah*) was previously located in the Faculty of Usul al-Din (principles of the religion) (UIN Sunan Gunung Djati 2007, 3–5).[1] The University's contemporary *dakwah* faculty offers two undergraduate degrees, *dakwah* and communications. The *dakwah* degree includes four specializations, each with its projected vocational outcomes: the Islamic counseling specialization qualifies students to work as counselors in hospitals, as therapists, social workers, and teachers; the communication and predication specialization prepares students to work as proselytizers through a wide range of media including *khitabah* (oratory); the *dakwah* management specialization prepares students to work in the development and administration of predication programs offered by government departments and private organizations; and the Islamic community development stream qualifies students to work in private and government community development programs. The communications degree has two streams, journalism and public relations. The faculty has been successful in attracting students. In 2006 more than five thousand of the State Islamic University's approximately thirteen thousand students were enrolled in the faculty. At that time, only the faculty of education and teaching, which prepares students for the relatively secure vocation of teaching, attracted more students (UIN SGD 2006; UIN SGD 2007).

The State Islamic University system was originally initiated within the republic's Ministry of Religious Affairs with the goals of creating the Islamic expertise required for an independent Indonesia, and of addressing what was perceived to be a neglect of spirituality in the existing educational system (Noer 1978, 24–41). In my experience as a guest in the Faculty of Dakwah and Communication, I sensed that its staff and the surrounding community expected it to play an active role as an agent of *dakwah*. This is reflected in a number of community outreach programs managed by the faculty (UIN SGD 2007, 354). The primary focus of the contemporary faculty, however, is academic. Its current mission statement foregrounds the goal of "serving Indonesian society through research and teaching about *dakwah* in its theoretical and practical aspects" (UIN SGD 2007, 7–8).

The *dakwah* faculties of the Ministry of Religion's universities have proved to be fertile environments for critical discussion of religion and pluralism in the Indonesian state. When *dakwah* became an academic discipline, its intellectuals began to inquire into the diversity of Indonesia's religious "audiences" and the boundaries between them (Millie 2012), raising important questions about citizenship and religious identity. Scholars of the Bandung Faculty of Dakwah and Communication play a leading role in these debates, responding to West Java's religious diversity with analyses that encourage respectful attention to the multiple Islamic interpretations produced in the province's diverse environments (Aripudin and Sambas 2007; Muhtadi et al. 2007). The serious consideration given to pluralism by the State Islamic Universities' academics has made these institutions key contributors to debates that are ongoing in contemporary Indonesia. They have also attracted criticism, for concepts such as pluralism and liberalism have their opponents in Indonesia (e.g., Jaiz 2005), and these opponents have characterized the universities under the Ministry of Religion as an ideological opponent in the struggle of Islam.

The question of whether *dakwah* is a religious or secular/scientific discipline is a topic of interest to *dakwah* academics, whose work reveals a range of interpretations of its methodological and epistemological constitution. The issue can be reduced to this question: should the proper framework for the study of *dakwah* be constructed out of the textual norms provided in the Qur'an and hadith or from the theoretical possibilities found within the social sciences, especially in the discipline of communications? In reality, both possibilities merge in the work of dakwah academics. Several national workshops held in 2003 established that Islamic *dakwah* was a social sciences discipline (Sambas 2006, 384), a decision that reflects the reality that many *dakwah* academics have qualifications in anthropology, sociology, or media studies and theorize *dakwah* using concepts from those disciplines (e.g. Muhtadi 2009a, 2009b; Muhtadi and Safei 2003). Others—for example,

Syukriadi Sambas (2009)—devise and employ scientific approaches based more closely on the Qur'anic verses and hadith about *dakwah*. Some scholars draw on both, unbothered by any suggestion that the two might not be compatible.

Bandung's State Islamic University is located within a society for whom Islamic listening is a preferred observance, so it is not surprising that the faculty includes many career orators. For these academic/*muballigh*, the faculty is a platform from which successful *dakwah* careers can be launched and sustained. West Javanese attach high social status to university graduates and public servants. The appellation M.Ag. (master of religion) and the title of *dosen* (lecturer) enhance a *muballigh's* viability in the dakwah marketplace. The name cards of lecturers such as Al-Jauhari, the best-known orator on the faculty, clearly display their qualifications and institutional affiliations.

M2KQ: Competing in Writing

Acep Hidayat, born in Bandung in 1961, is one of the high achievers among the Faculty of Dakwah and Communication. After a *pesantren* education in Bandung, he taught mathematics and religion to secondary-level students until he commenced undergraduate *dakwah* studies at the Bandung State Islamic University in 1982 and then took a master's degree at a university in the United States (1993–95). He completed a doctorate in the communications faculty of Bandung's best-known social sciences school, Padjadjaran University. His dissertation was an analysis of communication occurring within a political and religious movement of great significance to twentieth century Indonesia, Nahdlatul Ulama (Muhtadi 2004). He is an influential and prolific columnist and commentator in Bandung and acts as a consultant to West Java's provincial and regional governments.

One of Acep Hidayat's greatest achievements has been his creation and development of a competition in which participants compete in writing about the Qur'an. This is known as the Musabaqah Menulis Kandungan Al-Qur'an (M2KQ: Competition in Writing about the Contents of Al-Qur'an). As I show in the following, this initiative was motivated by perceptions about oratory that developed in Hidayat during his experiences as a Muslim educator and social sciences researcher in Bandung. The rationale for the M2KQ is an assessment of Indonesian Islamic society in which oral *dakwah* is an inferior medium to written *dakwah*.

The M2KQ has been added to the range of competitive events, known as branches, in the state-supported national Musabaqah Tilawat Al-Qur'an (MTQ: Qur'an Recitation Competition). In this giant tournament of Islamic skills, first held in 1968 and now held every three years, competitors represent their provinces by competing in disciplines such as Qur'anic recitation, memorization, interpretation, and calligraphy. Although the MTQ originated in the Indonesian government's desire to engage with Indonesia's Islamic public on favorable terms, it would be a mistake to overstate the top-down character of the event. As Anna Gade has shown, the competitive framework is eagerly embraced by many Indonesians who derive pious motivations from the competitive framework and enthusiastically participate against the background of shared dispositions toward the meanings and performance of Islamic revelation (Gade 2004, 216–66). Against this background, the admittance of Acep's innovation into the competition is a prestigious achievement on his part.

He first conceived of the competition in 2002 and developed the concept with Agus Ahmad Safei, his younger colleague in the Faculty of Dakwah and Communication. They promoted the event at regional level with such success that it was admitted as an exhibition event at the 2008 national MTQ in Banten. In June 2010 the M2KQ was staged as a new branch of the national MTQ held in Bengkulu.

In the M2KQ program, forty participants sit at computers, preparing ten to fifteen pages of writing on a given topic concerning the Qur'an. They do this within an allotted time of between ten to twelve hours. In the case of provincial or national competitions, the participants will have already been victorious in selection rounds held at municipal or provincial level. Equal numbers of male and female participants are selected by judges to progress to the next round, until six participants reach the final round. In the final round they are required to give an oral presentation about their work, but only 15 percent of their assessment is based on this oral presentation. The remainder of their result is calculated from their writing. The panel of judges measure the competitors against four criteria: the quality and strength of the content and its engagement with Al-Qur'an; style and correctness of language; coherence and logical clarity of thought; and the range and quality of references drawn upon. Selected essays are published by the organizers, and several volumes, edited by Hidayat and colleagues, have been published to date by the West Java provincial government.

Behind Hidayat's creation of the writing competition is his long-term project of studying and analyzing Indonesian Islam, politics, and media. His writings reveal two recurring preoccupations. The first is his observation that the politicized fragmentation of Indonesian Islamic society has prevented Islam from fulfilling its potential role in Indonesian political life.[2] Islamic communications genres could potentially serve as media for educating voters about meaningful participation in the democratic process. Instead, Indonesian voters display an irrational subservience to the symbols of whatever segment of Islamic society to which they are loyal. They respond emotionally to symbolic resources that are used by charismatic communicators from both secular and religious parties to manipulate the loyalties of their followers (Muhtadi 2004, 201) and, thus, Indonesian democracy displays a fragmented identity politics. Furthermore, Hidayat argues, contemporary Indonesians do not understand that civic participation in the political process should be more than just voting. Ideally, Indonesians should critically reflect on the democratic process. This political immaturity, he argues, represents a failure of *dakwah* in Indonesia.

The second theme, strongly linked to the first, is the state of Indonesian education and the nature of the subjectivities that should be cultivated within it. Hidayat's position on this is strongly shaped by his experiences as an educator at secondary and tertiary levels, which have made him strongly critical of Indonesian educational standards. His criticism turns on the model of agency to be developed in Indonesian youth. He sees Indonesia's national education system as weakened by its subordination to outmoded political and economic imperatives that shape Indonesian curricula and pedagogies. Ideally, the national education system should develop people in accordance with their dispositions as sovereign subjects. Education should be a liberating instrument to enable a person to discover an identity in the shape of her basic character and cultural environment (Muhtadi 2009b, 141–42). Instead, Indonesians have been disadvantaged by the pedagogical structures that reflected the New Order's monopoly on political participation and expression, and the country's economy has suffered from its failure to develop a class of knowledge workers (Muhtadi and Safei 2006). Hidayat approves of educational theories that take as their starting point the innate potential of students rather than the social conventions and structures that dominate their environments.[3]

These concerns construct a vulnerable democratic citizenship in need of specific communicative competencies for its strengthening. Hidayat's innovation was to connect democratic citizenship with styles of communication, and to implement an action program that was intended to cultivate those styles. The connection is revealed in the following three quotations:

[When considered] as a means for shaping society, and for shaping it as an autonomous political community, dakwah causes important issues to arise. Dakwah should not only be seen as a process of conveying religious teachings in ways which, in actual fact and without us realising it, amount to a process of making the Islamic community stupid. At a passing glance, dakwah that only touches the surface aspects of spirituality appears to have a refreshing influence in life. But from another perspective, without our realising it, this dakwah has weakened our competitive spirit, and has led the Islamic community to prefer an apolitical attitude that will bring it no benefit in the future. Ideally, and history reveals this to be true, dakwah should touch on society's weak points. If political knowledge is a weak point of the Islamic community, then dakwah should be oriented towards educating Muslims to enable them to participate in a proper and proportional way. This is preferable to the opposite, in which dakwah stays clear of political themes. The Dakwah we are used to at the present is indeed a "religious" phenomenon. We sense it is becoming ever more exciting, but it appears to have failed to convey its broader context. Considering that the society targeted by dakwah is experiencing increasing difficulty in facing up to life's challenges, where is the wisdom in merely inviting people to laugh and cry? They should not be pacified for the sake of their inner wholeness, when in truth this merely creates an attitude of social apathy. This failure to convey the broader context is seen in the increasing alienation of dakwah from political life . . . the process of political ignorance that occurred during the thirty years of the New Order has not yet gained attention in dakwah activities in general. (Muhtadi 2008, 115–16)

[Only] specialists develop the habit of reading, while our society in general prefers to listen. Moreover, we don't even express our opinions orally, no. We tend to be passive listeners. A congregation of thousands will attend a sermon. But quality writings are left lying around, never to be taken up.

Conveying Islamic teachings through the medium of orality is becoming more and more festive. They come to sit, listen, laugh or cry. Once they go home, the messages are easily forgotten. Only the stories are remembered, and this only happens because people hear them being played repeatedly on cassettes that become bestsellers. But [they do not encounter the stories] in reading materials. The results of this are less than satisfying. It is as if the "ritual" of conveying Islamic teaching is just a temporary stopping-place, something that comes in the right ear and out from the left. (Muhtadi 2012b, 97)

Up to now we have never known how many times in a month Imam Syafii or Imam Maliki received invitations to give sermons; we also do not know how many students Iman Hanafi or Imam Hambali had. We know these people through their works, from their books, from their writings. Yes, from their writings. (Muhtadi and Safei 2007, viii)

These statements create a hierarchy of communicative styles ranked according to their perceived value for national futures (see Salvatore 1998). The hierarchy emerges in four dispositions. The first concerns the outcomes that ideally should arise from *dakwah* activities. Hidayat is convinced that *dakwah* should empower Muslims to participate in the democratic processes for their own betterment. This is a transformative vision, exemplifying widely held convictions about the proper role of religion in society (see chapter 4). The second observation highlights his caricature of oratory as an affective medium. Listening is connected variously with passivity, emotional display, "surface aspects," and forgetfulness. The caricature downgrades the faculty of hearing in a manner characteristic of post-Enlightenment discourse and thus excludes the possibility that oratory could be a medium for rational deliberation.

Third, oratory is represented here as incapable of enabling the circulation that constitutes a cornerstone of idealizations of the public sphere. Ideas only touch the surface, or disappear in the bad memory of the listener, or travel in one ear and out the other without taking purchase and forming a base for future expression and circulation. In contrast to the informed circulation of ideas and rational-critical dialogue associated with genres of writing and reading, listeners are represented as being unable to act as nodes in the circulation of ideas. My final observation concerns his privileging of reading and writing, not speaking and listening, as the media that enable the formation of public opinion. A reading public is more efficacious than a listening audience.[4]

The M2KQ is a powerful indicator of the contrasting evaluations elites give to writing and listening as contributions to Indonesian democracy. Indonesia's democratic culture will not be furthered by its preachers, according to this critique, but by its writers. The M2KQ imagines a great distance between enlightened, reflective, creative reading and writing subjects, on the one hand, and thrilled, amused, inspired listening audiences on the other.

Democratic Citizenship and Its Obstacles

I argue in chapter 3 that the transformational ethos of Amien's preaching events located him closer to the center of public and civil life than Al-Jauhari. For similar reasons, Hidayat's M2KQ initiative has received a very positive reception from the governments and public bodies that have sponsored the competition. Its expansion has been enabled by a significant dedication of resources from governments. Hidayat's conception of *dakwah*'s role for Indonesian society merges favorably with governmental visions of Indonesian futures.

By supporting the M2KQ, West Javanese and Indonesian governments contribute to an ongoing tension between elite visions of democratic culture and the real preferences of Indonesians for particular styles. In postindustrial Western societies, similar discourses were created around the medium of television in its early days and found expression in what are widely called "media and democracy debates." Some academics and social commentators understood television as a lowest common denominator medium that appealed to the masses and was a servant of crass commercial interests rather than ideals of civic virtue (Hartley 1992, 101–44). Walter Lippmann (1889–1974), the renowned participant in the American media and democracy debate, urged broadcasters to give priority to what was "good" over what was "popular." Just as Hidayat is concerned about the effects of popular oratory, Lippmann was concerned that television could weaken the basis of popular democracy. In response, television programmers working for America's Public Broadcasting Service sought to "transform television viewers into active citizens" by implementing a code of civility in which rationality and a lack of emotion were key features (Ouellette 1999, 76). Hidayat is concerned with transforming the passive audiences of oral *dakwah* into active citizens who are identified as such by their skills in reading and writing.

Looking back, the critics of television are seen to have prioritized conservative notions of civic virtue over television's value as an accessible and democratic medium. An unsympathetic analysis could critique Hidayat in a similar way. Hidayat and the governments attracted to his programs elevate a particular concept of the role of religion in public life to become a universal norm, demonizing the mediating practices favored by many Indonesians in less privileged social spaces. In their wide-ranging study of the ways in which progressive movements in the west have taken issue with existing genres of communication and cultural expression, Richard Bauman and Charles L. Briggs (2003) have emphasized the social inequity enacted in processes of this kind; idealizations of the communicative modes inherent in one vision of public life result in the marginalization of contrasting modes.

But it would be a shallow analysis that represented Hidayat as the unreflective agent of a hegemonic modernizing project. To do so would be to take a selective perspective on the realities of West Javanese political and social life. The remainder of this chapter locates Hidayat's vision within the contexts that have determined it, revealing it as a reasoned and concerned response to his environment. His ideas are not intellectual caprices isolated from contexts that matter within his community. There are two inseparable contexts that need to be traced. The first is West Java's distinctive character as an Islamic public sphere. Hidayat's vision was shaped by his interpretation of Islamic society in the province. The second is the intellectual setting in which Hidayat studied. He draws on a lineage of Indonesian Muslim intellectuals stretching back several decades who have crafted responses to those characteristics. These intellectuals, whom Hefner (1998; 2000) has labeled "civil pluralists," have been pioneers in adapting concepts of the public sphere and civil society as solutions to real problems facing Indonesian society. In the following paragraphs I give an account of how his citation of these authors is a response to the Islamic environment in which he grew up.

Hidayat was a PhD researcher in Bandung in 1998, the year that saw the end of the Suharto regime. By that time, he held academic expertise in Islamic communication and media, and this specialization gave him insights into the new environment that was unfolding. His main concern was for the political and economic future of Indonesia's Muslims. Their interests were not being served, he felt, by a political class that played on their recognition of symbols in order to make political gains. Group identities were too easily manipulated by symbols (Muhtadi 2004). But after Suharto's fall, the public sphere became busy with expressions—previously prohibited—of Islamic programs and perspectives. The prospect of a unified Islamic politics in the new era quickly vanished. Fragmentation also emerged around disputes concerning public morality and religious diversity. Over recent years, issues that have triggered public action campaigns by activist groups include the granting of permits for church building; government policies on gambling; the operation of nightclubs and entertainment premises; the freedom to worship of the Ahmadiyah minority; the permissibility of cultural performances by musical performers whose moral value is questioned on religious grounds; the question of whether concepts such as liberalism and pluralism can be considered as permissible within Islam; and the relatively frequent rise of Islamic movements under the leadership of charismatic figures.[5]

The province is home to activist groups seeking to shape public life. As noted, PERSIS is a major player in advocating against diversity. Another activist organization dedicated to Islamic homogeneity was the Indonesian Council for Islamic Dakwah (DDII), the *dakwah* organization founded by Muhammad Natsir in his postpolitical phase. This group, which has an office in central Bandung, has been a consistent and vocal opponent of Christian expansion in Indonesia and opposes indigenous spiritualities, which it understands as "nativist" movements. It publishes these positions in various media (Liddle 1996; Siegel 2001), and organizes public action campaigns. The Indonesian Community and Clerics Forum (FUUI), based in Bandung's north, maintains surveillance of West Java for signs of deviant movements (*aliran sesat*), which it researches through its specially appointed investigatory team. It organizes media campaigns and works to establish coalitions of Muslim groups to agitate for government action against such groups (Muzakki 2007). The conflicts pursued by these groups rarely result in serious violence, but West Javanese Muslims witness constant outbreaks of conflict over religious difference. In 2009 the West Java / Banten region was named by the Jakarta-based monitoring organization Wahid Institute as one of the three provinces with the highest incidence of religious conflict in the republic (Wahid Institute 2009).[6]

Hidayat witnessed this outbreak of public conflict after digesting the works of Indonesia's major "civic pluralists." The academic and activist

Nurcholish Madjid (1939–2005) is heavily cited in his writing. Madjid's advocacy of a less sectarian and more inclusive Islamic political vision in the early 1970s (Madjid 1987, 62–75) was well-received because it validated a novel Muslim subjectivity that suited the developing republic's growing urban Muslim constituency (see Hefner 1998). Madjid's advocacy of the civil society concept was opposed by some Islamic movements because it seemed like submission to the Suharto government's prohibition of Muslim political representation. Yet it appealed to Hidayat, who must have appreciated the emphasis it placed on education. Madjid was an active educator and one of the founders of Jakarta's Paramadina University.

Another influential thinker frequently cited by Hidayat is Muhammad Hikam (b. 1958). This man was prominent among the NU activists who, in the wake of Madjid's advocacy, brought the civil society concept to broader audiences in the early and mid-1980s. Through the efforts of these activists, "civil society" became the "prevailing paradigm" of the time (Bush 2009, 97). Hikam was a pioneering scholar who translated the ideas of Habermas and Antonio Gramsci in the context of Indonesian political and sociological realities (Hikam 1994, 1996). One of the repeated messages in his writings is that Indonesians must be empowered to actualize their individual agency; political life should produce subjects able to overcome the constraints of their environment (Hikam 1996, 123–24). For Hikam, this empowerment program was a means to offset the damage to Indonesian political culture resulting from the Suharto regime's intimidation and cooption of elites. He was also concerned by the politicization of difference within Indonesia's religious communities. Hikam looked to the 1950s and 1960s as a period in which the politics of ideology and sectarianism caused harmful divisions within Indonesian society. The primordialism and fundamentalism implicit in those divisive affiliations would be overcome, he argued, by the recognition of the common good inherent in the civil society concept (Hikam 1996).

Hidayat saw a connection between the analyses put forward by these authors and the limitations he perceived in the oratorical routines so popular in his native West Java, and he created the M2KQ as an action plan aimed at improving Islamic political culture. It aims to convert West Java's Muslims from listening to writing. If enabled to write and read, Muslims will learn to bracket the interests of their own group for the sake of the broader public good. The themes assigned to writers in the essay competition point strongly to this aspiration. The thematic focus for the M2KQ held within the 28th West Java MTQ was "social transformation based on local knowledge in the context of a multicultural West-Javanese society" (Muhtadi and Safei 2007). In the following year, students produced essays on the topic "Multicultural Piety: Exploring the Values of the Qur'an in Local Cultural Practice" (Muhtadi and Safei 2008). These themes promote diversity in Islam as a positive value and make the Qur'an the platform for a program of Islamically legitimate tolerance.

Hidayat's commitment to the critique of oratory is extreme in comparison to the other activists and academics cited in my introductory chapter. He has gone beyond expressing a critical analysis to offer a practical solution. Looking to the future, there will be no way of measuring the success of this practical solution. For the moment, the M2KQ succeeds because it resonates so strongly against commonly held conceptions about the types of communicative competencies required for Indonesia to progress. But some idea of its prospects can be derived from the ambiguities the M2KQ strikes within the environments in which it is supported. I was very conscious of these as I carried out this research. The same governments that provide financial support for his writing competition are fully aware of preachers' value in communicating with publics (see chapter 1). They engage preachers constantly for various goals. Another ambiguity emerges from within the university that employs Hidayat. As noted, Hidayat is a professor in the Faculty of Dakwah and Communication. The faculty's staff includes preachers as lecturers, and among them is found Al-Jauhari, the preacher who causes more laughter than any other West Javanese orator. And finally, as narrated in the opening pages of this book, Hidayat first described his project to me while we were traveling to a routine preaching event that he felt obliged to attend. This was a typical event in his calendar. Hidayat appears trapped by the social power of the very thing from which he would like to free West Javanese Muslim listeners.

Chapter 6

A Feminized Domain

Acep Hidayat's vision is underpinned by three assumptions about contemporary Muslim subjectivity and media. First, Muslims' engagement with Islamic media should be dedicated to the goals of social and political progress. A second assumption is that individual subjects can and should be transformed into the rational-critical subjects implicit in the idea of democratic citizenship. A third assumption is that diverse media forms have different levels of efficacy in achieving this transformation. Taken together, these assumptions reflect negatively on the style of Al-Jauhari and preachers of his ilk. They remove Islamic mediations from the situations and routines in which they are embedded. Like the conceptions of proper mediation formulated by Bandung modernists of earlier years, they foreground an idealization of communication as a transparent and neutral means of conveying information, shaving off those aspects that distinguish preaching events as social interactions taking place in real environments.

This de-situated imaginary of human communication is my starting point in this chapter. I am particularly interested in the feminist version of this imaginary, for it gives rise to a special incongruity in West Java. In the course of my field research I observed that women attend a more diverse range of preaching events than men, and they attend them more frequently; from my regular head counts, I determined that women usually composed about 70 percent of the audiences at preaching events attended by both sexes. Many Bandung women told me that they attended preaching and pedagogical events up to six times a week, whereas men spoke of usually attending only once a week (at the Friday congregational prayer). Furthermore, there is a well-patronized oratorical/pedagogical frame attended only by women, known as *majlis taklim* (from Arabic, study gatherings), that has blossomed with the rise in Islamic participation observed over recent decades (Alawiyah 1997; Doorn-Harder 2006; Marcoes 1988). These events combine Qur'anic study and performance with other activities such as charitable fundraising, network marketing, and cooking. They are held according to fixed schedules in mosques, public spaces, and private homes, and Bandung preachers—male and female—are in constant demand to speak at them. The equivalent pedagogical or oratorical programs for men are infrequent and poorly attended in comparison.

Progressive critics, however, express doubt about the efficacy of these participatory forums. One of Indonesia's most prominent Islamic feminists, Siti Musdah Mulia (b. 1958), has stated that the pedagogical and oratorical forums so popular among contemporary Indonesian women have not advanced the interests of women at all (Santi 2005, 106). In her view, in these groups women "are entertained by beautiful rhetoric, captivating poetry, funny illustrations, accompanied by music and smutty jokes, and so on" (Mulia 2005, 503). They do not help women listeners develop autonomy and self-empowerment, things of critical importance in West Java, where poverty makes women vulnerable to various abuses. What is needed, she claims, is an expansion of the *dakwah* project into forms other than oratory, in which women will participate as active agents rather than as passive listeners, and in which they will be treated as "subjects, not as objects" (Mulia 2005, 508). Through these transformative *dakwah* forms, there will emerge "a society that can think critically about itself and its environment, and thereby be able to seek solutions to the problems it faces" (Mulia 2005, 508–9).

The feminist position on oratory is different in some respects from Hidayat's. Unlike his position, the feminist position is motivated by concerns about interpretations of Islamic norms that cast women as secondary servants of Allah beside men and about the perpetuation of those interpretations in traditions of observance and practice. It responds to problems not experienced by men. But Mulia and Hidayat are otherwise co-travelers in their critique of oratory. Both take the view that people who participate in the conventional oratorical forms will not achieve the personal transformations they view as being critical to progress.[1]

During my fieldwork, I had much cause to reflect on the incongruity just outlined. On the one hand, I was reading a compelling feminist critique of an Islamic observance; on the other hand, from my daily experience it was clear that this observance was especially popular among and important for Bandung women. Not only that, it appeared in some ways to be under their control, in that the conduct of oratory seemed to be shaped by their motivations, situations, and preferences (I explain this in the pages to follow). In other words, at the same time as I was studying the critical discourse and its assumptions about women's agency and autonomy, I was noticing how preaching events are frequently formatted and managed to cater specifically for their female audiences, even when both men and women were in the audience. I was not observing the transformative processes idealized by Mulia; the male dominance of religious authority in West Java makes that idealization seem unattainable. Yet I was witnessing women determine the nature of their religious practice—in this case, oratory—albeit in a way that was enabled and circumscribed by their social realities.

Wishing to establish the texture of women's understandings and experience of oratory and to find out how these could be understood against the realities of their lives as West Javanese women away from the preaching stage, I established discussion groups in two urban villages, one in the north (Karang Setra) and one in the east (Cibiru) of Bandung. The specific goal of the discussion groups was to determine the nature of the spectatorship within which women attend preaching events. Spectatorship is a perspective on viewing that treats it as something enacted within the social formations in which the subject is active not only as a viewer but as a participant in a broad range of undertakings.[2] This regard for the broader setting of oratorical attendance—for women's routines, in other words—is lacking from the negative evaluations produced by Hidayat and Mulia. Their perspectives exclude the possibility that oratorical events may in fact respond to the situated needs of their audiences. In Webb Keane's words (2007, 222), their perspectives "abstract the subject from its material and social entanglements in

the name of freedom and authenticity." An inquiry focused on spectatorship, by contrast, reverses the purifying effects of this abstraction. This
chapter discusses messages emanating from the preaching stage, but it also
considers oratorical participation as an embodied undertaking beside the
other embodied undertakings of the women participating in the discussion
groups. I observe how the constraints that shape their attendance at oratory
differ notably from those that accompany the sociability experienced by
West Javanese men.

My exploration of preaching and spectatorship highlights an irony concerning the pleasures of listening. The quotes from Siti Musdah Mulia are
clearly proscriptive about the delight and enjoyment women experience as
listeners; this is iconic of what is wrong with women's participation. Yet
when women's preaching participation is considered in the light of the sociability within which it takes place, it is clear that the pleasure element is a
significant benefit that women obtain from that participation. Furthermore,
as I argue at the conclusion of this chapter, the laughter is not a totally
distinct thing from the substantive mediation of norms. Preachers create
laughter out of respect for listeners in situation, and the same respect leads
to a less disciplinary mediation of Islamic norms than might be expected by
the critics of women's listening practices. The critiques unproblematically
separate the surface enjoyment of listening from its content, but my research
suggests that pleasure is not a sign that content is missing. Preachers' consideration of listeners' comfort shapes norms also.

Two distinctions need to be made before I proceed with my argument.
This chapter is not about participation in feminist Islamic projects but about
routine preaching events in which gender issues are not a specific focus of
interest. The women contributing to the discussion groups were not participants in the initiatives of reformist feminist movements, such as Malaysia's
Sisters in Islam or Indonesia's Rahima (Anitasari et al. 2010; Lichter 2009;
Ong 1999), and probably had little or no knowledge of those initiatives. Second, the range of events of interest to this research inevitably expands at this
point to include those that can accurately be described as pedagogical. The
routines of the women assisting with this research include activities that are
devoted to the acquisition and development of skills. From one perspective,
this matters. In pedagogical situations, the focus of the participants and
performer is trained more keenly on the acquisition and development of
skills, so the performer is often not subject to the stringent evaluation of

communicative skill through which preachers like Al-Jauhari find such success. From other perspectives, however, it matters little. Attendance by Bandung women in nonpedagogical events takes place through the same forms of collective participation displayed by women in their projects of Qur'anic learning. In other words, although pedagogical and nonpedagogical events can be regarded as contrasting embodiments of Islam, the spectatorship practices of their women patrons are correctly considered as sui generis. And, further, successful pedagogy needs skillful mediation, and the study groups so popular among Bandung women prefer their teachers to be skillful and attractive speakers.[3]

Accommodating Women's Spectatorship: An Example

In the first pages of this book I described my experiences at an oration delivered by the prominent Bandung preacher Abdurrahman in September of 2009. Abdurrahman faced an audience of about 140 listeners, 100 of whom were women. Most of these were middle-aged or older. Young men were conspicuously absent and there were few children. The audience was tired from two days of ritual, celebration, eating, and the labors implied by these. Lengthy formalities—a welcoming speech, an announcement of the aspirations underlying the event, singing of verses in praise of the Prophet, and a Qur'anic recitation—had been conducted even before Abdurrahman took the stage, giving the audience ample opportunity to feel their fatigue.

Abdurrahman commences with a greeting, a statement of praise for Allah, and a request to Allah to bless the Prophet Muhammad, all in Arabic. The audience recognizes these as formalities that key the performance as an Islamic one. He then begins a discourse in Sundanese around themes no different from those he has brought up at thousands of similar engagements in the past. He invariably focuses on the aspirations, successes, and disappointments of domestic life, especially parenting issues, and tells brief narratives to express this in pleasing and accessible ways. He calls on the Qur'an and hadith as foundations for his encouragements and advice. He maintains contact with his audience through backchannel cues, such as the verbal expressions of support that he constantly requests from his audience.

After about seven minutes of the sermon, the audience have relaxed into what appears as a pleasant state of boredom. Women are beginning to rest their heads on the bodies of their friends beside them. Other women are gently massaging each other. For some audience members, sleep is clearly not far off. Noticing this, Abdurrahman starts singing a popular, secular song in his pleasant baritone voice. He sings for less than a minute, but what happens at the conclusion of the excerpt is surprising. Rather than simply conclude with the final word of the song's chorus, Abdurrahman continues to deliver the melody in nonsense syllables: *Ning-nong, ning-nong, ning-nong, ning-nung, ning-nong.* After this cute-sounding coda, Abdurrahman returns to the themes of his sermon. The coda creates a ripple of responses through the audience, especially in the women's section. Bodies stiffen and move towards a more erect position. Some women look at each other in surprise. Others smile and renew their focus on Abdurrahman. Three minutes later, he sings another song, concluding with another nonsense coda. Some women giggle. Others use their arms to make contact with the person sitting beside them. Some turn to the person beside to share smiles or laughter. One woman gently strikes her friend's shoulder with a clenched fist. The men in the audience do not move so freely but merely smile.

The audience is now listening in expectation of hearing another song and nonsense coda, which are duly supplied five minutes later. Their attention is now sharply focused. Their gestural responses increase in volume and intensity. After about twenty minutes of this, women are singing along with the nonsense codas. They laugh together as they do so, and their bodies gently roll against one another. Affectionate slaps are exchanged. This participation enlivens the atmosphere of the sermon.

Nevertheless, Abdurrahman's style is a generally restrained one. Sudden changes in tone, tempo, or volume are rare. His body movements are minimal. Against this measured background, he uses the songs to refresh his audience and sharpen their attention on himself. In sharp contrast to an Al-Jauhari performance, the songs do not become a dominant feature of the performance. Abdurrahman never communicates with his listeners *about* his singing. He persists with the outbreaks of song for the first forty minutes of his seventy-minute sermon, but these are rare in its latter stages. All the while, he monitors the attention level and fatigue of his audience, employing refreshing strategies where necessary.

This event displayed contrasts between men's and women's participation that I frequently encountered in Bandung. I came to realize that orators and event organizers were very aware of these contrasts, and that they influenced

orators' choice of preaching strategies as well as the conduct and management of events. Thus, West Javanese preaching frequently appears to be a
feminized domain. In what follows I first provide an account of the responsive loop that structures successful interaction between a preacher and her
women listeners, drawing on the performance just described as well as my
attendance at other events. I then move away from the preaching stage to
contextualize preaching participation within other realities of women's lives
in Bandung, drawing largely on the discussion groups.

The Responsive Loop

When sitting in audiences before Islamic orators, women appear expressive
and unrestrained in their bodily reactions. They respond enthusiastically, for
example, to preachers' attempts to elicit verbal responses from the audience.[4]
Some orators, such as Al-Jauhari and Abdurrahman, make singing a prominent part of their performance. When doing so, they frequently employ a
trick in which they refrain from singing the last words of a song's lines and
point the microphone in the direction of female audience members at the
precise moment that they would have sung the words. Women will enthusiastically complete the line. Another example is to seek verbal affirmation
directly from them by asking "Is that right, ladies?" Preachers receive far less
enthusiastic responses to these strategies from men.

When stimulated by humorous, irreverent, or clever messages from the
preacher, female audience members often move their bodies expressively and
suddenly. They make contact with their friends with their arms. They often
lean on their friends or give them a friendly slap or punch. When listening
to risqué preaching, women will often bow their heads low and bury their
faces in the garments of their friends. Consequently, the women's section of
the audience can appear as a moving field of rolling bodies, whereas the men
generally move little from a basic sitting position.

It is important also to note the different seating patterns that women
form, especially in events involving large audiences. Women sometimes form
small groups within audience spaces, appearing to establish small chatting
circles made up of three or four women. Stimuli from the stage, such as Abdurrahman's engaging songs, often lead to the shared physical expression of
emotion within the small groups.

These characteristics of women's participation influence the conduct of performances as well as the layout of venues. In the performance described here, Abdurrahman directed his refreshing strategies primarily at female audience members not only because there were more of them but also because the lack of restraint in their responses helps make the event appropriately lively (Sundanese, *ramé*). Such an atmosphere is considered desirable at preaching events, although the appropriate level of liveliness differs according to the situation. This backchannel communication forms part of a communication loop in which priority is given to women's responses even though the audience consists of men and women.

This loop manifests in various ways, including preaching strategies that can appear as camp behavior. Several successful male preachers feminize their performance to accommodate their female audiences. One preacher, in constant demand for life-cycle celebrations, frequently replicates the voice of a complaining woman, producing a melodramatic caricature of a desperate or distraught woman. His largely female audience enjoys his overblown supplications, which are full of exaggerated expressions of the difficulties faced by women in contemporary West Javanese life. Another slightly different but no less successful preacher has a middle- to upper-class female following to whom he preaches regularly in the semiprivate setting of "pay for entry" sessions. In these sessions, he likes to circulate among his audience, moving fairly vigorously and expressively, yet consciously relaxing his upper body, wrists, and arms as he does so. This disarming style, which differs from his demeanor before mixed audiences, allows him to sustain a warm and intimate rapport with his female audience.[5]

As already noted, women's spectatorship also influences the physical layout of the spaces used for preaching events. When preparing the spaces for Al-Jauhari's preaching events, organizers do so in ways that facilitate the loop described earlier. On one occasion, I accompanied him to Garut, West Java, where he had been invited to speak at a celebration in a large, square mosque. Women occupied one half of the square, and men the other. There was no curtain or barrier between the two halves. The organizing committee placed the microphone and chair in the middle of the square floor space, facing the half occupied by the women so that Al-Jauhari faced the women throughout his performance while the male audience members watched his back. When I asked him why the audience had been arranged in this way, he gave the playful response that the women would complain if they had not

Figure 2. The responsive loop. Event organizers frequently arrange the preaching space
to enable close contact between women listeners and the preacher. Photo by author.

been arranged thus. Although his answer was self-aggrandizing, no doubt
it illustrates the recognition given to women's spectatorship in the conduct
of that performance.

At many preaching events, especially larger ones, the layout of the preaching space also recognizes women as shoppers. Around the location of
preaching events *pasar kagetan* ("surprise" markets) consisting of small stalls
are set up to sell products primarily of interest to women, such as clothing,
fabrics, cooking utensils, and perfume (see also Abaza 2004, 177–79).

Life-Course and Mobility

In my efforts to contextualize the differences between men's and women's
participation, I asked preachers for their perceptions of these matters. These
men and women have a well-developed knowledge of women's spectatorship, which is not surprising because they need to manipulate it to achieve

good outcomes in their performances. Their explanations generally revealed an essentializing tendency; women were more enthusiastic participants because they were more *peka* (sensitive) and *emosional* than men.[6]

From their point of view as keen observers of audience behavior, there is much to support this perception. Women's bodily responses are certainly less restrained than men's, making them appear more enthusiastic, but the preachers' sociobiological explanation is probably wrong as neither women nor men are inherently more emotional than the other (Shields 1987). The preachers postulated an inherent, feminine spirituality, but this obscures how women's participation in oratorical and pedagogical events is shaped by their embodiment in the specific terrains of West Javanese social and religious life. In other words, it obscures their spectatorship. For these reasons, in the analysis that follows, I do not ask about differences between men and women but about how preaching events provide the conditions for contrasting behavior along gender lines. The inquiry clearly does not involve women alone, for women's participation only seems enthusiastic in comparison with male participation. The influence of hegemonic masculinities on men's participation in preaching events is also relevant to this discussion.

The life-course experienced by West Javanese women is important for understanding their spectatorship: participation by women in preaching events does not display an even spread of women of all ages. Far fewer teenagers and young adult women attend in comparison with mature women. In the discussion group and interviews, it emerged clearly that women began to attend oratorical and pedagogical events frequently after the routines of caring for children became less demanding. In Bandung, this moment can occur quite early in a woman's life, sometimes in her mid to late thirties. Some women confessed to feeling that they were growing closer to death at this age and needed to become closer to Allah by improving their Islamic knowledge. According to one woman, some women began to worry about their social importance once their children were no longer dependent on them. Their range of social options decreased when they were no longer involved in school activities. She expressed this poignantly, saying that some women looked in their cupboards at their "good" clothes, previously worn when traveling out of the home for school activities, and wondered, "What are these clothes for?" When faced with this, she said, women found value in attending oratorical and pedagogical events (women generally wear their "good" clothes to study groups). In contemporary Bandung, they do not need to travel far to do so, for the city's Islamic infrastructure provides many locations. The women in the East Bandung discussion group could attend oratorical and pedagogical events at no fewer than five mosques within easy walking distance of their homes.[7] Most of the events they attend take place while men are at work.

The women emphasized that they did not undertake these activities on their own but in groups of women from their immediate neighborhood. This fits with a more general pattern in which women combine to carry out tasks related not only to the needs of their families but also to perform the backstage work that enables formal community events such as administrative meetings and ritual to take place (Sullivan 1994). They agree in advance to attend Islamic activities together, forming small collective units in which they repeatedly travel, participate, and learn together. They support each other in their study efforts, and sometimes test their skills by competing in activities such as Qur'anic recitation and sermonizing. In the discussions and interviews, women frequently referred to the capabilities of their friends, noting that so-and-so was a high achiever in this or that field of competence.

Most of their activities are located in their immediate neighborhoods, but women also attend events further afield. When doing so, they enjoy a greater mobility than that available for other kinds of activities. Going out from home requires permission from husband, and women find that husbands, supporting the pious goals motivating their travel and knowing the identities of their co-travelers on these trips, are unlikely to deny permission. Furthermore, many women, especially those from outside of the city, feel more comfortable being seen traveling in public without their husband when the goal of the travel is attendance at a study gathering (see Anitasari et al. 2010, 16). After obtaining permission from their husbands, the women travel in a group (Sundanese, *ngabring*) to hear the orations of well-known Islamic figures at larger mosques, such as the district mosques at Ujungberung (for the east of Bandung), at Cipaganti (north), or the great mosque at the Bandung *alun-alun* (central square). Visits to the larger mosques are made more interesting by the stalls set up around the mosque in anticipation of the larger crowds.

The women do not let their frequent attendance become a burdensome obligation, for they sometimes allow other activities to interrupt their schedules. Several women mentioned that caring for grandchildren takes precedence over attending an oratorical or pedagogical event. One North Bandung participant, interviewed in a mosque located in her neighborhood, expressed it thus:

> Where *pengajian* are concerned, it is up to the women themselves. If they wish to, there is one every day, this is what the women do in RW 3, RW 4, and RW 5 [points with her arm in different directions].[8] RW 1 also has many women. It depends on whether the individual is busy. For those women who are not busy and have time, on Monday it is in the al-Fitra mosque [points towards the mosque], or in the Barakah Mosque, in the al-Rahman Mosque. There are many here. It depends on the women. Sometimes the women wish to go to a *pengajian*, but their grandchild suddenly arrives, so they do not end up going out, see? They stop them from going. But for people like me . . . my grandchildren are far away . . . there are only two people here, my husband and I . . . I am free to go to a *pengajian* if I wish. We go here if we wish, we go there if we wish. On some Thursday nights, if it is raining, ah! we just go to the al-Huda mosque [close by]. If it is not raining, we might go to a mosque that is rather far . . . the al-Fitrah mosque . . . and sometimes many of our friends will be at that mosque on Thursday evening. So, the end result is that, where religion is concerned, Praise to Allah! All the mosques here make *pengajian* available to women.

Men's routines differ from this account. West Javanese society offers them a wholly different range of social activities. The difference reflects the dominant gender order in Bandung's urban villages, in which the domestic world is the women's domain, while men are protectors and providers. Men's free time is limited by work obligations, making it impossible for them to attend the events in which their wives participate. Men and women alike acknowledge that men are often too fatigued to attend oratorical and pedagogical events outside of work hours. When they do so, it is common for them to fall asleep during the event, something which is generally tolerated by preacher and audience, especially at smaller events where familiarity between listeners is high. Against this background, many men consider that attendance at the Friday congregational sermon is a sufficient engagement with Islam for a week.

Women and men stated that men do not attend many religious gatherings because they are lazy (cf. Frisk 2009, 161–67). This statement needs to be interpreted against the reality that women have fewer opportunities for socializing outside the home than men (Marcoes 1988, 6). Men are free to

Figure 3. Listener fatigue is an unavoidable reality of West Javanese
preaching routines. Photo by author.

engage in activities such as sitting in roadside stalls while smoking and
chatting or watching football on television with friends. For this reason, attendance at Islamic gatherings is less attractive for men because it cannot
compete with other possibilities in terms of enjoyment. The charge of laziness
arises because, although men can take advantage of a broader range of social
activities than women, religious activities are valued more highly by all because
they are judged to be more important and beneficial. Other activities seem
time-wasting in comparison.

Gendered Embodiments of Islamic Knowledge

In the two discussion groups, men and women participants frequently mentioned their obligation to acquire religious *ilmu* (from Arabic, knowledge).
It was striking, however, that men and women conceived the practical use-

fulness of Islamic knowledge differently and identified this practical useful-
ness in contrasting social domains. This emerged clearly when discussion
group contributors gave their accounts of the value of oratorical and pedagogical events. Women stated that attending these events enabled them to
nambah élmu (Sundanese, increase one's Islamic knowledge). They understand Islamic knowledge as including several capabilities, with Qur'anic
recitation being the most valued. Information about how to dress properly
as an Islamic woman was also highly valued, as was instruction and practice
in reciting supplications in Arabic.

But women do not acquire these skills solely for personal improvement.
Most women emphasized their role as mediators between their teachers and
their own children and grandchildren (and, in some cases, husbands). They
stated that, as they obtain skills in Islamic knowledge, they then "*membagi-
bagikan ilmu*" (distribute the knowledge) and "*memanfaatkan ilmu ke cucu*"
(pass its benefit to grandchildren). Women regard this mediation as an Islamic
obligation, but it fits seamlessly with a West Javanese convention that the
burden of educating children be shouldered by women (Marcoes 1988, 26).[9]

Men, by contrast, do not feel directly obliged to pass on Islamic knowledge within the domestic environment. Rather, their primary concern
appeared to be managing and supporting the infrastructure for Islamic
practice in their community. For men, the mosque was an extremely important materialization of Islamic knowledge. They placed great importance on
supporting the ongoing operation of the mosque and its activities as a means
for sustaining the religion in their communities.

In West Java, the organization and management of religious infrastructure such as mosques is a male-dominated activity. Mosques are managed
by *dewan kemakmuran mesjid* (DKM: management boards), and it is uncommon for a woman to sit on these boards. Membership of a board can pose a
substantial burden on a man, for it brings responsibilities and challenges in
connection with fundraising and maintenance. Several men spoke of the difficulties they faced in attracting people into the mosque and of the high
value of popular preachers who were able to do just that. Making the mosque
busy was important for honoring the legacy left by the ancestors and fore-
bears who had built and paid for it. For these reasons, men have ties of obligation and loyalty to a specific mosque.

In this way, the nexus between mobility and Islamic participation
emerges in contrasting patterns for men and women. West Javanese men are

responsible for and thereby tied to organizational duties within religious infrastructure at the various administrative levels at which it is managed, from the local neighborhood to the provincial level. Women, on the other hand, are excluded from the managerial level at which infrastructure is maintained and are mobile in their patronage of religious infrastructure. In harmony with their socially determined responsibility in the domestic rather than public sphere, women assume responsibility for passing on Islamic knowledge within that environment. They acquire this knowledge, especially after their children become independent, through spectatorship patterns that are mobile, flexible, intimate, and socially supportive.

Intra-Audience Relations

When Abdurrahman was navigating his way through his oratory in Sumedang, women's responses provided contextual cues that guided him in his selection of preaching strategies. Men's responses were far less instrumental in this selection. I follow this observation in two directions: the masculinities embodied by West Javanese men that restrain their bodily responses in crowds, and the sharing of pleasure through body contact and verbal responses that is permissible among women.

Indonesian men embody a hegemonic masculinity that valorizes headship. The ideal man is a provider for a dependent family, and his traditional role is bulwarked by legal and moral pressures to meet the family's *nafkah* (Arabic, material needs). The socialization of this role brings with it display rules, which are prescriptive norms that dictate how, when, and where emotions can be expressed by men and women in any particular culture (Brody 2000, 25). Expressive behavior by men in the presence of men and women at religious oratory infringes these rules. Sundanese men, like their Javanese counterparts, are subject to a status hierarchy that values control and restraint in verbal and physical expression (Keeler 1990; Lukmana 2005).

In contrast, Sundanese women are not under pressure to project an independent, hard demeanor, and the display rules differ accordingly.[10] Touching one's neighbor in an affectionate way is not improper. More importantly, this touching and sharing of pleasure takes place within a spectatorship collective that is formed not within the preaching audience but within the kinship and neighborhood relationships of women's social lives more broadly.

As already noted, before setting out women communicate with neighbors to form groups that travel together to an event. Consequently, when attending larger events, the groups of women create small spheres of communication with their regular companions, sometimes slumping or resting on each other, with their bodies not always aligned in the direction of the preacher. It often appeared to me that autonomous discussions were taking place within groups of women in the audience. These discussions can pose a challenge to a preacher, who must strive to attract listeners' attention to the sermon, and to prevent women from becoming engrossed in the conversations occurring within their clusters.

Women's spectatorship at preaching events, therefore, is exercised within a distinct social unit that is created not in the space of the preaching event but in the familiar and intimate spaces of family and neighborhood. The groups are social structures for sharing not just preaching events but all of life's triumphs and tribulations and enable women to import an intimacy into a larger audience that would otherwise be absent. In effect, larger audiences are composed of smaller units within which women can continue their daily discussions with neighbors, friends, and family members. The physical touching and reassurance that occurs within these groups makes their intimacy visible, and the unrestrained bodily responses within them appear as a socially permissible sharing of pleasure among intimates.

The women's formation of insulated circles of single-sex communication is enhanced, of course, by the segregation of audiences at preaching events. Because at most preaching events men and women sit in separate sections, women enjoy their intimate groups away from the possibility of interference by their male relatives and neighbors.

Oratorical Treatments of Gendered Norms

For feminist Muslims such as Mulia, the mediation and interpretation of textual norms (Qur'an and hadith) are matters of critical importance. They are concerned at traditions of interpretation that assume men's superiority over women, arguing that although the Qur'an offers an egalitarian perspective on human relations, its stipulations have been interpreted in such a way as to produce conceptions of women as secondary servants of Allah beside men. This concern has produced a body of critical Muslim feminist scholarship to which Mulia is a distinguished contributor. Of course, the concern that underpins this scholarship extends also to oratorical mediations. Muslims everywhere agree that the *muballigh* has responsibility for urging listeners to comply with Islamic norms. The danger arises, then, that women who participate in the conventional frames of oratorical mediation might be supporting something that contributes to their own subservience.

I draw attention here to some important aspects of oratorical mediations of gendered norms and the ways these are connected to the sociability of preaching. I emphasize that the arguments I make here need to be understood against the background of the general normative consensus prevailing in Muslim West Java. As stated earlier, West Javanese Muslims give support to a patriarchal hegemony, and oratory is clearly one of the social processes that buttress this hegemony. The norm of men's headship, for example, is generally interpreted by men and women as giving divine authority for male hegemony, and that interpretation is rarely challenged in a direct way by Bandung's popular orators. Yet as I became more familiar with the sociability that preachers create in preaching events, I noticed how it was partly created out of distinct forms and strategies for mediating norms. I had been initially concerned that by focusing on the sociability of listening, I might end up neglecting the message element of preaching events. Yet the sociability and the messages are not separate things, for the pleasing sociability within which preaching interactions succeed has its effects on the forms through which preachers convey gendered norms. After repeatedly observing preachers mobilize these forms, I came to realize that preachers' mediations of the norms concerning women do not consistently imply a female listener of secondary status.[11]

The starting point for this is the—rather obvious—observation that preachers and their listeners are usually not under any pressure to deliberate over interpretative possibilities (although some settings demand it, as we saw at the PERSIS event discussed in chapter 3). Preachers are not concerned with rivaling interpretations of norms, as is the case with the critical feminist scholarship. A potentially oppressive interpretation does not need to be dealt with but can be simply ignored. What cannot be ignored is the requirement of obtaining the attention and approval of listeners, and to do this, preachers will moralize in forms that are neither sharp nor potentially alienating for female (and male) audience members.

This style of moralizing is frequently expressed in narrative structures, which enable a pleasing appropriation of other voices into the sermon. Narrative structures enable preachers to neutralize what might otherwise be a gender-specific interpretation. If a norm is read in its source text as applicable only to women's conduct, Bandung orators often mediate the norm as one that makes undifferentiated demands on both men and women. In this way, orators avoid a dilemma that dominates written discourse on this issue, namely, that Islam's normative sources impose on women constraints that are more restrictive than those imposed on men.

Inversion is another method for softening normative messages; norms can be represented by the telling of stories in which they are violated. Preachers achieve good outcomes with audiences by affectionately narrating a Muslim's failure to comply with a norm. They display their storytelling skills in performing these narrations, often constructing them out of instantly recognizable aspects of daily life and inducing pleasure in audiences. These narrations are not prescriptive and can be frivolous and amusing. In this way, audiences are reminded of models for proper behavior but in pleasing ways that avoid negative self-reflection.

The example that follows, which is based on a preaching performance translated in part in appendix C, implements both these methods (narrating and inversion). It is a typical oratorical treatment of the norm concerning women's obligation to serve men, a topic of debate that has drawn conflicting interpretations from Muslims.[12] It is excerpted from a commercially available cassette recording of West Java's most popular preacher of the 1990s, A. F. Ghazali, who died in 2000.[13] The narrative falls into two parts. The first is set in the household of the Prophet Muhammad, which is depicted as a scene of perfect Islamic domesticity. The Prophet arrives home while his wife is engrossed in exemplary behavior: she is reciting supplicatory formulas. She does not notice his entrance. He wants to drink, but rather than disturb his wife's observances by asking her to do her duty and prepare him a drink, he pours it himself. After seeing him, the wife rushes to serve him the water while asking for forgiveness. Ghazali praises the behavior of the wife and the Prophet, stating that the wife's good conduct was formed by the Prophet's exemplary acts. He had not, after all, asked her to pour the water for him but had respected her recitation. At this point, Ghazali emphasizes his core theme: Muslims will succeed in cultivating

Islamic behavior in other Muslims through exemplary action rather than verbal admonition. This narrative does not contest the gender-specific effects of the norm, but it does express its prescriptive component as an equivalent obligation upon both sexes.

The second part of the narrative repeats the scene in a West Javanese household. Ghazali reveals that a Sundanese man had approached him after a sermon, telling him that he wished to follow the Prophet and set a good example for his wife. He deliberately wakes early one morning to do housework but feels resentful as he does so. He makes sure his sleeping wife knows he has woken early to do housework, banging the bucket on the sides of the well when drawing water and exclaiming, "In the name of Allah, the merciful and compassionate" very loudly before drinking. After making himself coffee, he places it in a prominent spot so his wife is sure to see it (and feel guilty), and so on. In the cassette recording, the audience can be heard responding to this part of the narrative with laughter. When the wife eventually wakes up because of the noise, she doesn't rush to help him in the manner of the Prophet's wife but shows herself just as incapable of attaining the standards of the Prophet and his wife. She turns to their son and says, "Ah! Finally! Since your father has been listening to the preacher, at last he knows his proper place in life!" This climactic moment of the narrative is greeted with tremendous laughter. In this second part of the narrative, the norm of women's service is still the central theme, but the contextualization of the narrative in the actual life setting of Ghazali's audience produces a travesty of its first part. In a pleasurable way, the audience identifies with this travesty.

With strategies of these kinds, preachers avoid taking critical positions toward the audience that would endanger the reception of their messages. In the example, Ghazali defuses the "normative pressures of morality" (Bauman 1986, 75–77) through performing a narrative that draws identification in two settings. One is the ideological setting, expressed in the example of the Prophet, representing an aspiration beyond challenge or question in this environment. In this idealized setting, the behavior of the Prophet and his wife replicate the normative texts about Islamic behavior with which the audiences are so familiar. The other setting is the everyday life of audience members, in which norms are represented through their violation. Audiences are confronted in an affectionate way by narrations of their own failings. They are not castigations. Rather, their humor and irony resolve the tension between the two settings of the ideal and the real. The narrative publicly states and reminds the audience of the norm, which is a basic task of the preacher's vocation, but avoids an overly monological mode of address because it "refuses to take ideal, normative moral expectations too seriously" (Bauman 1986, 75).[14]

The implication for women's spectatorship is that the disciplinary potential of the norm is avoided, and respect is shown for women's sensibilities and comfort. The feminist critique alerts us to a history of patriarchal interpretations of Islamic norms, yet oratorical mediations of this kind suggest something different. Through strategies such as narrating and inversion, women are not preached *to* as objects to be molded in the literal shape of the norms in question. Rather, preachers take care not to alienate listeners through focusing specifically on women's obligation but enjoin men and women equally in ways that recognize the situational requirement of providing a mediation that will capture listeners' attention in a way that avoids intimidating and alienating them.

Concluding Words

Preaching is clearly pleasing for women in Bandung. The word *pleasing* as I use it in the preceding sentence requires some elaboration, for its potential meanings include distinctions that are important for the deliberations of this chapter. Reflecting over this chapter as well as those that precede it, two understandings of pleasure emerge from preaching routines. One relates generally to Islamic practice, and that is the pleasure and satisfaction that comes with submission through pious action. Bandung Muslims, male and female, reflect positively on piety, and gain satisfaction from their individual and collective efforts to be pious people (*soleh*). Women obtain pleasure, for example, from their efforts to acquire Islamic skills and knowledge. But the preceding chapters reveal another pleasure, the one brought on through affective communication that creates surprise, laughter, sympathy, and feelings of comfort and belonging. This second mode of listening pleasure does not relate so much to shared convictions about the value of Islam as to the skillful performance of preachers, such as that of Abdurrahman described earlier.

This second kind of pleasure does not register positively in the analyses and opinions about preaching cited in this book. According to the PERSIS view, discussed in chapter 3, the medium of oratory is harnessed for strict programmatic goals, and communication strategies that lead to positive evaluations of the orator *as performer* are improper. In the progressive discourses of Hidayat and Mulia, manifest pleasure is a marker of oratory's anachronism. An audience's laughter marks it is as one whose members will not undergo individual transformation. In the cultural politics of feminism, for example, women's enjoyment of pleasure, when not accompanied by serious reflection on possibilities for advancement, is often interpreted as a sign of political passivity (Ang 1985, 130–36). Moreover, in the academic literature urging us to seriously consider traditions of religious practice "in relation to the practical engagements and forms of life in which they are embedded" (Mahmood 2005, 188), pleasure of this second kind is rarely highlighted among those practical engagements and forms. Charles Hirschkind (2006) argues that the members of the Egyptian *dakwah* movement should not be judged against the criteria of "superior reason" characteristic of the liberal public sphere but should be understood as subjects inhabiting a world in which the affective properties of rhetorical speech have the capacity to shape ethical subjects. Yet the affective communication to which Cairene cassette-listeners respond does not appear to include pleasure-giving capacities.

Al-Jauhari, Abdurrahman, Ghazali, and, to a lesser extent, Shiddiq Amien move into the frame here as mediators standing at, rather than above, the intersections of the diverse spheres of Bandung Muslims' religious, social, cultural, and political lives. While critics of oratory reveal a prescriptive ideal of an autonomous subject emancipated from the entanglements of West Javanese society, these orators mediate those very entanglements. While Hidayat and Mulia overlook the complex social realities determining women's attendance at oratorical and pedagogical events, Al-Jauhari and Ghazali creatively summon and mobilize those very realities in language, giving performances that actively reach out to the audience, mobilizing the constituent materials of their cultural worlds (language registers, social stereotypes, performance genres, etc.). As they reach out to listeners, what is striking is not the affirmation of the ideology of male superiority highlighted in the feminist literature. Rather, the preachers' mediations of norms are among the most inclusive, evocative, and creative moments of oratorical performances. They allow us to construct an audience subject that is not only a pious one in search of knowledge and desiring transformation but also one for whom pleasure and comfort matter.

Chapter 7

Public Contest and the Pragmatics of Performance

I started my field research in July 2007 by asking colleagues in Bandung for the names of the city's most prominent preachers and seeking introductions to them. If a preacher was agreeable, I traveled with him as he performed his engagements, familiarizing myself with his style and the environments in which he was invited to speak. At the same time, I was constantly reading the Bandung print media, including daily newspapers, specialist Islamic publications, Friday bulletins, and mosque newsletters.[1] In the process of simultaneously engaging with oratory and written genres, I encountered something I had not anticipated: in the printed media, I frequently read writing under the names of the preachers whose orations I was attending, usually in brief pieces of between 1,000 and 1,500 words. Often, the articles were accompanied by a small photograph of the *muballigh* above or below his or her name, distinguishing him or her as a figure of repute and standing in Bandung. At that early stage, I assumed that expressions in the two media would be similar. It seemed reasonable that a preacher would regard oratory and writing as different media for expressing the same content.

That turned out to be an incorrect assumption. The differences between the expressions encountered in these media, and the processes behind these differences, provide the background for this chapter.

My exploration of these differences recalls a conception that has been engaged with throughout this book: publics appear to exist when messages circulate in ways that give the impression of dialogue between concerned interlocutors. This conception has been given its most compelling analysis by Michael Warner (2002), but it is not something known only to academics. In West Java, Islamic activists have for a long while grasped the importance of creating the impression of circulation, and have made it the foundation of public action campaigns dedicated to Islamic transformation. The Indonesian Council for Islamic Predication (Dewan Dakwah Islamiyyah Indonesia, or DDII) has labeled the discursive contest in which it participates as a "war of ideas" in which media representations create dialogues that are instrumental in the battle for the hearts and minds of Indonesian Muslims (DII 2001, 61). The DDII seeks influence by joining in the circulation of representations. Importantly, oral preaching does not give much assistance to this circulation. Using the DDII's programs as examples, I reveal how preaching practice resists the logic of circulation that underpins this war of ideas.

The dual role of the writer-orator requires some background contextualizing. First, when reading the printed media referred to earlier, I was engaging with a particular process of authorship and publication that synergized in distinct ways with Bandung's preaching activity. The writings were not all products of an authorial process in which an original text is prepared by a preacher as a sovereign, autonomous creator. It would be impossible for these very busy people to produce so many pieces of writing through such a process. The process relies on helpers, often university students, who are engaged by the ideological, philanthropic, or commercial interests that own, produce, or sponsor the publications containing these articles. The helpers attend a sermon by a particular orator and record it. The sound recording is transcribed and edited as an article that is published under the name of the orator, often with the photo-autograph mentioned above. Sometimes the celebrity preacher is consulted as part of the process, but not always. To my knowledge, the protocol of this system does not require that the preacher be given a chance to read the piece before publication, and the preacher is not necessarily remunerated for his "work."[2]

Second, and more significantly for this chapter, I noticed that a good number of the written texts had a polemic orientation. The articles expressed positions on points of ideological contest and, when read alongside contrary positions expressed in other publications, revealed points of conflict among West Java's Muslim population. In the oratories delivered by the writer-orators before heterogeneous audiences, however, I rarely heard them express positions that allowed points of conflict to appear. I did hear such expressions in sermons held by activist groups for the audiences of their own constituency. In these sermons, the expression of distinct positions in polemic is part of what attracts listeners to the group's mission. But heterogeneous audiences rarely *hear* about the sociopolitical contests they might commonly *read* of in newspapers, bulletins, and magazines. The routines of everyday preaching are not sites for waging ideological conflict.

This contrast became especially obvious when I read some of the works written in the name of Nur Wahid, probably the most influential of all preachers in Bandung during my visits there between 2007 and 2011. Born in Cianjur in 1944, this man is an orator whose preaching practice combines deep knowledge of the diverse cultures of West Javanese society with high-level oratorical skills. His orations are favorably accepted by heterogeneous audiences in diverse social spaces such as workplaces, state utilities, private banks, and educational institutions. I came to realize that his success was derived in part from the way he shielded his oratorical audiences from content that could invoke the fault lines latent in those audiences, or that might be off-putting because it invoked conflictual dialogue that would not be well received by listeners. By contrast, in some of the writings that appeared in his name in print media, he took a clearly conflictual position in ongoing Indonesian polemics. The ways in which he negotiated these two modes—public contest in print and speaking to situated audiences—are explored in the following.

Wahid is unique for the amazing range of roles he plays in West Javanese society, all of them based on his authority as Muslim leader. These roles point to alliances with key actors in social, governmental, religious, and political spheres. Through these diverse roles, seven of which are named here, he has been able to position himself as the orator with the greatest access to government, civil, and religious contexts in Bandung. First, he is a *muballigh* renowned for his ability to speak to all social segments. During his early career, he was involved in activist groups (Muhtadi and Safei 2009) but at the same time was developing a reputation as a preacher for village audiences.

He later achieved popularity as a preacher at Bandung's Salman Mosque, which is noted for its urban, non-Sundanese following. By the time I had the opportunity to spend time with him, most of his engagements were at government institutions and utilities and at corporate events. In short, his preaching skill is recognized in a wide variety of environments, which places him in high demand as a preacher.

Second, his reputation as an *'alim* (from Arabic, scholar of Islam) has enabled him to play key public roles. At the time of my fieldwork he was the chairperson for the Bandung branch of the Majelis Ulama Indonesia (MUI, Council of Indonesian Islamic Scholars), a role that came to him because of his expertise in *fiqh* as well as his profile as a preacher. The Council of Indonesian Scholars is a quasi-governmental body created by Suharto in 1975 as a representative council for the country's Islamic scholars (see Ichwan 2005). Third, he has long been active as a lecturer in the civil education system, teaching Islamic studies at ITB, where he was appointed to a chair in Islamic studies in 2008. Fourth, he has long been the head of the Dewan Syurah (Consultative Board) of the Bandung branch of the activist group called the DDII, which has longstanding ties to the MUI (Husin 1998, 132–33). Fifth, he is the figurehead of a pilgrimage travel agency. His celebrity attracts customers to the agency, and he uses his oratorical skills and Islamic knowledge in training and preparing prospective pilgrims. Sixth, he is a public face for the Bandung branch of a national alms collection and distribution agency (Highlight 200–?). Seventh, he is known as an author. He has written at least thirty-five books, and a regular column appears in his name in a major West Javanese newspaper (Muhtadi and Safei 2009, 318–21).

The many roles he fills are proof of the high levels of faith and credibility with which he is regarded by state and nonstate groups in Bandung. They point to a celebrity status that is based on public recognition and positive identification with moral correctness and probity. This status encourages various interests within West Java—ideological, political, commercial, philanthropic, or a blend of these—to seek mutually beneficial alliances with Nur Wahid.

Pragmatism in Oratory

I attended a broad sample of Nur Wahid's orations to heterogeneous audiences, including sermons delivered at the Bandung Water Board, to the staff and students of the Bandung Manufacturing Polytechnic College, and at the corporate center where he trains aspirant pilgrims. I also accompanied him as he was filmed for a television program broadcast from the Bandung studios of the national state-run television station. In all of these situations, he and the event organizers placed high priority on avoiding fault lines in their audiences. Organizers of the Polytechnic event told me of their great concern that inviting an unknown preacher meant taking the risk of inflaming divisions within the audience. They had had positive experiences with Nur Wahid in the past and found it very reassuring that he had such close relations with West Javanese governments.

Wahid would always leave an audience feeling positive about him and about themselves. He achieves this by reassuringly speaking of Islamic teachings as resources to be called upon in the challenge of fulfilling one's daily responsibilities as a student, parent, employee, or whatever social role was relevant in any setting.[3] In accessible language interspersed with refreshing strategies, he translates Qur'anic concepts into generalized personal values, such as patience, self-awareness, tolerance, persistence, faith, and trust. It is difficult to conceive that a Muslim of any persuasion could object to these messages. At the same time, his audience members are not given any material that would make them mindful of the many groups into which the heterogeneous audience could potentially fragment. Wahid is pragmatic in this regard; the potential for division within the audience determines limits on what should be uttered. In other settings of their lives, audience members are free to engage with more specific mediations that set them apart from their workmates, neighbors, or fellow students, but under Nur Wahid's mediation, the student body or workplace will be free of specialized Islamic identities and affiliations. Programmatic goals are not allowed to overwhelm the sociability of the encounter between preacher and audience.[4]

Not all Muslims in West Java support the pragmatic approach. For counterpublic orators and commentators, it is objectionable, for it appears to run counter to the virtuous ideal that religious mediators should be resolutely consistent (Arabic, *istiqamah*) in their mediation of religious norms. Bandung is home to preachers for whom pragmatism registers as a misdeed.[5] These *muballigh* are not prepared to edit or calibrate messages to suit the needs of differing environments, and they do not aspire to the broad acceptance Wahid has achieved. Very few of these resolutely consistent preachers receive invitations to preach across the boundaries of Bandung's Islamic environments and, consequently, spend their careers preaching to limited audiences.

When discussing these issues with me, Wahid expressed this pragmatism as an imperative for a *muballigh* whose vocation lay in addressing heterogeneous audiences. He pointed out that there are traps lying in wait for the preacher, especially party politics, which can harm a preaching career. He himself had avoided party affiliation throughout his career, even though he had been requested to nominate for candidacy by various groups.[6] Preachers rely on repeat invitations, he said, and open affiliation with a particular party reduces the likelihood of invitations to preach in contexts connected with rival parties. Furthermore, organizing committees are often reluctant to invite *muballigh* with political affiliations into workplaces and educational institutions for fear of being accused of favoring or campaigning on behalf of that *muballigh*'s party. Nur Wahid mentioned the career of Zainuddin M.Z. as an example of one that had been impeded by involvement with party politics. In the 1970s and 1980s, Zainuddin was a pioneer of preaching to stadium size audiences. He surprised observers when he began campaigning on behalf of the United Development Party (PPP). In Wahid's view, Zainuddin's massive support base was weakened by his involvement in politics.[7]

Given Wahid's avoidance of contentious content in his preaching, I was surprised to encounter his book *Dakwah Is Not Just Oratory* (Sundanese, *Da'wah Lain Saukur Ceramah*) (Faridl 2008). This book was prepared and circulated by DDII, a group dedicated to advocating an Islamic position in the war of ideas. In this book, he unequivocally takes sides in sensitive public contests.

Putting Preaching into Writing

Although attracting a very small following, the DDII is one of the highest profile groups participating in public Islamic contest in Indonesia. It is a national body, but the trajectory leading to its establishment in 1967 gives the group a special place in West Javanese Islamic society, for it was the initiative of Muhammad Natsir. After serving as prime minister of Indonesia and representing the Masyumi political party, Natsir was excluded from politics under the governments of Sukarno and his successor, Suharto. When

Natsir realized that his desire to maintain an Islamic presence in Indonesian party politics would be fruitless, he opted to continue the struggle of creating a more Islamic Indonesia through community activism. The DDII was to be the vehicle for this *dakwah* project (Hefner 2000, 109; Husin 1998, 67–77; Kahin 2012). As noted in chapter 3, Natsir saw *dakwah* as an obligation that devolved to every Muslim after the conclusion of the Prophet's task as messenger. Based on the Qur'anic verse of Ali 'Imran 104, this obligation required Muslims to support a "corps" that would represent the community in the "field of conflict" being waged between Muslims and their opponents. In the present, DDII assumes this role of special corps, and its grounding philosophy justifies confrontation with those it perceives as internal or external threats to the community (Husin 1998, 123–46). It opposes the reduction of religion to a distinct, privatized sphere of spirituality, which it sees as a component of the secularizing process, and is very sensitive to the proselytizing of religions other than Islam, especially Christianity and Hinduism. It campaigns to remedy the economic weakness of Indonesia's Muslims in comparison with other groups and seeks to strengthen the Muslim community after what it perceives to be the weakening effect of the New Order government. It warns Indonesian Muslims away from what it perceives to be the errors and misconceptions of locally inflected Islams (DDII 2001). In other words, DDII was designed to defend Muslim interests, and on this basis, it has entered decisively into public contest under the *dakwah* banner.[8]

As noted, the concept of *al-ghazw al-fikri* (Arabic, the war of ideas) motivates the group to compete through the circulation of competing discourse (Husin 1998, 140–42; Natsir [1996] 2000, 101–19). It sees the media as tools for the formation of public opinion and social engineering and laments that the mass media has thus far been successfully exploited by the opponents of Islam.[9] Its publishing arm is productive and well resourced, and even produces a magazine in Sundanese for West Javanese audiences, *Bina Da'wah* (Development of *dakwah*). In contemporary Bandung, however, there is no high-profile orator among DDII's leaders. Nur Wahid is sympathetic to DDII, having been involved with the group for a long period. The group hoped to make a forceful contribution to public contest by publishing a collection of his writings/orations under his name.

Publishing ventures of this kind are common in West Java, and their benefits do not accrue only to the activist organization or publisher. They can also benefit the preacher, generating prestige and helping to spread a preacher's reputation into contexts beyond the audiences who attend orations. Not surprisingly, then, the bookshops of Indonesia and West Java offer many titles written by or in the names of orators, many of which are adaptations of materials originally presented as oratory. Some of these have made important contributions to public discourse in West Java. During the period when preaching was a highly valued medium for party-political propagandizing, from before the 1955 election to the early years of the New Order, books in the names of high-profile orators were valued tools in political campaigning. *Mujahid Da'wah* (*Dakwah* strugglers; 1967) by the Masyumi and PERSIS leader Isa Anshary (1916–69), a Sumatran who lived for much of his life in West Java, is an example. Another is *Sikap Muslim* (The Muslim position; 1968), containing the prison sermons of the Sundanese E. Z. Muttaqien (1925–85). Both works are collections of orations transcribed and adapted for writing, in which the authors take sides in contests on social and political issues relevant at the time of publication.[10]

The motivations for these publishing projects are not always ideological. Financial considerations also play a role in the decision to publish. An illustrative example in Bandung is the popular orator, Islamic intellectual and media studies expert Jalaluddin Rakhmat, born in Bandung in 1949. In the late 1980s and through the 1990s, he led a series of weekly *pengajian* at his home in Bandung, and then later at a mosque located behind his house. Participants recorded these sessions and, subsequently, Bandung-based publishers released a series of transcripts of the recordings.[11] The books serve several purposes. First, they are a means for Rakhmat's supporters to disseminate the ideas of an intellectual whom they regard as having insights and perceptions that will be of value to Islamic society in Indonesia. Second, very large numbers of some of the books have been sold, indicating the economic value of the recordings; in 2010 *The Road to Allah* (Rakhmat 2007) was being sold with a "bestseller" sticker affixed by its publisher, Mizan. Third, Rakhmat's reputation is maintained through the circulation of these materials, adding value to his ongoing endeavors.[12]

The publications resulting from these partnerships display editorial processes of reduction. The jokes, humorous asides, refreshing strategies, and affective markers of oratorical discourse are removed, especially from the ideologically motivated publications, for where the shaping of public opinion is the desired result, cultural particularism does not register as a high priority (see Warner 2002, 82–83). DDII, for example, imagines the war of ideas as a rational discussion conducted through silent reading by strangers, and the affective-poetic-performance aspects of oratory are considered to have lesser value in that process. In other words, after transformation into print, an oration loses those features that reference the situated interaction of its delivery and is shaped instead by the conventions of written genres (Goffman 1981, 177–79). Strategies of affect are not completely excluded, of course, for written works necessarily create affect through the stylistic traits of their genres. Furthermore, some strategies employed in oratory, such as narrating, are effective across different media, including print publication. It is generally true, however, that in the perceptions of public contestants hoping to sway publics, it is not necessary to make readers laugh or cry. Rather, reading subjects need to be presented with a rational-critical argument.[13]

Taking a Stand in Writing

Nur Wahid's *Dakwah Is Not Just Oratory* is a book of forty-one chapters in the Sundanese language. The publisher is Bina Da'wah. Each of the chapters appeared originally in *Bina Da'wah*, with a "photo-autograph" of Nur Wahid and a credit acknowledging the work of Alma, one of the magazine's editorial staff. It is likely that the book's chapters originated as edited transcripts of his orations. It is also possible that he wrote some of them himself.

Some chapters are striking because they were clearly intended as contributions to debates on sensitive issues in the national discourse at the time of publication. In other words, the book is not simply a statement of religious positions per se but an attempt to engage in a national dialogue.[14] The key issues covered in the chapters are first new Islamic movements (Indonesian, *aliran sesat*, literally, misguided currents) and second the ongoing problems surrounding the Ahmadiyah sect. At the time of publication of *Dakwah Is Not Just Oratory*, these topics were subjects of a national dialogue about evolving Indonesian notions of pluralism and social inclusion, and they underpinned outbreaks of minor violence that occurred while I was in West Java.

During my first fieldwork period, in 2007, an apparent upsurge in the number of new Islamic movements caused a mild panic to sweep West Java, bringing on introspection among Islamic leaders about the underlying reasons for what appeared to be an explosion in their number.[15] One such movement, Al-Qiyadah Al-Islamiyah (The Islamic Leadership), caused particular concern. After a period of heavy press coverage, its premises were destroyed by a mob and its leader, Ahmad Mushaddeq, was imprisoned. *Dakwah Is Not Just Oratory* warns against harms being caused to the public by several new movements, including Al-Qiyadah Al-Islamiyah. In Nur Wahid's view, these groups are promoted by unnamed agents pursuing political goals, and they reflect the inadequacy of contemporary *dakwah* projects. As the government has failed in its responsibility to monitor and manage such groups, it is argued, Wahid encourages Muslims to be on the lookout for them and to take active steps to report them (Faridl 2008, 35–40).

The second topic of contest is the Ahmadiyah issue (Faridl 2008, 196–202). The Ahmadiyah are an Islamic sect of Pakistani origin whose missionaries first commenced activity in Indonesia in 1925 (Beck 2005). Nevertheless, at various times, a number of the doctrinal positions of one branch of the Ahmadiyah have attracted disapproval for their divergence from Sunni orthodoxy, and West Java has been the site of strong opposition to the sect. PERSIS, since its founding in 1923, has consistently expressed and publicized its theologically based disapproval of the group (Federspiel 2001, 61–63, 150–58). West Javanese municipalities including Cimahi, Tasikmalaya, Cianjur, Kuningan, and Bogor have been active in passing regional resolutions purporting to ban or restrict the group (Crouch 2009, 10–12). Mob violence directed at the group's infrastructure has been common in West Java over recent years, and the state has been reluctant to intervene to protect the group's property and safety. An apogee appeared to be reached in February 2011, when mobs murdered three Ahmadiyah followers in the village of Umbulan, in the municipality of Cikeusik, Banten (*Tempo* 2011). At the time of this writing, the national government has not banned the sect but is under strong pressure to do so.

Dakwah Is Not Just Oratory argues vigorously in favor of the prohibition of the sect, blaming the recent violence on the provocation enacted by the sect and on the government's reluctance to ban it. It expresses sympathy and understanding toward groups who have committed violence against Ahmadiyah property. Nur Wahid establishes several discursive battle lines, blaming Ahmadiyah's continuing existence not just on the government but also on a number of other individuals, groups, and concepts, including former president Gus Dur, who was a vocal defender of the group's rights to exist, the Jakarta-based Liberal Islam Network (Jaringan Islam Liberal, or JIL), and the concept of human rights (*hak asasi manusia*, or HAM) (Faridl 2008, 196–202).

In this way, Nur Wahid expresses a clear stance in ongoing Indonesian polemics about religious freedom, constitutional rights, the role of the government in religious affairs, and social inclusion.[16] Analysts have used various labels to locate participants in these contests. One labeling understands the opposition as contest being waged between "scripturalists" on the one side, arguing for the literal interpretation of Islamic norms, and "substantialists" on the other, who consider the Qur'an and hadith as sources of generalized norms that need to be interpreted for contemporary conditions (Liddle 1996; Mulkhan 2005). PERSIS, which shares many positions with DDII, refers to their own part in these struggles with a term that points to its history of oppositional stances—*mujahidin* (strugglers) (for example, Anshary [1967] 1995). For Hefner (2000), the contest is between a shared commitment from state and society groups to a public culture of "civility" on the one hand, and "uncivil forces" that oppose democratic culture on the other. The text of *Dakwah Is Not Just Oratory* does something that Wahid's orations do not. It enables him to be located within this spectrum of positions emerging in ongoing Indonesian contests. His listening audiences, in contrast, are given nothing that would enable this process of differentiation.

Concluding Words

This discussion enables further elaboration of two themes engaged with at length in this book. The first is the idea of "the public" and its compelling authority (chapter 5). *Dakwah Is Not Just Oratory* is an icon of the respect activist groups have for the concept that public opinion is formed through circulation of written discourse among strangers. Activist groups arguing from both sides of the contests mentioned in this chapter prosecute their positions by circulating them in writing to stranger publics, imagining them as a site of contest or even *ghazw* (war) within which opposing ideas vie for supremacy. To these groups, this process appears as a rational dialogue in which readers critically consider ideas, so the humor and warmth typically found in oratory is redundant. The affective signs of human contact are literally deleted from the documents that originated in living performance. This is the poetic of "stranger sociability," and a part of this imaginary is that publics can rise up, revolt, repent, or do something if they could only be persuaded to do so (Warner 2002, 81–85). DDII's ongoing project is premised on the hope that it might succeed in persuading Indonesian Muslims to such an end.

The second theme is the pragmatic shaping of oratorical mediations in accordance with realities inhering in the context of the event. The concept of the public as a space of circulation is of secondary relevance for Nur Wahid when he faces heterogeneous audiences in Bandung's workplaces, state utilities, corporations, and educational institutions. These audiences are not abstractions in the way reading publics are but are bound groups of actual humans requiring appropriate mediation. Audience members can become disengaged, impatient, irritated, hungry, and disinterested. Of course, readers can also experience these states, but the writer does not have to deal with them when they do so. Wahid responds to the risk of listeners falling into these states by using the set of skills that distinguish him as a performer in the oratorical medium, and he receives ongoing invitations to preach because event organizers are aware of how well he can do this (as well as because of their perceptions of his importance in West Javanese society). He is not invited because of the ideological positions he expresses in writing, of which the organizing committees of events are unlikely to be aware.

For the critics of oratory discussed in previous chapters, Nur Wahid's differentiation between these two media would surely confirm the negative impression they have of sociable oratory. They would see his adroit navigation of the two communication forms as proof that oratory in its routine forms is incapable of enabling Muslims to achieve the transformations required if social and political progress is to be made.

The fact that preachers tend to avoid polemic when delivering sermons to heterogeneous audiences has been beneficial for the recent expansion of public Islam in Indonesia. As noted, Wahid delivers sermons in workplaces, corporations, and state institutions. These are emergent settings for Islamic observance, and the holding of sermons in them represents an expansion of Islam into novel environments. Orators are the Islamic agents capable of accommodating the dynamic shifts that this expansion entails. Clever speakers like Wahid are not left behind by the constant change that is ever reshaping everyday life, and new contexts in urban centers are not beyond oratory's reach. This resilience has enabled oratory to become and remain a core Islamic medium, not only in the past but also throughout the global developments of recent decades labeled the "Islamic resurgence." Oratory, the most ancient of media genres, is also a medium for the present and—it seems certain—for the future.

On one level, this is good news for activist groups involved in the contests described here. DDII, for example, has long desired that Islam should have such prominence. The writings in which the group expresses its strategic goals have bemoaned the distancing of Islam from the diverse spheres of contemporary life. DDII is distressed at the compartmentalization (Indonesian, *dikotak-kotakkan*, literally, being placed in a box) of Islam into a distinct sphere named religion, identifying it as a sign of secular society's marginalization of religion and of its increasing subservience to capitalist and developmentalist agendas (DDII 2001, 9–14). The group has advocated for the integration of Islamic teachings into contemporary social, political, and cultural settings.

Bandung's *muballigh* have high access to such settings, but have not advanced the DDII's activist program in them. Islamic preaching transforms contemporary spaces into religious environments but in ways that affirm the integrity and cohesion of the listening employee body, village community, neighborhood, extended family, student body, prospective pilgrimage cohort, and so on. This involves the avoidance of those discourses that threaten cohesion within the context, insulating it from the war of ideas being waged by public contestants. Consequently, while Bandung's contemporary spaces are not out of the reach of oratory, they are usually out of reach of the contest-oriented programs of activist groups.

The recent public revitalization of Islam in Indonesia has materialized through these complementary but mutually exclusive trajectories of heterogeneous oratory and circulations aimed at publics composed of strangers. Since the relaxation of the censorship and public surveillance that characterized the Suharto regime, activist groups have been busy addressing their rhetoric to these publics. At the same time, public participation has risen, creating contemporary audiences displaying enthusiasm for the satisfying, affective engagement provided by the practiced performers who are Indonesia's career preachers. The written products that circulate express an aspiration for sociopolitical transformation while oratorical routines prioritize the congeniality and pleasing affect of embodied sociability. Nur Wahid's success is based on his awareness of this difference.

Chapter 8

Standing Up for Listening

The Indonesian public Islamic sphere is not dominated by modernists. The preceding chapters might have given this impression, giving close attention to a largely modernist critique that argues that Islamic communications should enable Muslims to move beyond their existing realities. In fact, there is considerable support in Indonesia for an Islamic view that aligns specifically in opposition to some of the core ideas of Islamic modernism, which compels us to ask a question: among supporters of this view, does anyone stand up for the listener? Are there discourses which construct a counter image for listening? In the introduction I briefly described some defenses put forward by star preachers in which they argue for the propriety of what they do, but those defenses are not about the public value of listening. They are attempts to recuperate preachers' personal reputations by providing answers to the accusation of "selling the verses." In this chapter I explore understandings of listening that contrast with the caricatures encountered in the preceding chapters.

For two reasons, there are no defenses of listening that address the specific terms of the modernist critique. Charles Hirschkind (2006) wrestled with the first of these, which is the paucity of discursive resources for explaining how affective communications benefit the public sphere. Where does one turn to mount an argument that affective oratory can provide the kinds of benefits commonly associated with genres of print publication? Those genres—not spoken ones—have provided the basis on which widely received understandings of the public sphere have been constructed. The second reason is that the assumptions that underpin critiques of oratory are so broadly authoritative in contemporary Indonesia and other postcolonial societies. Hidayat, Natsir, Mulia, and others are expressing ideals that many Indonesian Muslims understand to be national aspirations affecting core concerns such as public health, education, economic development, and literacy. No one will disagree with the idea that citizens need to be equipped with certain skills through formal education in order to participate in the democratic process. By extension, no one will argue against the proposition that writing and reading are superior *dakwah* options to listening and speaking. And when it is claimed that something is amiss when Islam's potential as a vehicle for progress is "subverted" by orators and audiences who laugh or cry rather than think, no one is prepared to argue against that. The autonomous, empowered subject so fundamental to understandings of democratic modernity emerges from critiques of oratory, and cannot emerge from defenses of it.

Hirschkind described a community whose members could articulate the public value of listening. He spent a lengthy period with Muslims in Cairo who were connected by, among other things, the circulation of cassette recordings of orations by well-known Cairene preachers. These listeners stand apart from Cairo society for their dedication to a program of *dakwah* that challenges basic tenets of the liberal public sphere. For example, they consider the shaping of ethical selves to be a legitimate motivation for public action, and these practices aspire to outputs achieved not in the form of public policy but in the cultivation of Islamic public virtues (Hirschkind 2006, 140). These listeners share ties of publicness founded not on the supremacy of rational/critical reasoning but on shared appreciation of cassette technology "as a device for the reanimation, modulation and embodiment of pious sensibilities" (74), and of the "ability of ethical language and exemplary behaviour to move human beings towards correct modes of being and acting" (113). They rate ethical interventions in public life so highly that they come into conflict with other social and political actors. For this reason, Hirschkind labels them a "counterpublic"—"a domain of discourse and practice that stands in a disjunctive relationship to the public sphere of the nation and its media instruments" (117). In this *dakwah* counterpublic, affect is construed as a public resource, and the affective and poetic aspects of sermonic discourse are meaningful in its deliberations about the public good.

Hirschkind provides a way of thinking about orations as efficacious contributions to public spheres, but he and I have encountered different species of affect. The listeners described by Hirschkind are entitled to argue for the public value of affect because they tether it to an oppositional project characterized as ethical, and ethical motivations, it is argued, serve the common good. They provide an acceptable basis for claims to social utility. The sermons delivered to Bandung's heterogeneous audiences are also mediations of an ethical program shared by listeners, but when facing audiences strongly tending to disengagement, preachers communicate affect to sustain audience attention. Success is measured by the engagement of the listener. Affect of this kind does not have such a legitimate claim to be considered as a contribution to the public sphere, and the preachers do not do so. In fact, we could at this point envision a hierarchy of affects, in which ethical listeners occupy a higher place than laughing ones.

So, if not in the ethical motivations of the counterpublic, where does one find support for the public value of affective oratory? Where does the listening subject find validation and buttressing? In Indonesia, it finds it, I argue, in a publicly acceptable self-identification under the banner of *tradisi* (tradition). This banner is borne most prominently by the organization known as NU (Nahdlatul Ulama, the Rising of the Scholars). NU has a monopoly over a space that it itself refers to as "traditional" and accommodates a subject to rival the transformational one emerging from critiques of oratory. Indonesian traditionalism does not defend the listening subject with justifications of oratorical convention, for reasons just stated. Rather, the rival subject takes shape in NU's practical and ideological validation of a subject that is not obliged to achieve empowerment but is in fact permitted to rely upon the mediations of authoritative leaders and is encouraged to enjoy those mediations in forms that are shaped by situated conditions of sociability. In other words, "passivity" is given religious legitimacy, providing normative bolstering for a subject that challenges the universal claims of the liberal public sphere. In the following pages, I sketch out this subject, using NU's theological reasoning and communicative practices as references.

In most of the academic accounts of the traditionalist/modernist dichotomy, it is represented as rival social segments preferring contrasting mediations appropriate to their respective situations.[1] I would add that the dichotomy is also determined by contrasting assumptions about the human subject and its agency, and forms of communication and mediation operate as signs of these contrasting assumptions.[2] Especially for modernists, these forms provide materials for recognizing and denying the quality of modernity. The effect is to locate forms of media and communication in a narrative of modernity, and this narrative, just like the dispositions toward mediation held by the Protestant reformers discussed by Webb Keane (2007), makes anachronisms out of the forms that are shaped by the routines of West Javanese life. In contrast, NU advocates a counternarrative that provides different meanings for Islamic forms of mediation and communication. These meanings create a space that accommodates the listening subject. In what follows, I trace this accommodation from two angles: first, by examining NU's religiously justified prescriptions about the level of knowledge Muslims should ideally hold, and second, by observing the sociability inherent in the organization's preferred forms of mediation.

NU: Defending the Listening Subject

NU's important functionaries are Islamic elites in the overlapping categories of *ulama* (Arabic, scholars) and *kyai* (Javanese, Islamic leader, usually of a religious school). In many cases, these elites are leaders of the Islamic schools that form an important segment of Indonesia's education system. Al-Jauhari, whose preaching was discussed in chapter 2, identifies himself as a *kyai*. These elites mediate Islam in forms that Indonesians commonly refer to as *tradisi* (see below). The size of NU's following is debated, but support for its elites and the Islamic worldview they espouse is undoubtedly massive. When the 1955 and 1971 elections were held, NU was a political party, and estimates of its present-day following, based on the number of votes it won in those contests, exceed 40,000,000. If its support base is calculated as the number of people whose religious observances and social situation match those of typical NU constituents, then a higher figure could be claimed. Many contemporary Indonesians identify themselves as "Islam NU," affirming themselves as traditional in contradistinction to other Islamic identities.

There is nothing irregular or controversial about this identification as NU affiliation is mainstream and neither antisystemic nor malcontent.

NU's genesis occurred at a moment—already described in this book's introductory chapter—when the *ulama* class felt threatened by a burgeoning Islamic reform movement.[3] Some Muslim reformers, including PERSIS ideologues, focused their critiques on the traditional clerical elite, accusing them of being self-interested agents of religious and social atrophy. These errors, they argued, had contributed to Muslims' degraded states of material prosperity and technological progress. Practical observance was central in their discourses—modernists told Muslims that respected observances such as grave-visiting, supplication for the dead, intercession, and ritual commensality had no Islamic value. This polarized Muslim communities in the Indies. In 1925 'Abd al-'Aziz ibn Saud came to power in what we now know as the Kingdom of Saudi Arabia and thereby became custodian of the sacred places of Islam. Indonesian traditionalists were concerned by the regime's ideological opposition to traditionalist practices and doctrine. Ibn Saud organized a World Islamic Congress, but traditional *ulama* were refused participation. At the same time, Java's modernist organizations were attracting economic and political support that posed threats to the future of the *ulama*. As a response, a leading *kyai* invited several of the foremost traditionalist leaders to meet in Surabaya in 1926. At that meeting a committee was formed to oversee the sending of a representative delegation to Mecca, and the NU organization was formed to defend traditional Islam. In other words, NU's original mission was to defend the "traditional" space in a narrative of progress created by their modernist rivals. Resistance to versions of Islamic modernity that it perceives as threatening has been one of its constant characteristics since 1926.

Indonesia may be unique for the way in which the traditional/modern dichotomy is an established fact of public life. Many contemporary Indonesians associate NU and Muhammadiyah, its rival modernist organization, with contrasting subjectivities. These associations are so strong that the names of the organizations have become metaphors for distinguishing between "traditional" and "modern." "NU" is frequently used as a metaphor for "traditional." Likewise, a person might refer to a neighbor as "Muhammadiyah," or "very Muhammadiyah," even if the neighbor is not affiliated with the group, in order to differentiate that person's religious outlook and social identity in a way that is easily recognized by all Indonesians.

Muslims and Knowledge

The ideal subject emerging from critiques of oratory is empowered through its acquisition of knowledge. NU's religious prescriptions reveal something different as NU subjects are not faulted for their low levels of knowledge. To explain this, it is necessary to reflect on the continuing relevance, in NU circles, of the four *madhab* (legal schools) as sources of Islamic authority.[4] These schools (and others that are less well known today) developed in the Middle Eastern centers of Islam in the three and a half centuries after the death of the Prophet. Each is preserved in a corpus of doctrinal literature based on the canonical texts of Islam, the Qur'an, and hadith. This literature has for centuries been respected as a source of authority on important questions of Islamic life. Given that the literature of the legal schools is written in Arabic and requires lengthy study from those wishing to master it, it follows that a specialist class is required to mediate it. This mediating role provides a foundation for the power and prestige of the religious scholars who lead NU.[5]

One of the specific challenges that motivated the formation of NU was the modernists' derogation of the authority of the legal schools and the scholarly mediation of their textual corpus. Modernist Muslims such as those of PERSIS and Muhammadiyah argued that the legal schools were accretions on top of the core sources (Qur'an and hadith); the texts themselves were a problem because they had not responded to social change; Muslims could resolve most of the relevant questions by using their own faculties of interpretation; and the *ulama* class was conservative and anachronistic (see Federspiel 2001, 158–62; Noer 1973, 233–34).

The tension between the "modernist" and "traditionalist" positions manifested clearly in their respective responses to this question: How should Muslims properly respond to problems for which answers are not immediately apparent in the explicit words of the Qur'an and hadith? The methodology for resolving such problems is referred to as *ijtihad* (Arabic, effort, endeavor). The NU position was that the literature of the Shafi'i legal school provided the solutions. Even members of the scholarly elite were obliged to submit to the authority of this literature, and the limited number of scholars with authority to formulate answers to novel problems in fact obtained their qualification to do so through mastery of that literature (Hosen 2004).

According to the modernist position, the reverence in which the traditionalists held the legal literature impeded the formulation of adequate responses to contemporary problems. For them, the authority to perform *ijtihad* is not dependent on mastery of the textual corpus. The position of the modernist organization Muhammadiyah, for example, is frequently stated as follows: the "Muhammadiyah takes the position that the gate of *ijtihad* is always open" (Nasri, Nashir, and Sudjarwo 2009, 61). Accordingly, when Muhammadiyah holds deliberations prior to the production of a fatwa, these deliberations are open to people with specializations in secular sciences appropriate for the subject matter at hand. From Muhammadiyah's perspective, Muslims possess agency to search for solutions in the light of contemporary conditions (Hosen 2002, 234–39).

The dispute about deliberation over new problems cannot be separated from the concept of *taqlid* (Arabic, imitation). One authoritative NU ideologue defined it thus: "According to the majority of knowledgeable scholars, it is obligatory for every person who does not have the capacity to strive for solutions to matters not mentioned in the Qur'an and hadith [*ijtihad*] to follow the opinion of a scholar who can arrive at solutions in such matters, and to accept their adjudications [fatwa]" (Asy'ari 2005, 187). The concept of imitation structures a hierarchy elevating those who deal in knowledge above those who are not in the position to do so. It recognizes a category of Muslims without knowledge and provides a religious legitimization for this lack. Here emerges a subject not countenanced by Hidayat (chapter 5), who, against the background of Indonesia's developing democracy, envisages education—religious and secular—as an imperative for all. NU theology, however, acknowledges a space for Muslims without it.

For Indonesian modernist groups, a religiously legitimate state of reliance was an unsatisfactorily passive subject position. Muslims should position themselves actively in relation to Islamic knowledge and reasoning. So modernists advanced the concept of *ittiba'* (Arabic, following of precedent). Those without the capability of *ijtihad* were allowed to accept or follow the fatwa of another person, "but with the condition of knowing or understanding the principle on which the fatwa is based" (Hosen 2002, 236).[6] Muslims are required to understand the rationale underlying a proposition. For modernists, it is not enough to simply rely on the mediation. Rather, the subject must have a substantive understanding of the issues at stake.

As Hirschkind (2006, 117) has noted, it is striking how much the specifications of proper subjectivity produced by modernist groups correspond with the ideal subjects imagined to occupy the bourgeois public sphere. The historian Deliar Noer, a determined Indonesian modernist, characterized *ijtihad* as follows: "Idjtihad demands continual research, the confrontation of one's opinion with others, the readiness to lay down one's judgment for another which has been based on stronger arguments" (Noer 1973, 94). This definition projects the modernist Muslim as the same subject as the informed citizen of the modern public sphere; both participate in the circulation of ideas among informed citizens, balance possibilities, and are prepared to bracket their own interests for the benefit of the common good. By contrast, NU projects a hierarchy in which expert mediators communicate opinions and judgments to Muslims who are not faulted for their reliance on them. Even though this hierarchy is not argued as a specific response to critiques of oratory, it nevertheless presents an alternative normative vision of the model position a Muslim should take in relation to mediations of the religion.

Communicating Embodied Authority

A second resource for constructing the NU listening subject arises from the organization's authority structures and from the forms of communication these entail. NU authority is to a great degree embodied in its elites. Even today, although not to the extent of the early days of the organization, power is exercised and transferred mainly through informal kinship and patronage networks, and advancement in the organization is dependent on personal ties within the networks (Fealy 1998, 46; Muhtadi 2004). Many Indonesians recognize an NU leader's distinction because of special qualities they identify in his or her genealogical lineage. It is a mode of authority that contrasts with the transparency and merit-based procedures implied by bureaucratic models. It would be incorrect, however, to overstate the extent of this traditional authority in NU, which has, for example, been highly successful in asserting its interests through members who have achieved high positions in the state bureaucracy (Fealy 1998). Nevertheless, NU authority is clearly centered in individuals who ascend to their status through patronage networks, genealogies, and complexes of spiritual value.[7] In NU, authority is recognized as something inhering in individuals rather than in systematic abstractions of its mission and program.[8]

This authority has its appropriate communication forms and media. Oratorical events are a routine form of participation for NU followers and are core channels for the expression of the authority of its leaders. In a wide-ranging interview published in 2002, NU elder statesman Abdul Muchith Muzadi discussed the importance of NU's "traditional communication channels," meaning oral communications at events "such as death commemorations (*haul*), celebrations to mark the end of the scholastic year (*imtihanan*), wedding receptions (*walimah*) and so on" (author's translation of Muzadi 2002, 30; see also Muhtadi 2004, 51–53). The centrality of preaching events to NU practice reveals a clear reordering of the hierarchy of communications media proposed by oratory's critics. While the critics of oratory seek to purify religious mediations of situated realities, NU subjects are accustomed to listening to oratorical expressions of religious authority at the significant, routine junctures of religious, life cycle, and civil calendars. While oratory's critics idealize a subject free from social entanglements, NU's preferred mediatory forms presume a subject that dwells within them.

Oratory's critics idealize the exchange of information and mutual comprehension as primary efficacies of communication events. In contrast, preaching events taking place in the routine spaces of local lives imply a plurality of meanings and outcomes: famous religious leaders are frequently regarded as bearers of blessings that can be accessed through contact with or proximity to them, and this motivates attendance at oratorical events (Muhtadi 2004, 205–6); group supplications are often a core component of oratorical events, making them highly attractive to many NU followers (Millie 2008); NU audiences are known also for their liking for preachers with virtuoso performance skills such as Al-Jauhari, which indicates the acceptability of pleasure and affect as benefits of oratory; and attendance at oratorical events for many Indonesians, especially women, is a routine observance conducted in groups that provides a socially pleasing experience as well as religious merit. All these functions are encouraged and facilitated by NU preachers and event organizers, so NU subjects are justified in experiencing religious mediations in events that are deeply embedded in social realities, often of a highly localized nature.

While NU retains oral/aural communication as a core participatory form for its followers, its critics valorize written genres as transformative media. Indeed, historians (Laffan 2004; Roff 1967) have documented the efflorescence of Islamic reformism through networks of journal publication and translation. The days when literacy within NU was the sole preserve of its leaders have passed, but for many NU followers, the postindependence democratization of writing and reading has not reduced the value of oratory. NU's dispositions and practices of mediation continue to favorably accommodate a context-dependent listening subject that is reliant on and affected by the mediations of others.

NU's Empowerment Project

The background to NU provided here has so far ignored major changes that have affected the organization since its founding in 1926. Some of the initiatives that have emerged within the organization in recent decades complicate the "black and white" distinctions I have presented. As discussed in chapter 5, NU intellectuals and activists such as Muhammad A. S. Hikam were prominent in promoting a civil society concept as an antidote to particular problems that the Indonesian nation faced, especially in the 1980s and early 1990s. At that time the work of younger NU activists made "civil society" the "prevailing paradigm" (Bush 2009, 97).[9]

Their elaborations of this concept emphasize that Indonesians must be empowered to actualize their individual agency; Hikam (1996, 123–24) argued that a democratic political culture would be sustained by subjects able to overcome their political, social, and economic constraints through their own resources. Positions such as this were promoted in practice by organizations established within NU or in affiliation with it. The Association for the Development of Pesantren and Society (P3M), founded in 1983, pursued a program of *pesantren*-based social transformation. NU-affiliated development activists formed the Institute for Human Resources Studies and Development (Lakpesdam) as a branch of NU in 1985. Lakpesdam implemented grassroots programs for the empowerment of village society in areas such as health, education, and economic self-sufficiency. It propagandized the concept of civil society as a program that would enable, among other things, the political and economic empowerment of the NU community. The Institute for the Study of Islam and Society (LKiS) was formed in 1993 by university activists of the 1980s and promoted a theme of transformative Islam that would allow for the liberation of Muslims through reworkings of canonical Islamic sources. It established a major publishing house that published the works of authors, including Hikam. Some of these works placed the issue of pluralism and interfaith relations on the NU agenda (Bush 2009, 87–110).

The civil society movement brought with it practical innovations affecting the forms of media and communication encountered at NU events. The idealization of the empowered, democratically literate subject appeared with a new lexicon to describe its mediations and forms of communication. Robin Bush's description of the NU gatherings she attended in the late-1990s exemplifies this new lexicon: she was attending "workshops," not oratorical events. The gatherings were led not by scholarly elites (*kyai* or *ulama*) but by *fasilitator* and *aktivis* (Bush 2009, 95–100). In their writings, NU's civil society activists of the time do not use the conventional lexicon for describing NU's gatherings: *tabligh* (sermons), *pengajian* (study gatherings), or *ceramah* (speech). Rather, the words they use reflect the discursive modes of nongovernment organizations, labeling the program's events as *training, diskusi, seminar,* and *workshop.* The programs implemented at these are not pious renewal, supplication, or spiritual betterment, but *advokasi, pemberdayaan* (empowerment), *penguatan* (consolidation), *penyadaran* (consciousness-raising), *emansipasi,* and *pengembangan diskursus* (discursive development).[10] The embodied authority of NU tradition appears very distant from these events, as does the validation of subjects who may properly keep their distance from ideas and their circulation. Passivity is gone. Instead, the speaker and listener participate on equal footing with a shared commitment to individual empowerment and autonomy.

These developments do not signal the end of NU's culture of preaching and listening. Rather, they point to dichotomies within the contemporary NU. Open conflict materializes in contrasting religious interpretations of social issues such as those involving women's rights, religious freedom, and family law. The conflict is described as a clash between *muda progresif* (young progressives), many of whom are active in organizations such as the LKiS, and a *sayap konservatif* (conservative wing) consisting of heads of *pesantren* (see Zada and Sjadzili 2010).

Concluding Words

NU poses challenges to the dominant normative conception of the public. From its beginning, NU has embraced the traditionalist label, thereby agreeing to a designation that fixes the group at an earlier stage of a linear progression in which their reformist colleagues will always appear more advanced. Followers do not sense the label as a negative one, for they hold traditionalist Islam to be an essential resource for creating a prosperous and just Indonesian modernity. NU is not against progress, for its elites hold goals for the national future that are similar to those held by leaders of Muhammadiyah and other modernist organizations. But the arguments I present here indicate that NU does not have an ideological commitment to the project of purification within which the critiques of oratory derive their logic. Its theology and embodied modes of communication undercut the supremacy of autonomy, resistance, and empowerment as necessary characteristics for an Indonesian Muslim subject. They render unproblematic Muslim preferences for mediating forms that are determined by the localized realities in which they are embedded.

This position is surely conducive to Indonesians' sense of belonging within the national project. Oratory is a favored Islamic observance because it is highly amenable to listeners' ways of life and religious dispositions. The critique of oratory, although justifying itself by aspiring to economic and social improvement of the masses, passes over the economic inequalities and diverse histories that correspond to these ways of life and dispositions. Against this, NU stands as a bulwark against the universalizing momentum of widely accepted norms about proper ways of being Islamic in the age of Indonesian modernity. Many Indonesians find Islamic oratory so amenable because of its embeddedness, its familiarity, and its lack of strangeness, but it is precisely this embeddedness that the normalizing critique of oratory problematizes. It is significant, then, that aspects of NU doctrine and practice provide defenses of a listening subject that would otherwise appear as illegitimate and anachronistic. In other words, if the narrative of (post-oratorical) modernity privileges an emancipated and empowered subject, NU's Islamically based ideologies concerning mediation and knowledge project a Muslim subject that should not be characterized as merely the opposite of emancipated and empowered.

CONCLUSION

Connections between forms of Islamic communication and public spheres have for good reason been the object of scholarly attention in recent years.[1] Preaching events are significant among forms of Islamic communication because they draw mass participation to mediations of symbols and ideas held in the highest regard by Muslim listeners. The forms of sociability and publicness arising from this communication are not well understood but gain extra importance in the present when they are under such stress in several Islamic populations. Indonesia is not suffering the same fragmentations as are unfolding in some countries in the Middle East and Central Asia, but this contrast of itself makes Indonesia's Islamic publicness an important focus for comparative conversations.

Researchers have only recently made progress in considering the place of listening in Islamic public life. The listener has not been taken seriously in the discourses of secular modernity and, as the preceding chapters indicate, has even been an object of suspicion and derision (Hirschkind 2006, 13–18). Large groups of rapt listeners signify the obduracy of public religion when faced with what secular modernists hold to be a universal, natural evolution away from it; listening audiences seem to have refused to acknowledge the superiority of autonomous personhood. A powerful expression of such a perception is Roland Barthes's description of a 1955 sermon delivered in Paris by the American evangelical Billy Graham. The father of poststructuralism noted "the systematic eviction of any rational content" from Graham's attempt at "magical transformation." He likened the evangelist's performance to two other social phenomena—namely, the "savage cults" of "primitives" such as that of the "Papuan" and the professional arts of deception such as hypnotism (Barthes 1979, 63–66).

The preceding chapters engage with Indonesians whose outlooks on preaching and listening resembles Barthes's (minus his contempt for religion). Their critiques, especially those of Acep Hidayat and Siti Musdah Mulia, deserve close attention because these figures grew up in communities where oratory is a preferred medium. They have lived within the routines in which clever speaking is so prominent. Yet they also hold to a conviction that Indonesians will benefit from democratic governance and the progressive social outlook that comes with it, and this conviction has spurred them to reflect and comment on those routines. By doing so, they initiate conversations very similar to those initiated by Dale Eickelman, Armando Salvatore, Patrick Gaffney, and Charles Hirschkind as well as thinkers such as Jürgen Habermas and Michael Warner, who developed ideas about communications and publicness without reference to specifically Islamic spheres. A basic question of interest to all these figures is, what do genres and styles of public communication mean for collectives and public life? In the remaining pages, I respond to this question, drawing together strands emerging in the preceding chapters.

The question is important for several reasons. First, for an influential segment of Indonesians, the most popular forms of preaching imply a subjectivity that is inadequate because it appears to be incompatible with contemporary idealizations of Muslim subjectivity. Popular genres of face-to-face verbal communication create an impression of "antipublicness," and this demands interrogation. The second reason runs counter to the reasoning of the first: recent decades have seen serious efforts by Bandung Muslims to broaden the range of sites in which preaching events are held and to increase the frequency of their occurrence. More preaching, from this perspective, is a good thing. These efforts are justified based on their public benefit, and this justification should be taken seriously in that vein. And third, academic theorizations that connect face-to-face communications with public spheres are in the developmental stage. It seems almost impossible to speak of publicness without giving central position to writing and reading as the foundational processes in the emergence of contemporary public spheres (Hirschkind 2006; Salvatore 1998; Warner 2002). The unfortunate result of this is that contemporary listeners are constructed as participants in something that seems to belong to collectives of the past. Charles Hirschkind's *Ethical Soundscape: Cassette Sermons and Islamic Counterpublics* was such a welcome intervention because it addressed that very problem. The title itself opens the plausibility of connections between listening and concern for the wellbeing of collectives extending beyond the setting of the interaction.

The starting point in evaluating preaching's contribution to publicness must be the re-embedding of listeners in the situations of individual preaching events. In recent years a good part of the literature on Islamic publics has disembedded Muslim listeners by constructing them as consumers of Islamic media products and commodities. Dominant ideas about publicness have pushed analysis in that direction. Media are considered to have the special property of creating relations between absent receivers, and these relations over distance are recognized to be the foundation of its public-creating capabilities (Schlesinger 2000; Thompson 1995). It has also become clear that, in the era of heavy mediatization and consumption, Islamic communications successfully attract public support when their authors anticipate and appropriate contemporary forms of publicness wider than religious ones (Salvatore 1998). Thus, the absent receiver of mediated communication has become isomorphic with the Islamic consumer. We know of this absent receiver because of the Islamic commodities that circulate in the culture market, especially books and recordings marketed under the brand of individual celebrity mediators (e.g., Eickelman 1992, 1998; Fealy 2008; Muzakki 2008; Salvatore 1998; Starrett 1998). This perspective is undoubtedly important because it reveals the novel Islamic subjectivities and changing forms of Islamic authority brought with mediatization, but it also disembeds Muslim subjects by abstracting them as consumers, an abstraction that obscures the ongoing realities of face-to-face listening.[2]

In the early stages of my field research, I was working under the influence of this disembedding, thinking that the sermon as text and performance provided the limits of the investigation, for the audience could surely be assumed to be consumers of these products. When attending preaching events, my attention was primarily focused on the preacher. It was only after a few months that I realized that almost all of the audiences that I was joining had assembled for undertakings other than listening to a sermon. I first realized this while attending a sermon in the Bandung Milk Producers' Association, a state-owned corporation. As I listened to the sermon, I looked around the audience, an assortment of people with diverse backgrounds and specializations, and realized that the attendance of these people was grounded in two shared attributes: they were Muslims and they were present at this event because they were employees of the association. From then on I was aware that participation as listener is most often based on a relationship of dependence such as an employment relationship, family tie, client–patron relation, enrolment status and so on. Thinking about listeners as consumers would lead me to ignore the actual conditions of listeners' participation in the event. From then on, I realized that the core competencies of the successful Bandung preacher include the capacity to negotiate variations between such situations. Preachers understood full well the embeddedness of their listeners, and I had to attempt to develop the same competency in order to properly carry out this research.

It is a crucial feature of routine, face-to-face verbal communication that acceptance of the mediation is negotiated at the site and during the temporal parameters of the interaction. Written genres are nothing like this. Books can be embraced, rejected, discarded, laughed at, and so on, without the knowledge of the writer. By contrast, the preacher's success or failure is determined at the moment of speaking. For that reason, analysis of preaching should follow the method of the successful preacher and treat listeners as subjects embedded in the situation at hand. It should acknowledge that, when taking up the microphone to preach, preachers fail if they treat their listeners as generic public subjects or pious consumers. There is no general category of listener but only contextually bound listeners, all linked by some common status or social tie, and all capable of disengaging from the interaction.

Once I realized these things, my inquiry expanded beyond a narrow focus on the preacher as privileged mediator. I noticed women sitting in small circles of friends and family, chatting and pinching each other while the preacher was speaking. In workplace sermons, I noticed some employees taking notes in exercise books at the front of the audience while others with minimal commitment to the sermon were dozing off, to be brought back to a state of attentiveness by a joke or song from the preacher. At other events, I watched women enthusiastically respond verbally to cues from the preacher while their fatigued husbands, sitting elsewhere in the audience, resignedly stroked unlit cigarettes in expectation of leaving the mosque at the sermon's conclusion. These are not just observations of audience behavior but are elements of situation that determine the communicative interaction. Therefore, understanding the success of Islamic oratory requires a re-embedding of Islamic speaking in the specific settings in which it occurs.

A Successful Project of Public Islam

Despite all the objections to the preaching practices I encountered in Bandung, they can rightfully be considered as forming a successful project of public Islam. One achievement best illustrates that success, although in stating this, I do not mean that the project provides one benefit only. In fact, a number of public benefits can be identified. For example, this is a project that, to some degree, develops in listeners the faculties of the idealized, rational-critical citizen-subject. A baseline civic publicness is expressed in all of the preaching interactions that I observed in Bandung: preachers affirm dominant values concerning citizenship, gender, family roles, and so on. Yet this feature cannot be understood as a dominant benefit; the same effect is achieved through many secular media and communications genres, and furthermore, preachers succeed by appropriating many genres, among which those enabling the crosscutting of voices and rational critique associated with the bourgeois public sphere are not prominent. Nor can the project's contribution to the cultivation of pious subjects be claimed as its primary success. There is no doubt that preachers are influential among the agents responsible for cultivating personal and public piety, but a mutual commitment to pious self-development is not sufficient of itself to explain the high acceptance by listeners of their preferred preachers. The high volume of preaching activity in West Java is sustained also by verbal skill and artifice that frequently have little connection with pious themes.

The distinctive success of the preaching project described in the preceding chapters is found in the high level of public acceptance that it attracts. In an era when the seemingly irresistible progress of secularism appears so threatening to Muslim societies, and when divisions among Islamic societies are leading to such devastating fragmentation, it is remarkable that so many religious, social, and political actors support the frequent holding of Islamic preaching events. West Javanese society displays an extraordinary public consensus that the constant restatement of Islamic messages through listening is a desirable thing. In what follows, I wish to reflect on the social realities within which public listening has become such an acceptable practice, and on the conditions and limits that constrain the listening project in order that it be successful as a public one.

Four overlapping features distinguish this successful project of public Islam. The first is routines. By routines, I mean those abstract sequences against which people coordinate the movement of their bodies, resources, and energies to form, in concert with others, a Muslim audience. Routines cause audiences to form and signal the embededdness of listening subjects more than anything else, for they are always performed in formations structured from relationships created through work, family, or community obligation. In Bandung, the sequence incorporates several cycles, including the Islamic calendar, the human life cycle, learning schedules, and the civil calendar. In West Java, these cycles provide a schedule for the public performance of Islam, and in many of the events that comprise them, skillful speech provides the primary focus around which audiences assemble.

The second feature is a development of the first. In recent times the routines just mentioned have expanded in the range of contexts in which their preaching events are implemented. An especially notable example of this is the transplanting of preaching routines into contemporary places of work (see also Rudnyckyj 2010). It was only in the late 1960s, when the Suharto regime opened the door to Islamic actors prepared to support its development programs, that Islamic messages entered the spaces of modern labor. This extension of routines of observance into the specialized contexts of urban life cuts across borders that characterize spaces as private and public, secular and sacred. It is not so remarkable that schedules of Islamic observance continued to structure collective life in rural communities, where the effort required to hold events can be summoned through collaborations between domestic households. But it was a surprise for me that "rational actors" in modern places of work and study supported the attempt to cultivate the routines of Islamic observance in spaces that would otherwise, following the logic of secular modernity, be free of collective Islamic expression and performance. It is unremarkable that the Bandung preacher Nur Wahid preaches to audiences at weddings and calendrical celebrations (chapter7), for preachers have been invited to perform at these for centuries, but it is noteworthy that he also receives invitations to preach at the Bandung Polytechnic, the state-owned Water Board, the governor's office, privately owned banks, and so on. Bandung preaching routines display a shared conviction that all spaces can be dignified by Islamic speech and therefore contrast with the secular idealization that prefers public places to be neutral in their religious meanings. This is achieved through the willingness of a broad range of social and political actors to support Islamic listening by organizing preaching events in the spaces under their management (families, neighborhoods, mosque committees, Islamic organizations, governments at all levels, corporations, political parties, and educational institutions).

The third feature is the plasticity of speech and the wide access that is enabled by it. Skillful speech is the Islamic medium that provides the most appropriate vehicle for the nurturing of routines of observance in a society such as Bandung, where life is constantly becoming further differentiated into specialized spheres. Hosts take risks when they try to obtain support from heterogeneous audiences for ritual performance such as supplication, for by doing so they run the risk of offending audience members' dispositions about correctness in observance or of causing awkwardness to listeners not accustomed to them.[3] By contrast, an experienced preacher can verbalize messages acceptable to all. Preachers are skilled at affirming the integrity and cohesion of the structure they address, be it a body of employees, village community, military corps, neighborhood, extended family, or student body. By doing so, they help transform the disparate spaces into which humans are taken by the exigencies of contemporary life into Islamic environments, giving the religion greater salience in the public and private spaces of West Javanese society than at any other time in the history of the province. This capability distinguishes preachers as important contributors to the contemporary Islamic public sphere.

Final among the features distinguishing West Java's public compact about preaching is the regulatory mechanism that forms a condition on preachers' access to diverse settings and underpins career success. The public commitment to Islamic speech in diverse spaces, public and private, succeeds because of agreements between preacher, audience, and organizer that ensure sermons are appropriate to context. Organizing committees represent the interests and preferences of listeners and hosts and create understandings with preachers about what kinds of mediations are necessary for the environment. Complying with these understandings is an imperative for a preaching career, for the alternative is to be "struck off the schedule" (*dicoret dari jadwal*). This mechanism guarantees preaching performances are appropriate for the specific settings in which they take place.

Ambivalence

This public Islamic project succeeds despite a contradiction inhering within it. Preaching events succeed when good relations between copresent subjects are affirmed and maintained and when listeners' attention is engaged throughout the communication. But oratory's critics have aspirations for Islamic communication as a tool for programs of social and political progress. They hope it might contribute to a public sphere in which communications are conducted for the benefit of the common good.

I was in a privileged position to observe the incongruity between the realities of sociable oratory and the criticisms it attracts, for I spent lengthy time with both Al-Jauhari and Acep Hidayat. The former generated more laughter than any other preacher in West Java while, for the latter, laughter symbolized all that was wrong with oratory. I could not help thinking that the M2KQ program would not achieve its aspirations (chapter 5) even though many Indonesians recognize its logics and support them. Al-Jauhari's high energy multivocality remains popular. At the time of this writing, he continues to appear on up to three stages per day. And there are many other preachers who have similar appeal. Their styles find disapproval in the critiques of their oratory, which promote empowered, capable subjects in charge of their own destinies. Yet to what extent does this idealization of contemporary subjectivity resonate with the realities of life for Indonesia's 210 million Muslims? Does it resonate for women, especially older women who, in many Indonesian communities, enjoy fewer social and economic opportunities than men and who are enabled to enjoy a greater public mobility and sociability through engaging in routines of Islamic listening and learning? Does it resonate with the multitudes of poor Indonesians? For these people, preachers extend the possibility of participating in public Islam on a "come as you are" basis. For these reasons, the critique of sociable preaching seems to make no dent on the problem it identifies. The critics of festive oratory aspire to turn laughing and crying listeners into thinking Muslims participating in the democratic process, but the laughing and crying continue unabated.

This tension should be recognized as more than a culture war between frustrated progressives and audiences determined to enjoy their preferences. I argue that the critiques of popular oratorical styles and routines are important for maintaining the integrity of Islam in the public imagination. They are a necessary element of the public consensus sketched out earlier. Preaching is happening in spaces of all kinds, with the inevitable consequence that preaching performances—although recognizable as Islamic speech—will blend into and take forms appropriate for those environments. This is how it succeeds. In the process, it moves further away from the idealizations of Muslims who care about the quality and potential of Islamic communication. For PERSIS, for example, the danger is that preachers mingle the worldly and religious spheres too liberally. For political and social activists, Islam's potential as a tool for transformation is wasted. Even ordinary listeners who enjoy popular preaching in multivocal styles acknowledge that these styles have less value than constrained preaching styles that index national publicness (chapter 4).

Putting aside the specific objections produced by the critics of oratory discussed in the preceding chapters, a public discourse that recognizes these threats to Islam is functionally valuable at a more popular level because it supports the collective's commitment to Islam's other-worldliness.[4] There is an obvious irony in this: the more Islam materializes in everyday life, the more it seems to require protection from everyday life. Yet it is impossible for Muslims of Bandung to give fulsome recognition to preachers like Al-Jauhari, no matter how much they relish listening to them, for their mutual commitment is to Islam and the routines through which it is performed publicly, not to its clever mediators. This is what distinguishes Islamic communications from other genres of expression. West Javanese Muslims like to publicly recognize the province's famous puppet masters (*dalang*) as individual geniuses, yet they cannot publicly acknowledge that Islamic messages are more acceptable and inclusive when they are delivered through the skills of a clever mediator. This would reduce Islam's value to oratorical virtuosity. When a preacher verbalizes and translates hadith and Qur'an, he points directly to revelation and Allah's Prophet. By contrast, the multivocal strategies that make preaching such an effective medium for keeping Islamic meanings in circulation point to something far less noble: individual preaching skills and the affective responses they help create. They point to the economics of celebrity preaching, the ephemeral thrill of humor, and the shifting appeal of trends in popular culture.[5] Concealing these realities is important for the integrity of Islam as a public resource. When academics, activists, and many ordinary Muslims agree on the differences between good and bad preaching styles, they create a layer of ambivalent reflection that affirms the dignity of Islam in a time when it is threatened by its popular uptake. It is a necessary counterpoint to the enjoyable artifice that underpins preaching's popularity.

One of the preachers discussed in the preceding chapters provides a fitting example for this conclusion. The example clearly expresses how public consensus on the differing values of oratorical styles protects Islam from the realities of actual preaching performances. In chapter 3 I discussed Shiddiq Amien's 2009 oration dealing with matters forbidden to women during menstruation. Like all his sermons, that one was full of verbalizations, translations, and interpretations of hadith. Amien verbalized the following excerpt amid his translations of hadith about matrimonial conduct. The sermon was delivered in Indonesian, but this example is one of his switches to Sundanese. Only the underlined text was delivered in Indonesian:

> "A year of drought . . . how do we say it? Is soaked by a day of rain. <u>After all, there are wives who say to their husbands,</u> 'All you do is cause me pain!' [audience: laughter] 'What do you mean I cause you pain?' 'You never make me happy.' Her husband says, 'If you want to be happy [*senang*], fart in the steamer. [audience: laughter] The sound will be "*senang*".' That's what he says" (appendix B, segment 15).

The rice-steamer, one of the most recognizable items in a Sundanese home, forms a resonating chamber of sorts because of its metal fabric, shape, and depth. It is a common joke that breaking wind in the steamer will produce the sound "se-nang," which resembles the Indonesian and Sundanese word *senang*, meaning to be happy.[6] Through materials such as this, Amien's scholarly messages become highly acceptable to listeners. Yet as explained in chapter 3, Amien did not only communicate through the spoken word. Being a public figure and Islamic authority, his sermons were published as short articles by the general media as well as the media produced by the organization to which he dedicated his life, PERSIS. While I was in West Java I read many of these articles, all of them prepared as serious contributions to public discourse.

Earthy humor of this kind, as well as other multivocal strategies through which he achieved success with face-to-face audiences, were absent from the written versions of his sermons. They were removed in the editing process. The same thing occurred in the redactions of sermons by other preachers. Very little of the artifice by which Bandung's preachers create good outcomes in performance survived the transition from oral to written text.[7] When an orator consents to the transformation of an oration into a published piece of writing, he is aware that the circulation of that written text has implications that differ from the effects of the statements he utters before face-to-face audiences. An oration is a negotiation between a speaker and a willing, copresent audience. Speaker and audience attend with more or less matching conceptions of what is proper for the situation. Within the oratorical situation, the preacher has some measure of control over the communicative interaction, but this control is lost when the preacher's text enters the circulatory flows of the print media. A newspaper article can circulate into contexts that cannot be foreseen. If the wrong kind of material—such as the kind of humor just excerpted—were to circulate in written form, the preacher risks appearing as a buffoon or disrespectful of Islam. Furthermore, the publication would risk being implicated in this. In other words, the protocols of the paradigmatic public-forming medium—print publication—conceal the fact that preachers like Amien are not only learned in religion but also skilled verbal performers. These protocols protected Shiddiq Amien, whose supporters would, for reasons stated in chapter 3, be shocked to see him remembered here for this example. They also protect the public image of Islam.

In practice, West Java's preachers fill their mediations with recognizable realities of daily life through inversion, narrative, wordplay, profane genres, travesty, jokes, and vernacularisms. These enable the frequent circulation of Islamic messages through preaching. But public approval of this would threaten Islam's otherworldliness. Thus, Islamic mediators cannot be recognized as the performers they actually are. By ensuring that impious multivocality is kept away from public recognition, the domain of religion is protected from the cultural realities that sustain participation within it.

Appendix A

Wedding Sermon by Al-Jauhari

The following is a transcript and translation of an excerpt from a typical wedding sermon by Al-Jauhari.[1] The excerpt commences at the opening of the sermon and comprises sixteen minutes of a performance lasting one hour and seven minutes in total. The source recording is an unauthorized, commercially produced video recording purchased in VCD format at a stall in a bus terminal in Bandung (Junaedi 2008). The opening frames of the video, all in Sundanese, give the title of the performance as follows: "Wedding advices of Kyai Haji Al-Jauhari [delivered] at the celebration of the birth of the Prophet Muhammad, peace and blessings be upon him, and the wedding banquet of Titi Martini and Yudi Anwari." The event took place on April 8, 2007, in the area known as Pasar Inpres, Sumedang, West Java.

The analysis in chapter 2 is based on this performance. In that chapter, the radical intertextuality of Al-Jauhari's style is used as the starting point for a discussion of the conception of oratorical appropriateness supported by him and his audiences. Presenting the sermon in written form involves challenges. In performance, the preacher moves rapidly between voices and performance genres, most of them within the knowledge of his listeners. For listeners gathered at a festive event, this is highly acceptable. For a reader not familiar with contemporary Sundanese and Indonesian culture, or for a reader searching for thematic coherence, the written transcript of such a performance might appear chaotic and incoherent. The excerpt is presented in a way that addresses these difficulties. It is broken into segments, presented in between two and four components. Two components are used constantly throughout the excerpt—namely, the Sundanese text of the sermon and the English translation of Al-Jauhari's words (with audience reaction interspersed). At times, additional information is conveyed through two other components, one that explains and comments on variations in speech, preaching techniques, and intertextual references and one that describes body movements and gestures. The "Comments on Variation in Speech" are provided to help illustrate the diverse range of ways of speaking he mobilizes and how these underpin his efforts to maintain involvement with his audience. They are not intended as a complete descriptive account of his use of diverse speech genres, voices, languages, registers, speech-act types, discursive structures, and performance genres. Rather, they draw attention to the generic variation that forms such a central element of his oratorical style and translate it for readers unfamiliar with the cultural contexts. The information given in the fourth component about the preacher's frequent body movements and gestures, which are sometimes a part of planned routines in his sermons, is important because it conveys the broad range of expression mobilized by Al-Jauhari. It also conveys an impression of his strategy of addressing individual segments of his audience, especially the respective segments occupied by men or women. At the event, women were seated on his right side, men on his left. The organizers provided him with a swivel chair so that he could turn to face different segments of the audience even when seated.

Sundanese was the dominant language used in the oration. In the English translation and in the Sundanese text, words and phrases in languages other than Sundanese—Arabic, Indonesian, and the youth variant of Indonesian known as *gaul*—have been italicized. Arabic or Indonesian loanwords that have been accepted into regular Sundanese usage are not italicized. Al-Jauhari frequently translates his Arabic into Sundanese in the immediately following utterance. In places where he has done so, we have preserved his Arabic usage in the English translation. The translations of the Qur'an are those of Marmaduke Pickthall (1930).

Al-Jauhari often uses rising intonation to elicit affirmation from his audience and frequently requests audience members, for example, to complete his own utterance of words or phrases. I have indicated his use of rising intonation with the symbol ◀.

Segment 1

[**English translation with backchannel cues:**] *In the name Allah the most merciful, the most beneficent. May the peace and blessing of Allah be upon you.* [audience, subdued: *And may Allah's peace be upon you.*]

[**Comments on variation in speech:**] Formulaic invocation and greeting in Arabic.

[**Sundanese text with backchannel cues:**] *Bi-'smi 'llahi al-rahman al-rahim. Al-salamu 'alaikum wa rahmatu 'llahi wa barakatuhu.* [audience: *wa 'alaikum al-salam*]

[**Body movements and gestures:**] Al-Jauhari is seated on a swivel chair above a small stage.

Segment 2

Those who answer *salam*, may you go [on pilgrimage] to Mecca. [audience: amiin!] For those who didn't answer, I hope their husbands find another wife. [audience: laughter]

Anu ngajawab salam sing ka Mekah. [audience: amiin!] Anu henteu ngajawab salam, salakina sing kawin deui. [audience: laughter]

Looks to the side where the women are sitting and smiles.

Segment 3

May the peace and blessing of Allah be upon you. [audience, this time louder: *And may the peace, mercy and blessings of Allah be upon you!*]

Al-salamu 'alaikum wa rahmatu 'llahi wa barakatuhu. [audience: *Wa 'alaikum al-salam wa rahmatu 'llahi wa barakatuhu!*]

Segment 4

When threatened, you respond more loudly! [audience: laughter]

Diancam mah tarik euy! [audience: laughter]

Segment 5

In the name of Allah, the first before all firsts, and the last after all lasts,
He is the first and last, the outer and inner.

We seek refuge in Allah, the All-hearing and All-knowing, from the accursed devils. In the name of Allah, the merciful and beneficent.

Arabic invocation and supplication

Bi-'smi 'llahi al-awwal qabla kulli al-awwal, wa al-akhir ba'da kulli al-akhir
Huwa al-awwal wa al-akhir wa al-dzahir wa al-batin
Audzu bi-'llahi al-sami' al-'alim min al-shaitani al-rajim
Bi-'smi 'llahi al-rahman al-rahim

Segment 6

And We said: O Adam! Dwell thou and they wife in the Garden [audience: *Allah*]*, and eat ye freely [of the fruits] thereof where ye will; but come not nigh this* *tree* [audience: *Allah*], *but come not nigh this tree lest ye become wrongdoers* [audience: *Allah*]. *Almighty Allah speaks the truth.*

Melodic Qur'anic performance (Qur'an 2:35). The audience responds by saying "Allah" at the end of each phrase.

Wa qulna ya adam uskun anta wa zaujuka al-jannah [audience: Allah], *wa kula minha raghadan haithu shi'tuma wa la taqraba hadhihi al-shajarah* [audience: Allah], *wa la taqraba hadhihi shajarah, fa takuna min al-dzalimin* [audience: Allah]. *Sadaqa 'llahu al-'adzim.*

Segment 7

Marriage, according to folk etymology, is an abbreviation for a bounty that feels warm. [audience: laughter] Or, according to the mischievous Islamic students, marriage means sleeping on something big. [audience: laughter] These are only folk etymologies; speculations that are apparent.

Folk etymology (Sundanese, *kirata*); double entendre

Nikah, ceuk kirata mah, nikah téh singkétan, nikmat karasa haneut. [audience: laughter] Atawa ceuk santri lenger mah, nikah téh nindihan nu beukah. [audience: laughter] Éta mah kirata; dikira-kira tapi nyata.

Segment 8

Whatever the terminology, marriage is the *shariah* of Allah revealed to humans. For this reason, humans shouldn't be ruled by their basic instincts, like animals. If people here in Sumedang just follow their basic instincts in releasing their sexual desires, then they are animals. Human sexual drives should be channeled *bi 'aqdin sahihin*, that is, through a legal marriage.

Naon waé istilahna, ari nikah téh syaréat Allah nu diturunken ka jelema. Matak jelema mah teu maén kéclak. Nu sok maén kéclak mah sato. Lamun di Sumedang asal hayang maén kéclak nyalurkeun syahwat, maka éta sato. Ari jelema mah kudu disalurkeun *bi 'aqdin sahihin*, maké akad nikah anu sah.

Segment 9

To whom was the law of marriage first revealed? To the prophet Adam, *be upon him* ◀ . . . [audience: *peace*]

Through requests for completion of phrases and words, Al-Jauhari obtains affirmations of support from his audience. He frequently uses contrived questions like this one as structuring devices.

Ka saha ari nikah pangheulana disyaréatkeun? Ka nabi Adam *'alaihi al-s* ◀ . . . [audience: *salam*]

Segment 10

So, the prophet Adam also got married, just like Yuda and Titi. The difference is, Yuda's dowry to Titi is gold, a diamond, a set of clothing for prayer, and other things. Whereas Adam's dowry to Eve was the recital of a blessing one hundred times in one breath.

Jadi nabi Adam gé jiga Cép Yuda ka Néng Titi. Ngan bédana, ari Yuda ka Titi mah mas kawinna emas, inten berlian, saperangkat alat sholat jeung sajabana. Ari Nabi Adam ka Siti Hawa mah, mas kawinna maca solawat saratus kali teu ngarénghap.

Segment 11

But the prophet Adam was not up to it. He could only recite it fifty times, and postponed the other fifty. Since then, it has been permissible to postpone the payment of dowries. "I accept to marry Titi, with the dowry being four kilograms of metal to be paid in the future." [audience: laughter]

Al-Jauhari delivers the final sentence in a voice that the audience readily identify as "Yuda's."

Ngan nabi Adam teu kuateun. Ngan kuateun 50 kali, anu 50 kali dianjuk. Matak ti saprak harita tepi ka ayeuna meunang lamun mas kawin dianjuk. "Tarima abdi nampi nikah ka Néng Titi kalayan mas kawin 4 kilogram beusi dianjuk." [audience: laughter]

Segment 12

But this is only allowed if the bride agrees. Ladies, do you mind being asked to marry with a postponed dowry? [audience: No way! With laughter.]

Éta téh meunang asal awéwéna daékeun. Ibu kersa upami mas kawinna dianjuk teu? [audience: Aliim! With laughter.]

Rotates to face the female listeners

Segment 13

Material girl . . . material girl . . . [audience: laughter]

Al-Jauhari sings this phrase, which is an excerpt from a popular song that heavily references Indonesian youth culture: *Cewek Matre* (Material Girl) by 8 Ball.

Cewek matre, cewek matre [audience: laughter]

Segment 14

So you can understand how marriage has become difficult, even though it is a simple thing. Marriage is easy and needs only five things to happen: a groom, a bride, the bride's guardian, a witness, and acceptance. Then it happens. Nowadays it seems so difficult. Tonight, I have found the reason. . . . The people of Sumedang have made it more difficult.

Paingan atuh nikah anu gampang jadi susah ayeuna mah. Da nikah mah cukup aya lima gé jadi: calon panganten lalaki, calon panganten awéwé, wali, saksi, ijab kabul. Jadi. Ayeuna mah ternyata susah pernikahan ayeuna mah. Kapanggih wé peuting ayeuna. . . . Nu sok mempersulit pernikahan téh urang Sumedang.

At the final sentence, he points his finger accusingly at the audience

Segment 15

What's the reason? You answered me earlier: you don't want to postpone your dowries. Because of that, people nowadays want to postpone their marriages, for they think about the yenom . . . [audience member: money!] . . . yenom. That's right . . . yenom.

Wordplay: *duit* (money) is reversed to become *tiud* (yenom)

Naon sababna? Ternyata bieu ngajawab, embung dianjuk. Matak ayeuna mah jelema diengké-engké rék kawin téh, sabab mikiran tiudna . . . [audience member: duit!] . . . tiud. Heueuh . . . duit.

While speaking, Al-Jauhari removes his mobile phone from his pocket, and reads a text message. This is not intended as part of the performance. Al-Jauhari regularly reads and responds to text messages during his sermons.

Segment 16

Money for someone to put up the decorations, especially decorations like this, they look very expensive to hire, right? Right? [audience: right!]

Duit jang nyéwa tukang riasna, komo tukang rias jiga kieu mah, jigana mahal nyéwana gé, bener? [audience: bener!]

Points to the decorations on stage

Segment 17

Money for hiring the chairs. Money for Al-Jauhari's envelope. [audience: laughter] [interjector: That's number one!] [Al-Jauhari: laughter] Money for this and for that.

Duit keur nyéwa korsina. Duit keur ngamplopan Al-Jauharina. [audience: laughter] [Interjector: Nomor hiji éta mah!] [Al-Jauhari: laughter] Duit keur itu keur ieu.

Segment 18

But it is strange that nowadays marriages are postponed because people are thinking about money, but when a young person is invited out to have fun with her boyfriend and comes back at 11:00 at night, we just ignore it! That is why we shouldn't be surprised that many girls claim to be virgins *but on their wedding night* there's nothing there.

Ngan anéh ayeuna mah, ari nikah diengké-engké gara-gara mikiran duit, tapi lamun budak diajak ulin ku kabogohna, balik jam sabelas peuting, di-arantep! Matak tong kagét lamun ayeuna loba awéwé nu ngakuna parawan *ternyata malam pertama* euweuh nanaonan.

While saying these words, Al-Jauhari is typing into his mobile phone with the hand that is not holding the microphone.

Segment 19

The groom sings on his wedding night: *Tell me, who is the one who preceded me?* [audience: some murmurs of surprise]

Al-Jauhari is here performing the Indonesian *dangdut* song: *Air Mata Perkawinan* (The Tears of Marriage), by Mansyur S.

Salakina nyanyi malam pertama: *Katakanlah, siapakah orang yang telah mendahului aku* [audience: murmurs of surprise]

Types into his mobile phone then returns it to his shirt pocket.

Segment 20

Be quiet! I sing because my voice is good. If you don't like it, don't oppose me! The reason you don't like it is because your own voice is ugly! Be quiet! [audience: laughter]

The indignation is contrived.

Cicing! Da nyanyi sotéh alus sorana, ulah sok nentang yeuh ka nu teu beuki. Matak teu beuki gé manéh mah goréng sorana! Cicing! [audience: laughter]

Motions dismissively at the audience generally.

Segment 21

*The first night I have so looked forward to has ended in disappointment
and is full of regret.* [audience: hoots in appreciation]
*The most sickening thing . . . the most sickening thing for my heart
is that someone else has eaten the jackfruit, while I have been splashed by
the sap,
I have been splashed by the sap . . .*

Continues singing *Air Mata Perkawinan*. Al-Jauhari chooses his profane songs carefully so that they harmonize with the themes of his speech. His performance of these songs is highly expressive of whatever emotion is relevant for the textual moment (see also segments 44 and 54).

*Malam pertama kudambakan telah berakhir dengan kekecewaan
dan penuh penyesalan* [audience: hoots in appreciation]
Yang paling menyakitkan . . . yang paling menyakitkan hatiku ini,

orang makan nangkanya aku kena getahnya,
ku kena getahnya . . .

Segment 22

That grandma looks confused. "What song is that?" [audience: laughter] That, Granny, is the song of a groom who has obtained a *parabola*. Do you know what *parabola* means? A maiden worn out from before. [audience: laughter]

The dialogue is contrived. *Parabola* is a contrived acronym.

Nini-nini ngahuleng, "Lagu naon cenah éta"? [audience: laughter] Éta téh, Ema, lagu lalaki nu meunangkeun parabola. Naon parabola téh? Parawan jebol ti heula. [audience: laughter]

Points his finger in the direction of the "grandma."

Segment 23

For that reason, Haji Aklani did something different. When he saw someone becoming close to his daughter, Titi, he did not delay. He called him. Yuda! Titi! *Come here! Come here!* Come here. Get married! And they were married.

Matak pak haji Aklani mah henteu kitu. Ninggal Néng Titi aya anu nyakétan henteu diengké-engké. Digeroan. Yuda! Titi! *Come here. Ta'ala!* Ka dieu! Nikah! Ditikahkeun wé.

Waves his hand, as if summoning someone.

Segment 24

So, this marriage is a big thing, ladies. Not because the stage is big. Not because there are three preachers here. And not because the audience is so big. I call this event a big one because it changes an unlawful relationship into a lawful one. Before now, Yuda was forbidden to be with Titi, but because of this proper marriage, their relationship has become lawful. So, this is considered a worthwhile act in the sight of Allah.

Tah ieu pernikahan téh perkara gedé, ibu. Disebut gedé lain pédah gedé panggungna. Lain pédah kiyaina satilu-tilu. Lain pédah balandonganana gedé. Lain pédah nu hadirna loba. Ieu perkara disebut perkara gedé sabab ieu perkara ngahalalkeun anu tadina haram. Tadina Cép Yuda ka Néng Titi haram bergaul, ku akad nikah anu sah jadi halal. Maka ieu perkara di-pandang ibadah di sisi Allah.

Addresses the female segment of the audience.

Segment 25

May all the effort and expenditure of Haji Aklani and his in-laws in hold-ing this event and all it entails be rewarded by Allah many times over! [au-dience: amiin!]

Audience members understand the preacher to be leading them in a *doa* (supplication) at this point.

Mudah-mudahan sagala rupi anu dikaluarkeun ku Pa haji Aklani sareng bésanna kanggo ngayakeun ieu acara sapuratina, sing digentosan ku Allah anu berlipat ganda. [audience: amiin!]

Segment 26

Yup, this event, ladies, really needs money. It could not take place without money. No way. The wedding parties of nowadays, as Haji Hasan told me before, have so many guests. Can you imagine? Ooooh! How many hun-dreds of millions for this kind of thing? These days, everything needs ye-nom, doesn't it?

Heueuh da kikieuan téh, ibu, maké duit. Teu maké duit mah moal jadi atuh, heueuh. Hajat jaman kiwari kieu, coba tamuna gé cenah tadi béjana, ceuk Haji Hasan, mani loba. Bayangkeun coba brrreuuh! Sabaraha ratus jutaeun meureun kikieuan? Make tiud ayeuna mah nanaon ogé heueuh.

Facing female section.

Segment 27

This stage needs . . . [audience: yenom], the decorations also . . . [audience: yenom], the sound system also . . . [audience: yenom], Al-Jauhari also . . . [Audience: yenom]

Al-Jauhari sings these prompts in a children's melody. The audience members complete each prompt in melody also.

Nyieun panggung maké . . . [audience: tiud], balandongana gé . . . [audience: tiud], sound systemna ogé . . . [audience: tiud], Al-Jauharina ogé . . . [audience: tiud]

Segment 28

I'm a human, not money! [audience: laughter] . . . money. You Sumedang people are really frank! If it is the case that the host gives the preacher some money, don't mention it so blatantly. I am really offended. [audience: laughter]

Frame jokes such as this are common in Al-Jauhari's work. In segment 27 he established a frame of expectation in the audience, leading the audience to expect the statement *Al-Jauharina ogé tiud* (lit: Al-Jauhari is money, but in the context: The wedding is expensive because of the money paid to Al-Jauhari). In this segment he creates surprise and humor by suddenly reorienting the frames contrary to expectation.

Jelema aing mah, duit! [audience: laughter] . . . duit. Pararoksang urang Sumedang nya! Dina enyana ogé anu hajat méré duit ka ajengan, tong sok bulutak-beletuk teuing atuh. Meuni tersinggung aku. [audience: laughter]

Segment 29

Think before you say something, ladies. Don't just say anything without considering it first. . . . Think first, Ijah! [audience: laughter] And you also Anah! [audience: laughter]

Al-Jauhari is here making humorous use of typical village names.

Méméh ngomong téh mikir heula, ibu. Tong sok dikira, lamun ngomong téh beletuk-beletuk wéh ngomong téh. . . . Pikir heula, Ijah! [audience: laughter] Si Anah tah saruana! [audience: laughter]

Swivels his chair to face the women's section.

Segment 30

Before you say something, don't just follow the ◄ . . . [audience: buffalo] . . . money! [audience: laughter]

Another frame game: *tuturut munding* (to follow the buffalo) is a Sundanese expression equivalent to the English "to follow the herd."

Méméh ngomong téh, ulah sok tuturut ◄ . . . [audience: munding] . . . duit! [audience: laughter]

Segment 31

Why say buffalo when we are talking about money? Sundanese people are like that. They speak first, then think afterward. That's why they often say the wrong thing. Answer this, ladies: For what do you buy a mattress? [audience: for sleeping!]

Keur ngomong duit kana munding. Kitu urang Sunda mah. Ari ngomong diheulakeun ari mikir dipandeurikeun. Matak saralah ngomongna téh. Jawab ibu: Ari ibu meuli kasur keur naon? [audience: keur bobo!]

In the direction of the women's section.

Segment 32

For sleeping? Sumedang people are amazing, for they can buy a mattress for sleeping. I can't do that. I usually buy a mattress while I am awake. [audience: laughter] How can you buy a mattress when you are sleeping? Arggh! [audience: laughter]

Another frame game. The joke relies on *keur saré* which can mean either "for sleeping" or "while sleeping." The audience initially interprets Al-Jauhari to be using the first meaning, until they hear the words *keur beunta* (while awake). The audience is surprised and amused by Al-Jauhari's sudden and unexpected switch to the other meaning of *keur saré*.

Keur saré? Jagoan urang Sumedang mah, bisa meuli kasur keur saré. Uing mah teu bisa. Uing mah mun meuli kasur téh keur beunta. [audience: laughter] Moal enya meuli kasur keur saré, waah! [audience: laughter]

Segment 33

How do you walk to the market? People usually buy a mattress when they are awake, and the mattress is used for slee—◀ [audience:—ping]. How can you buy a mattress while sleeping? You must be day-dreaming! [audience: laughter]

Aing mah kumaha leumpang ka pasarna. Meuli kasur mah biasana keur beunta, ngan kasurna sok dipaké sar—◀ [audience:—ré]. Meuli kasur keur saré, ngalindur manéh mah, ah! [audience: laughter]

Segment 34

"Are you sure, Mr. Al-Jauhari, that the prophet Adam was married to Eve?" That's right. "How do you know it?" The Qur'anic verse I read to you just now. *Wa qulna ya adam uskun anta wa zaujuka.* That's the one.

This question and answer marks the commencement of a lengthy, highly embellished replay of the Adam and Eve story, which ends at segment 61.

"Bener Pak Al-Juhari, nabi Adam ka Siti Hawa téh nikah?" Bener. "Mana buktina?" Ayat nu dibacakeun ku kuring tadi. *Wa qulna ya adam uskun anta wa zaujuka.* Éta.

Segment 35

"Hi Adam, live with your wife *al-jannah*, in paradise, *wa kula minha ragha-dan haithu shi'tuma.* You can eat together, do whatever you wish. You are free to choose what you want. Only one thing is not allowed. *Wa la taqraba had-hihi al-shajarah.* Do not approach this tree. If you keep trying to approach it, to climb it to pick its leaves and take its fruit, *fa takuna min al-dzalimin,* you will be considered among the wrongdoers."

"Hai Adam, geura cicing manéh jeung pamajikan manéh, *al-jannah*, di surga, *wa kula minha raghadan haithu shi'tuma.* Manéh duaan rék dahar rék naon gé pék. Bébas pék kumaha kahayang manéh. Nu teu meunang mah ngan hiji. *Wa la taqraba hadhihi al-shajarah.* Manéh tong coba-coba ngadeukeu-tan tangkal ieu. Lamun coba-coba ngadeukeutan naék metik daunna ngala buahna, *fa takuna min al-dzalimin,* maka manéh kaasup jelema dzalim."

Segment 36

The Prophet Adam went right on enjoying his life together with Eve. That's the meaning of *uskun anta.* *Uskun* means living a peaceful life, we can also call it *sakinah.* While the prophet Adam was enjoying paradise, along comes Satan. If we tell this as a story it could go like this:

Nabi Adam ngeunah wé jeung Siti Hawa duaan. Ngaranna gé *uskun anta, uskun* mah cicingna gé cicing tengteram, ngarana gé sakinah. Genah di surga, ari torojol téh Iblis. Mun didongéngkeun mah meureun kieu:

Segment 37

"Hi, what's your name?" "Adam." "And you?" "Eve." "I'm Satan." [audience: laughter] *"You are new residents here, aren't you?" "Yes." "I'm your senior,"* Satan said. "What are you doing here, Dam?" *"I am free* to do whatever I want. One thing is not allowed; approaching that tree."

In this mimicry of the register typically used for informal introductions, Al-Jauhari switches to Indonesian.

"Kenalan siapa namanya?" "Adam." "Kamu?" "Hawa." "Iblis." [audience: laughter] *"Penduduk baru ya?" "Iya." "Senior,"* ceuk Iblis téh. "Naon waé ceunah di dieu, Dam?" *"Bebas saya* mah cenah rék naon-naon. Nu teu meunang mah éta wé ngadeukeutan tangkal éta."

Motions with his hands as if he were Iblis introducing himself to Adam and Eve. Points to "the tree."

Segment 38

"Aaah! That's a test from Allah. That tree is the *shajarat al-khuldi*, the tree of eternity. If you eat its fruit, you'll live here forever. If not, you will be ousted from here at any time." The Prophet Adam said, *"No way!* If Allah says I am not allowed, I am not allowed."

"Eisss! Éta mah tés ti Allah. Éta tangkal téh ngaranna *shajarat al-khuldi*, tangkal kaabadian. Mun manéh ngadahar buahna, manéh abadi di surga. Mun can ngadahar buahna, isuk-pagéto gé manéh diusir ti surga." Ceuk nabi Adam, *"No way!* Aing mah, ceuk Allah teu meunang, teu meunang."

Segment 39

History proves that the Prophet Adam was not persuaded. But Satan did not keep still. When Adam was not persuaded, he persisted in tempting Eve. After a while, Eve was the first to be tempted. Because of that, the descendants of Eve, like those wearing the head-covering here [audience: laughter] are easy to tempt.

As is the case with much of the narrative material presented in this excerpt, these details about Adam and Eve far exceed the sparse information found in the Qur'an.

Teu kagoda Nabi Adam mah na sajarah. Ngan si sétan teu cicing. Adam teu kagoda, Hawa dirayu terus. Lila-lila Siti Hawa pangheulana karayu. Matak turunan Siti Hawa mah, tah ieu tah, awéwé nu ditariung [audience: laughter] gampang dirayuna téh.

Points at the female section of the audience.

Segment 40

Are there any young males here who haven't yet got a fiancée? [audience: Yes] They must be very stupid. They can't persuade a girl. [audience: laughter] Eve was persuaded.

Aya pamuda nu can boga kabogoh calon pamajikan, aya? [audience: Aya] Éta téh belegug, teu bisa ngarayu éta téh. [audience: laughter] Siti Hawa karayu.

Rotates to his left, where the men are sitting.

Segment 41

After Eve was tempted, then Satan started to persuade Adam. If I tell it as a story, it could go like this: *"Adam, come here!" "What's up, Honey?" "Do you still love me?" "Of course, I do, Eve. I love no woman but you."* Of course, there weren't any other women then, just one. [audience: laughter]

In this parodic stylization of the romantic dialogue Indonesians hear in television romance, Al-Jauhari speaks in an exaggerated caricature of a women's voice.

Nah siti Hawa géus karayu, ngarayu Nabi Adam. Mun didongéngkeun mah kieu meureun: *"Kang Adam, sini!" "Ada apa, sayang?" "Kang Adam masih cinta nggak sama Hawa?" "Ya cinta dong Hawa. Tidak ada lagi wanita yang kucintai kecuali engkau."* Da euweuh deui awéwé na ogé karék hiji. [audience: laughter]

Segment 42

"If you really love me, *how do I appear to you?*" If the Prophet Adam acted like a youngster of today, he might have sung it [like this]:

"Lamun bener Kang Adam cinta ka Hawa, saperti apakah Hawa di hadapan Akang." Mun cara budak ayeuna mah meureun ngalagu:

Segment 43

You are like a song in my heart
That summons my longing for you, ooh . . .
Like the air I inhale, you are always there, ha . . . ha . . . .

Indonesian pop song: *Dealova* by Once of the group Dewa

Kau seperti nyanyian dalam hatiku
Yang memanggil rinduku padamu, oohhh
Seperti udara yang kuhela, kau selalu ada, ha . . . ha . . . .

Segment 44

That grandma looks confused again. She doesn't know the song! [audience: laughter] That song is Dealova, Grandma, the singer is Once.

Geus ngahuleng deui waé. Teu nyahoeun. [audience: laughter] Éta mah lagu Dealova ibu, nu ngalaguna ogé Once.

Looks in the direction of "the grandma."

Segment 45

Do you know everything, Al-Jauhari? *Hang out, man! So what, that's how it is . . .* ! [audience: laughter]

Al-Jauhari uses *gaul* language here. *Gaul* literally means sociability and is used as an inclusive term for the linguistic forms and cultural trends preferred by Indonesian youth. *So what gitu loh!* is the title of a popular hip-hip song of 2005 by Saykoji.

"Na Pa Al-Jauhari mani sagala apal?" *Gaul, man! So what gitu loh . . .* ! [audience: laughter]

Holds hands out in expression of indifference.

Segment 46

"If you really love me, prove your love for me?" "How can I show my love to you? Do you want my life? Or can I give you the life of a duck?" [audience: laughter] "No. I only want that fruit," said Eve. "I want you to pick that fruit for me."

"Lamun bener Kang Adam cinta ka Hawa buktikeun rasa cinta akang ka Hawa." "Kudu ku naon Akang ngabuktikeunana Hawa? Hayang nyawa? Dibikeun ku Akang nyawa éntog." [audience: laughter] "Ah embung, pokona mah Hawa mah hayang buah éta," ceuk Hawa. "Hayang gé dipangmetikeun buah éta."

Segment 47

"Don't ask me to pick that fruit. You know Allah has forbidden it. Ask for something else." "No . . . I only want that. If you don't pick it for me, I will commit suicide. I will kill myself with a lost knife." [audience: laughter]

Al-Jauhari uses a common form of Sundanese humor here, which is to state an intention along with a condition that makes its achievement impossible.

"Ulah, ménta éta. Pan ku Allah teu meunang. Ménta nu séjén." "Ah Embung Hawa mah hayang éta. Lamun teu dipangalakan ku akang Hawa rék bunuh diri. Rék mencit manéh ku bedog nu leungit." [audience: laughter]

Segment 48

Of course, she won't die, will she? The thing is, if we tell it as a story, it's got to be like that, however it might unfold. Finally, the Prophet Adam gave up. Strange. Adam could not be tempted by Satan, but was tempted by Eve, once she had been tempted by Satan. Because of that . . . the sons of Adam, all you men here . . . Your weakness is women.

Moal paéh-paéh meureun nya? Pokona mah kitu lamun didongéngkeun mah meureun, kumaha prosésna. Akhirna nabi Adam léah. Anéh. Ari ku iblis bungkeuleukan teu kagoda. Ari ku Siti Hawa anu geus kagoda ku iblis kagoda. Matak turunan Adam mah . . . tah ieu lalaki tah turunan Adam . . . kalemahanana ku awéwé.

Rotates to face the male section.

Segment 49

Come on, confess your weakness is women! Ask a soldier. Even though they might be colonels, their wives act like they are brigadier-generals. Women are like that. When Mike Tyson punches his opponent, in three rounds, wham! Knockout. Wham! The third round, knockout. But with his wife, he comes after fifteen minutes! [audience: laughter]

Sok lah, ngaraku kabéh ogé ku awéwé mah. Tanyakeun ka TNI. Pangkatna kolonel, pamajikana mah brigjen. Kitu, awéwé mah. Mike Tyson neunggeulan jelema, jebrod tilu ronde. Ngajungkel! Jebrod, tilu ronda, ngajungkel! Ku pamajikanna mah 15 menit géh ngacay! [audience: laughter]

Facing the male segment of the audience, he makes punching motions with hands, then he turns to face the female side to deliver the punchline.

Segment 50

The Prophet Adam gave up. Up the tree he goes. He didn't pick two, just one, and broke it in half. A half for Adam, a half for Eve. They eat it, and before it even reached their stomachs, Allah was angry.

Léah nabi Adam. Térékél téh kana tangkal. Teu ngala dua, hiji buahna gé, dibeulah dua. Adam sabeulah, Hawa sabeulah. Dituang, can tepi kana patuangan, Allah bendu.

Points to his stomach.

Segment 51

But Satan caused them to deflect therefrom and expelled them from the [happy state] in which they were.

Qur'an 2:36

Fa azallahuma al-shaitanu 'anha fa akhrajahuma mimma kana fihi.

Segment 52

The Prophet Adam and Eve were expelled, thrown out of paradise. Cast into the world and separated. Where was Adam? And where was Hawa? Adam looked for Eve, and Eve looked for Adam. They were used to being together, so they were sad. The young people of today might put it like this:

Nabi Adam jeung Siti Hawa diusir, dialungkeun ti surga. Dipiceun ka alam dunya mangkaning dipisahkeun. Adam di mana Hawa di mana. Adam néangan Hawa, Hawa néangan Adam. Mangkaning babarengan biasa meureun, sedih. Mun cara budak ayeuna mah meureun:

Segment 53

Only when you were gone did I feel
the true value of your presence.
It feels truly hard to lose you.
It feels truly hard to live without you.

Performance of Indonesian *dangdut* song: *Kehilangan* by Rhoma Irama

Kalau sudah tiada, baru terasa
bahwa kehadirannya sungguh berharga.
Sungguh berat aku rasa kehilangan dia.
Sungguh berat aku rasa, hidup tanpa dia.

Segment 54

The Prophet Adam searched over there, but he could not find her. He searched over here, but didn't find her. And so did Eve, they searched for each other, but didn't find each other. Finally, Adam prostrated himself, and prayed for repentance.

Nabi Adam geus nguriling ka ditu teu kapanggih, kuriling ka dieu teu kapendak. Siti Hawa néangan, patéangan-téangan teu kapanggih waé. Rumpuyuk wé Nabi Adam téh sujud, bari ngado'a bari tobat.

Points in various directions.

Segment 55

I am sure you know the Prophet Adam's prayer for repentance, don't you? *Our Lord! We have wronged our* ◀ [audience: *selves*]. *If Thou do not forgive* ◀

[audience: *us*] *and have no mercy on* ◀ [audience: *us*] *surely* ◀ [audience: *we*] *are of the* ◀ [audience: *lost*].

Al-Jauhari recites a supplication from the Qur'an (7:23) with which his audience is familiar. The prompting and answering pattern follows the patterns of the text of the supplication.

Pan apal tobatna Nabi Adam, kumaha do'ana? *Rabbana dzalamna anfu*——◀ [audience: *sana*] *wa in lam taghfir* ◀ [audience: *lana*] *wa tar*——◀ [audience: *hamna*] *lanaku*——◀ [audience: *nanna*] *min al-kha*——◀ [audience: *sirin*].

Segment 56

Sumedang people know this, don't you? You have studied Islam, haven't you? And also, this is the prayer that your grandfather used to sing in the early hours.

Apal kabéh urang Sumedang mah atuh? Nyalalantri atuh? Jaba ieu mah sok dilagukeun ku aki-aki geuning ari janari.

Segment 57

"*Our Lord, Our Lord*," in a small prayer-room. "*We have wronged ourselves, and if You do not*, cough, cough!" . . . he can't finish it! [audience: laughter]

Al-Jauhari commences repeating the supplication in a stylized parody of the voice of a very old man, who then collapses into a fit of coughing.

"*Rabbana, ya rabbana*," di tajug. "*Dzalamna anfusana, wa in lam*, eh heu!" . . . teu tamat! [audience: laughter]

Segment 58

For how long did the Prophet Adam lie prostrate while saying this prayer of repentance? He did it for two hundred years. Try to imagine, audience members, the prophet Adam committed one sin but repented for two hundred years. He was not like us. We commit sins every day, tens of them, but we never repent, and keep on asking Allah for things.

Sabaraha lami Nabi Adam sujud bari tobat ngadoa éta? 200 tahun lamina. Coba, hadirin, Nabi Adam mah nyieun dosa sakali, 200 tahun tah tobatna. Béda jeung urang, nyieun dosa unggal poé, puluhan kali, tobat tara, barang pénta wé beuki.

Segment 59

The Lord might say: "*EGP, why should I care?*" [audience: laughter]

Gaul language.

Ceuk Pangéran: "*EGP, emang gue pikirin?*" [audience: laughter]

Segment 60

After Allah had accepted Adam's repentance, he reunited him with Eve. Then their children sprang out, one after the other. New human beings. And it's come to this, all you Sumedang people staring at me now.

Saatos nabi Adam ditampi tobatna ku Allah, ditepangkeun deui sareng Siti Hawa. Perejel waé geuning jul-jel anak. Jelema téa. Nepi wé marolotot urang Sumedang ka uing ayeuna.

Segment 61

Praise be to Allah! So, we share the same ancestors, Adam and Eve. We are siblings, audience members. My grandma and your grandmas are both grandmas. [audience: laughter] *So, there are no longer any reasons for us to consider our differences to be a problem.*

The final sentence is in Indonesian.

Al-hamdu li-'llah. Jadi Urang téh sa-Adam jeung sa-Hawa, urang téh dulur, hadirin. Pan Nini akang jeung nini abdi téh nini-nini éta téh. [audience: laughter] *Jadi sudah tidak ada lagi alasan kita untuk saling membedakan sesuatu.*

Appendix B

Sunday Study Sermon
by Shiddiq Amien

The following is a transcript and translation of an excerpt from an oration delivered by Shiddiq Amien at the PERSIS Sunday Study of May 3, 2009. The source is a DVD produced and circulated by PERSIS (Amien 2009).[1] The excerpt below commences at the sixty-third minute of the seventy-eight-minute oration. It provides the basis for the analytical discussion in chapter 3, which, together with chapter 2, enables a comparison of two conceptions of preaching appropriateness accepted by Bandung audiences. Generic variation/intertextuality provided the starting point for this comparison, thus, the text segments below include comment and translation of Amien's use of diverse speech genres, voices, languages, registers, speech-act types, discursive structures, and performance genres.

Amien's body movement onstage was subdued in comparison with Al-Jauhari's, and his gestural repertoire far less expressive. His style was unhurried, and his delivery measured. He never moved from his position behind the lectern. For most of the oration, his head moved between two orientations: one toward the notes on the lectern and the other toward the audience. His bearing was solemn to the point of melancholy, although during regular moments of animation he would gesture emphatically with his right hand. Because of his lack of body movement and limited gestures, information about his use of body movement is not included in each segment as it was for Al-Jauhari's sermon in appendix A.

Indonesian was the dominant language used in this oratory. In the English translation and in the Indonesian text, languages other than Indonesian (namely, Arabic and Sundanese) have been italicized. Amien frequently translated his Arabic into Indonesian immediately after he had spoken the Arabic word or phrase. When he has done this, we have preserved his Arabic usage in the English translation. At times, Amien did not translate the Arabic word *Qala* (meaning "he said"), a frame marker of hadith discourse, into Indonesian. Because it is such a recognizable sign of hadith entextualization, I have retained its Arabic form in the translation.

During this sermon, Amien made frequent reference to written notes he held on the lectern. Because of his close concentration on the notes as he spoke the hadith, he appeared to be using them for guidance in reading the Arabic text of the hadith. The majority of his sermon, however, appeared to be created as he delivered it. At times, he used rising intonation (indicated in the transcript by the symbol ◀) to elicit affirmation from his audience.

Segment 1

[**English translation with backchannel cues:**] Some things are forbidden to women during their menstruation. Sexual intercourse is the first. The second is circumambulation around the House of Allah.

[**Comments on variation in speech:**] [no comment for this segment]

[**Indonesian text with backchannel cues:**] Ada hal-hal yang terlarang bagi wanita yang sedang haid. Yang pertama tadi adalah *jima'*, yang kedua *tawaf* di *baitu 'llah*.

Segment 2

This is based on hadith number 10, *'an 'aishah taqulu* Siti Aisyah said, *kharajna* we went out, *la nara illa al-hajj* with no intention other than to do pilgrimage. Siti Aisyah left Medina in the direction of . . . to perform her pilgrimage. *Fa lamma kunna bi sarif hidtu* when we arrived at Sarif, this is the name of a place, *"Hidtu"* said Siti Aisyah, "I was menstruating. *Fa dakhala 'alayya rasulu 'llah* and the Messenger of Allah came, into my tent, *wa ana abki* and I was crying."

Much of Amien's oratory consists of his simultaneous carrying out of a number of processes: verbalization in Arabic of hadith and Al-Qur'an (never in melodic or rhythmic style); translation of these materials into Indonesian within elaborated replays of the source text; interpretation of and reflection on the textual sources. "Number 10" refers to the number on the sheet distributed among the audience.

Ini berdasar hadis nomor 10, *'an 'aishah taqulu* Siti Aisyah berkata, *kharajna* kami keluar *la nara illa al-hajj* tidak ada tujuan kecuali mau menunaikan ibadah haji. Siti Aisyah keluar dari Medina menuju ke . . . untuk ibadah haji. *Fa lamma kunna bi sarif hidtu* ketika kami tiba di daerah Sarif, nama tempat, *"Hidtu"* kata Siti Aisyah, "Saya haid. *Fa dakhala 'alayya rasulu 'llah* Rasulullah datang, masuk ke kemahku, *wa ana abki* dan saya sedang menangis."

Segment 3

Qala nabi the Prophet asked, *"Ma laki* why are you crying? *'Anafasti* Are you giving birth?"* But he meant menstruation here, not giving birth. *Qultu* Siti Aisyah said, *"Na'am* [yes]." *Qala,* then the Prophet explained, "You should not cry because of menstruation, *inna hadha* for indeed this, this menstruation, *amrun,* is something, *katabahu 'llahu* that Allah has decreed, *'ala banati adam* for all women" [literally, for the daughters of Adam].

Qala al-nabi bertanya, *"Ma laki* mengapa engkau menangis? *A nafasti* apakah engkau *nifas?"* Maksud *nifas* di sini haid, bukan melahirkan. *Qultu* kata Siti

Aisyah, *"Na'am."* *Qala* lalu nabi menjelaskan, "Gak usah ditangisi kalau haid itu, *inna hadha* sesungguhnya ini, haid ini, *amrun,* suatu perkara, *katabahu 'llahu* yang telah Allah tetapkan, *'ala banati adam* kepada setiap wanita."

Segment 4

"Fa aqdi [go ahead and do the pilgrimage]!" Perhaps Aisyah was crying because she had come so far from Madinah to perform pilgrimage, but when near to Mecca, she began menstruating. Siti Aisyah imagined, "That means I cannot do my pilgrimage," probably.

"Fa aqdi!" Tadi mungkin Siti Aisyah itu nangis jauh-jauh dari Madinah datang ke Mekah mau haji, sudah dekat ke Mekah malah haid. Bayangan Siti Aisyah, "Berarti saya tidak bisa haji," gitu.

Segment 5

So the Prophet made it clear, *"Fa aqdi,* carry it out! *Ma* whatever, *ya'malu ul-hajju* the pilgrims do, *ghaira* except, *'ala tatufa bi al-bait* you may not walk around the House of Allah." This means that all the procedures and journeys of the pilgrimage may be performed by a menstruating woman except for *tawaf.* When will she perform *tawaf?* Later, when she is ◄... [audience: ritually pure] . . . ritually pure. [That is the] second [forbidden thing].

Like Al-Jauhari, Amien frequently asks questions on behalf of his audience as a device for structuring his ongoing discourse.

Maka Nabi menjelaskan, *"Fa aqdi* kerjakan olehmu! *Ma* apa-apa, *ya'malu ul-hajju* yang dikerjakan oleh jamaah haji, *ghaira* selain, *'ala tatufa bi al-bait* kamu tidak boleh tawaf di *baitu 'llah."* Artinya semua perjalanan manasik haji boleh dilakukan oleh wanita yang sedang haid kecuali *tawaf.* Kapan tawafnya? Nanti ketika dia sudah ◄... [audience: bersih] . . . bersih. Dua.

Segment 6

The third and fourth things forbidden to menstruating women are *ritual prayer* and *fasting.*

Yang ketiga dan keempat, yang dilarang bagi wanita yang sedang haid adalah *salat* dan *saum.*

Segment 7

'An abi sa'id bin khudri qala [According to Abu Said bin Kudri, the Prophet said], *kharaja rasulu 'llah* the Messenger of Allah left his house, *fi adha au fitrin,* probably forgetting whether it was the festival of Adha or Fitri, but it was certainly a feast day, *ila al-musalla* and went to the *musalla.* We often translate this among ourselves as "went to the mosque," but in fact *musalla,* in this context, is the name of a field in the eastern part of Medinah.

'An abi sa'id bin khudri qala, kharaja rasulu 'llah Rasulullah keluar dari rumah, *fi adha au fitrin,* rupanya lupa ini, apa Idul Adha atau Idul Fitri, yang jelas hari raya, *ila al-musalla* ke musalla. Ini suka sering diartikan di kita itu "ke mesjid," padahal musalla itu, di sini, nama sebuah lapang di Madinah sebelah timur.

Segment 8

Fa marra 'ala al-nisa', the Prophet then went toward the place where the women were. Ladies, at that time it was probable that, because there were no sound systems, or because he had special advice for women, after giving his sermon to the men, the Prophet descended from the rostrum then went to the back rows to give a special sermon for the women.

Fa marra 'ala al-nisa', Nabi kemudian pergi menuju ke tempat ibu-ibu. Mungkin Bu, waktu itu, karena tidak ada speaker atau karena ada nasihat khusus buat ibu-ibu, jadi Rasulullah setelah khutbah di hadapan bapak-bapak turun dari mimbar lalu ke belakang mengkhutbahi khusus ibu-ibu.

Segment 9

The content of that sermon, "*Ya ma'shar al-nisa'* Oh women! *Tasaddaqna* increase your alms, *fa inni* for verily, *uritukunna* it was revealed to me that you all, *akthar ahl al-nar* will be the majority of those in hell." *The Messenger of Allah said, "Women! Increase your alms,* for I have seen into hell, and most of its inhabitants are women."

Isi khutbahnya itu, "*Ya ma'shar al-nisa'* Wahai kaum wanita! *Tasaddaqna* perbanyaklah sodakoh, *fa inni* sesungguhnya aku, *uritukunna* diperlihatkan kepadaku kalian ini, *akthar ahl al-nar* kebanyakan masuk neraka." *Ceuk Rosulullah téh, "Ibu-ibu sing saleueur sodakoh* sebab aku lihat di neraka, penghuni itu kebanyakan wanita."

Segment 10

In reality, don't be shocked, ladies! For we need to pay attention to the first sentence, *tasaddaqna* [give alms], only that one. If you don't wish to dwell in hell you must increase your alms.

In this and the following segments, Amien creates a conversation with his female audience members in which he reflects with them on the meaning of the hadith under discussion.

Ibu-ibu sebenarnya jangan, jangan terkejut sebab yang harus diperhatikan itu kalimat pertamanya itu, *tasaddaqna-* hanya itu. Kalau ingin, tidak ingin menjadi penghuni neraka harus memperbanyak sodakoh.

Segment 11

At this point, the women were surprised, "*Fa qulna,*" so they asked, "*wa bima ya rasulu 'llah* why is that, Oh Messenger of Allah?" *Qala* the Prophet explained, "Firstly *tukthirna al-la'na* you often speak ill of others, women often speak ill of others. They curse people." Perhaps because their thoughts, not feelings, come first. *They feel a bit of resentment, so they wish misfortune upon someone else.*

Ibu-ibu waktu itu kaget, "*Fa qulna,*" kemudian mereka bertanya, "*wa bima ya rasulu 'llah* kenapa Rasulallah?*" qala* Nabi menjelaskan, "Pertama *tukthirna al-la'nah* kalian ini banyak melaknat. Wanita itu mudah melaknat, mengutuk orang." Mungkin karena yang mengedepan sering bukan pikiran tapi perasaan, *aya kakeuheul saeutik ngadoakeun goréng wéh ka batur téh.*

Segment 12

"I pray that your life be full of misfortune! That a cockroach will crush you! That your wajit will stick to its wrapper!" [audience: smiles and mild laughter]

Amien here verbalizes—in the "voices" of his female audience—Sundanese formulas for expressing ill will toward others. The cockroach is regarded as being especially disgusting to females. The sticking of the sweet *wajit* to its wrapper is used as a metaphor for poor outcomes generally. Amien does not imitate female voices here but utters these lines in his regular speaking voice. Even though this sermon was delivered in Indonesian, this excerpt is rich in Sundanese idiom.

"Pék siah didoakeun sing tong jamuga, sing ditubruk cucunguk, sing rapet kana wajit!" [audience: smiles and mild laughter]

Segment 13

"Secondly, *wa takfurna al-'ashir,* they frequently *disobey* their husbands." *Disobedience* to husbands, not to Allah. This has been explained in another hadith, ladies, where the Prophet explains what he means by *disobedience, wa lau ahsanta ila ihdahunna al-dahra kulla* if a husband behaves well toward his wife for a whole year, *thumma ra'at minka shai'an qatt* and then she sees the smallest mistake from him, [she acts as if] all the goodness of the husband is then erased.

"Yang kedua *wa takfurna al-'ashir*, mereka itu sering kufur kepada suami." Kufur kepada suami, bukan kufur kepada Allah. Jadi sudah dijelaskan dalam hadis lain, Bu, yang disebut kufur kepada suami itu oleh Nabi dijelaskan bahwa, *wa lau ahsanta ila ihdahunna al-dahra kulla* kalau suami itu berbuat kebaikan setahun penuh kepada istrinya, *thumma ra'at minka shai'an qatt* kemudian terlihat ada kesalahan sedikit saja dari suami, kebaikan suami yang banyak itu kemudian dihapus.

Segment 14

A year of drought . . . how do we say it? Is soaked by a day of rain. After all, there are wives who say to their husbands, *"All you do is cause me pain!"* [audience: laughter] *"What do you mean I cause you pain?" "You never make me happy."* Her husband says, *"If you want to be happy [senang], fart in the steamer.* [audience: laughter] *The sound will be 'senang'." That's what he says.*

The audience members' laughter after the word "pain" is partly brought on by "the wife's" use of the coarse second pronoun *sia* (you) to address her husband. There is a hint of parody here: Amien uses an exaggerated ascending tone in the pronunciation of the last syllable of *disenangkeun* (makes someone happy). This is the only hint of stylized parody in the excerpt. The *sééng* is the bronze water receptacle for steaming rice, which is resonant because of its shape and depth. It is a common joke that breaking wind in the *sééng* will produce the sound "se-nang," close to the Indonesian and Sundanese word *senang*, meaning to be happy.

Halodo sataun . . . naon cenah? Lantis ku hujan sapoé. Suka ada istri kan yang ngomong sama suaminya, *"Aing téh ngan dinyenyeri wé ku sia téh?"* [audience: laughter] *"Piraku dinyenyeri waé?" "Can ngajaran disenangkeun aing téh."* Ceuk *salakina téh, "Hayang senang mah hitut wé dina sééng.* [audience: laughter] *Disada geura 'senang'," cenah kitu.*

Segment 15

In fact the husband has done many good things for his wife, but it is as if all of that would be erased. That is a danger, ladies, and can cause you to be *plunged* into hell.

Amien and some of his audience members share smiles here, indicating the warning is not intended to be interpreted literally.

Padahal suaminya sudah banyak berbuat kebaikan tapi seakan dihapus semua. Nah itu bahaya Bu, bisa mengakibatkan Ibu *tikecemplung kana* neraka.

Segment 16

Then, "*Ma ra'itu* I have never seen, *min naqisat 'aqlin* a person with little knowledge, *wa dinin* and only little religion, *adhaba li lubb al-rajul al-hazim* who could defeat or conquer the heart of a man of strength, of strong faith, *min ihdakunna* except from among you." The Messenger of Allah said, "I find this strange. Women are less rational," the Prophet said, "they are less religious, but they can conquer the heart of a man strong in faith." Many men encounter misfortune because of a woman's *flirtatious* tempting. [audience: laughter] Now there are even cases of murder that involve women.

Kemudian, "*Ma ra'itu* aku tidak melihat, *min naqisat 'aql* dari orang yang kurang akal, *wa din* dan kurang agama, *adhaba li lubb al-rajul al-hazim* bisa meluluhkan, mengalahkan hati seorang lelaki yang kuat, kuat iman, *min ihdakunna* selain salah seorang di antara kalian." Kata Rasulullah, "Aku ini aneh. Wanita itu," kata Nabi, 'akalnya kurang, agamanya kurang, tapi bisa mengalahkan lelaki yang kuat iman." Banyak lelaki yang celaka, karena rayuan *gombal* [audience: laughter] dari seorang wanita. Sekarang juga ada kasus pembunuhan yang melibatkan wanita juga.

Segment 17

Qulna, the ladies asked in surprise, "We are called irrational? Does irrationality mean idiocy?" So they asked, "*Wa ma nuqsan dinina wa aqlina ya rasulu 'llah* what are our deficiencies in religion and rationality, Oh Messenger of Allah?"

Amien's affective embellishment of the hadith narrative through direct reported speech is noticeable here.

Qulna, nah ibu-ibu itu bertanya, kaget, "Disebut kurang akal. Apa kurang akal itu gila?" Maka mereka menanyakan, "*Wa ma nuqsan dinina wa aqlina ya rasulu 'llah* apa kurangnya agama dan akal kami wahai Rasulullah?"

Segment 18

Qala, the Prophet explained, "*Alaisa shahadat al-mar'ah* is not the testimony of a woman, *mithla nisf* equal to half, *shahadat al-rajul* the testimony of a man? The testimony of two men is sufficient, but four women are required." "Now *this*," *qulna* the women said, "*Bala* is true."

Qala nabi menjelaskan, "*Alaisa shahadat al-mar'ah* bukankah kesaksian wanita, *mithla nisf* seperti setengah, *shahadat al-rajul* kesaksian lelaki? Kalau laki-laki saksinya cukup dua, tapi kalau perempuan harus empat." "Nah *ieu*," *qulna* kata ibu-ibu, "*Bala* benar."

Segment 19

Qala "*Fa dhalik min nuqsan aqliha*. That is what is meant by irrational." It does not mean that irrational is ignorance. No. But it is a decree of Allah that the testimony of a woman is worth half the value of a man.

Qala "*Fa dhalik min nuqsan aqliha*. Itulah yang dimaksud dengan kurang akal." Bukan kurang akal itu bodoh. Bukan. Tapi ketetapan Allah, wanita itu kesaksiannya dinilai setengah kesaksian laki-laki.

Segment 20

"And what is the deficiency of our religion?" The Prophet answered, "*Alaisa idha hadat* is it not the case that when a woman menstruates, *lam tusalli wa lam tasum* she may not perform ritual prayer, she does not perform it, and does not fast?" *Qulna* the women said, "*Bala* that is true." *Qala* "*Fa dhalik min nuqsan diniha.* That is what is meant by lacking in religion."

"Lalu apa kekurangan agama kami?" Nabi menjawab, "*Alaisa idha hadat* bukankah apabila wanita haid, *lam tusalli wa lam tasum* tidak boleh salat, tidak salat, dan tidak saum?" *Qulna* kata ibu-ibu, "*Bala* benar." *Qala* "*Fa dhalik min nuqsan diniha* itulah yang dimaksud dengan kurang agama."

Segment 21

For a week *they do not perform ritual prayer at all.* So, balance it by increasing alms! From the sentence, *lam tusalli wa lam tasum,* number three and number four, the prohibitions on ritual prayer and fasting, it is only fasting that has to be *compensated,* whereas the ritual prayer does not.

Seminggu *teu salat pan.* Nah imbangi dengan memperbanyak sodakoh. Dari kalimat, *lam tusalli wa lam tasum* nomer tiga dan nomer empat, tidak boleh salat tidak boleh saum, hanya saum harus diganti dalam bentuk *qadla,* sementara salat tidak.

Segment 22

And finally, the fourth thing that is forbidden for a menstruating woman, apart from the special discussion to follow about "stockpiling," if Allah wills it, that will follow in this morning's discussion, relates to the touching and reading of al-Qur'an by a menstruating woman. So the textual proofs are clear: first *sexual relations,* second *ritual prayer,* third *fasting,* and fourth *circumambulation,* and the fifth is being present in a mosque.

Yang terakhir yang keempat yang terlarang bagi wanita yang sedang haid, selain nanti ada pembahasan khusus mengenai "tabungan" insya'allah dari pembahasan pagi ini, terkait dengan menyentuh dan membaca al-Qur'an bagi wanita yang sedang haid. Jadi sudah jelas dalilnya, pertama *jima',* kedua *salat,* ketiga *saum,* keempat *tawaf,* dan kelima tinggal di dalam mesjid.

Segment 23

Based on the verses in the chapter of Al-Nisa, verse 43, *ya ayyuha alladhina amanu* Oh people of faith! *La taqrabu al-salat* you may not approach the place of ritual prayer, *wa antum sukara* while in a state of drunkedness, *hatta ta'lam ma taqulun* until you, *ta'lam* are aware of what you are saying. For if a person is drunk, he doesn't know his own words and deeds, does he?

Berdasar ayat al-Quran surat Al-Nisa ayat 43, *ya ayyuha alladhina amanu* wahai orang-orang yang beriman, *la taqrabu al-salat* kalian tidak boleh mendekati salat, *wa antum sukara* sedangkan kalian dalam keadaan mabok, *hatta ta'lam ma taqulun* sehingga kamu, *ta'lam* sadar atas apa yang kamu omongkan. Sebab kalau orang yang mabok, kan dia tidak sadar punya omongan dan perbuatannya sendiri?

Segment 24

The next sentence is the expression, *wa la junuban* [nor ritually impure]. The intention of this is *wa la taqraba al-salat wa antum junuban*, you are not allowed to be close to the ritual prayer when you are in the state of *junub* [ritually impure]. We translate *junub* here as causes of ◄[audience: impurity] . . . impurity. Including menstruation.

Nah ke sananya itu ada kalimat, *wa la junuban*. Ini maksudnya, *wa la taqrabu al-salat wa antum junuban* tidak boleh mendekati salat ketika kamu sedang *junub*. *Junub* itu di kita diartikan berhadats ◄[audience: besar] . . . besar. Termasuk di dalamnya haid.

Segment 25

You may not be close to the *salat* when you are ritually impure, *illa* except for *'abiri sabil*. *'Abiri sabil* means a passerby, *hatta taghtasilu* until you have bathed, until you have bathed. Someone may ask, "We are not allowed to go close to prayer except in passing? *What is this about?* We are not allowed to perform our ritual prayer except in passing?" *Salat* here means mosque, *salat* in the second meaning.

The question "What is this about?" was spoken in Sundanese. (He is discussing a syntactically ambiguous phrase in Al-Qur'an 4:43.)

Tidak boleh mendekati salat ketika junub, *illa* kecuali, *'abiri sabil.* *'Abiri sabil* itu lewat, *hatta taghtasilu* sampai kamu mandi, sampai kamu mandi. Ada yang nanya, "Tidak boleh mendekati salat kecuali hanya lewat? *Kumaha ieu téh?* Tidak boleh *ngadegkeun* salat kecuali lewat?" Nah, salat di sini maksudnya masjid, salat yang kedua itu.

Segment 26

In Indonesian language, this could be called a compound sentence with two predicates. So, the first is *wa la taqraba al-salat wa antum sukara*, and *wa la junuban* also has the same understanding as *wa la taqraba al-salat*, you are not allowed to be close to the venue of *salat*. In *Arabic semantics*, this is called *majaz mursal* [figurative meaning].

Jadi kalau dalam bahasa Indonesia mungkin ini kalimat majemuk rapatan sama predikat. Jadi, *wa la taqrabu salat wa antum sukara* satu, *wa la junuban* itu juga mengandung pengertian *wa la taqrabu al-salat* kamu tidak boleh mendekati tempat salat. Di dalam *ilmu balaghah* disebutnya kalimat *majaz mursal.*

Segment 27

How do [the two] differ? *Salat* is used when what is intended is the venue of *salat* which is the mosque. You are not allowed to be close to the venue of *salat*, which is the mosque, when you are in a state of *junub*, being ◀ [audience: ritually impure] . . . ritually impure, including having menstruation, *illa 'abiri sabil* except if you are only passing.

Bénten? Disebut salatnya padahal yang dimaksud adalah tempat salat yaitu masjid. Tidak boleh mendekati tempat salat, yaitu masjid, *wa antum junuban* ketika kamu sedang junub, punya hadats ◀ [audience: ritually impure] . . . besar, termasuk haid, *illa 'abiri sabil* kecuali hanya lewat.

Segment 28

For instance, ladies, you are menstruating and enter the mosque to pick up something then exit again. That is allowed, according to this verse. *Illa 'abiri sabil* only in passing by, *hatta taghtasilu* until you have bathed. So, remaining inside the mosque is not allowed. Many other hadith support the prohibition on menstruating women and men in a state of *junub* [ritually impure due to sexual intercourse or semen discharge] from staying inside the mosque, except for passing by.

Misalnya ibu-ibu sedang haid masuk masjid, ngambil sesuatu lalu keluar lagi, boleh menurut ayat ini. *Illa 'abiri sabil* itu hanya lewat, *hatta taghtasilu* sampai mandi. Berarti diam di dalam masjid tidak boleh, dan pasti banyak hadis yang menunjang terhadap larangan wanita yang sedang haid dan laki-laki yang sedang *junub* tinggal di dalam mesjid, kecuali hanya lewat.

Segment 29

A man, for instance, is sleeping in the mosque and has a wet dream, [audience: scattered laughter] and when he wakes he realizes that he is in the mosque and that he has to go out, bathe, come back in, and go back to sleep. [audience: laughter] He can't postpone his bath until morning prayer, for he has already realized [what has happened]. Remember, this verse prohibits it. People in a state of *junub*, including women who are menstruating, are not allowed to stay inside the mosque.

Bapak-bapak misalnya tidur di masjid, mimpi basah di masjid, [audience: scattered laughter] lalu dia sadar bahwa dia sedang tidur di masjid, maka dia harus keluar, mandi, balik lagi, tidur lagi. [audience: laughter] Ya, nanti saja sudah subuh, tidak boleh karena sudah sadar. Ingat menurut ayat ini tidak boleh. Orang yang *junub*, termasuk wanita yang sedang haid, tidak boleh tinggal di dalam mesjid.

Segment 30

So, there are five things prohibited: first *sexual intercourse*, second performing *tawaf*, third *prayer*, fourth *fasting*, and fifth staying inside the mosque. Meanwhile, matters relating to touching and reading the Qur'an require their own discussion.

Jadi ada lima perkara: yaitu *jima'* satu, dua *tawaf*, tiga *salat*, empat *saum*, lima tinggal di dalam mesjid. Sementara menyangkut masalah menyentuh dan membaca al-Quran perlu ada pembahasan tersendiri.

Segment 31

That's all, *brethren in faith*, for our study this morning. I hope this has provided some benefit. Again, I thank you: Forgive me. *That is what I have to say. I beg Allah's pardon for me and you all. I seek your forgiveness, and may the peace and the blessing of Allah be upon you.*

Concluding formula is in Arabic.

Itulah *ikhwatu iman* kajian kita pagi ini, mudah-mudahan bermanfaat adanya. Sekali lagi terima kasih. Mohon maaf. *Aqulu qauli hadha. Wa astaghfiru 'llah 'alayya wa 'alaikum. Wa al-afwa minkum wa al-salamu 'alaikum wa rahmatu 'llah.*

Appendix C

TRANSLATION OF EXCERPT OF SERMON BY A. F. GHAZALI

This text supports the discussion in chapter 6. It is an excerpt from the cassette *Tugas Risalah* (Ghazali n.d. [1990?]) and is part of a larger excerpt published, along with the original Sundanese text, in Ghazali (2008).

When arriving home, the Prophet liked to take a drink. Picture this, ok? Those of you who haven't been to Mecca won't know, and won't be able to feel what this was like. In Mecca, ladies, not to mention at the time of the Prophet, even now in modern times the temperature can reach 57 degrees. In the Prophet's time a glass of drinking water like this would be drunk by seven people. There was no air-conditioning, no refrigerators, no fans. I've been to Mecca in modern times, recently, and it was 100 metres from the hotel to the Sacred Mosque. The fridge in the room had the girth of a buffalo. The air-conditioning fan up above was as big as a bamboo tray. I took some iced water with me, two bottles for the journey to the mosque. Glug, glug! I drank it on the way and then got thirsty again, and after arriving at the mosque we performed our worship, but not many *ruku'*.[1] Two before midday, four for the midday prayer, after midday two, then we rushed back to the hotel because we had such dry throats.

It was even worse in the time of the Prophet. When the Prophet arrived home, he wanted to drink but found his wife performing supplications. Picture this, she is reciting *subhana Allah, subhana Allah* [Praise be to Allah]. That creates difficulties, doesn't it? It's difficult. What's the difficulty, Pak Ghazali? The wife! If I told her to stop her supplications she might turn her head away in anger. But if I let it go, it could go on for too long. For example, if the Prophet said, "Eh! Too much supplicating, bring me some water!" Our wives would answer, "On the one hand you tell me to perform supplications, on the other hand you forbid it!" [audience: laughter]

Our wives would do that for sure. How would the Prophet face a situation like that? He wouldn't give orders or forbid verbally. If he wanted to drink, he would go to the back by himself, taking the water with him. He wouldn't drink the water in the kitchen. My habit is to sprint to the kitchen, glug, glug, drinking straight from the jug so that even my nose if filled up with water, then I walk into the main part of the house while letting off a burp and shouting at my wife! [audience: laughter]

The Prophet was different. He took the water but didn't drink it in the kitchen, taking it to the main part of the house. The house was only four by six metres, so it took only two steps to get there. He had to take it past his wife, who was performing her supplications.

His wife looks away in embarrassment, saying "Oh! Messenger of Allah! You've come home!"

"Yes."

She didn't see him earlier because she was engrossed in her supplications. "You've come home?"

"True."

"Why did you get that water by yourself and not order me to do it? Are you angry?"

My goodness! What beautiful behavior! What a beautiful thing to hear those words from a wife like that! My goodness! If there is such a woman here, if there was a woman who spoke like that to her husband, I'd pay five million for her dowry! [audience: laughter] It's not that I have the money: I can say that because there's no one here like that. [audience: laughter] Like a rare antique.

She said, "Why, oh messenger, did you get the water yourself? Why didn't you order me to do it? Are you angry?"

"No!"

"Why didn't you command me to do it? What now?"

Her husband answers her, "You were reciting your formulas, weren't you? Continue on with your supplication, and leave the water, I can do it myself later."

That's the sincere way, without any grimacing. Not like us. Our reply would have a sting in it: "No problem, darling, you were performing your formulas, keep on with it, and you're an idiot for behaving like that!!" [audience: laughter] It'd be like that, perhaps?

No, this was done sincerely; "You were reciting formulas, so continue!"

What does his wife say? "No, supplicating is simple, it's *sunnat*. Caring for one's husband is *wajib*, so let me do it."[2]

The messenger gives the water to her before taking his next step. If it was me, I wouldn't give it to her, I'd be angry, "Don't stop me now, there's only one more step!!" [audience: laughter]

I'd be like that, wouldn't I? No. The Prophet says, "Please, take it."

He had taken the water by himself because he wished to show the greatness of Islamic teaching through his actions. He takes the [final] step, and as he sits down his wife hands the water back to him, while asking her husband for forgiveness. "Forgive me, oh messenger of Allah, forgive me, oh noble one! I wasn't thinking straight and didn't see you come in. Forgive me, forgive me."

"It's nothing," says the Prophet.

Now, that is called *syahidan* [giving witness]. What happens the next day? Without being ordered, on the next day the water is ready before the Prophet has arrived home. When did he give an order? She wasn't ordered, but was given an example the day before. *Syahidan*. Rip! The Prophet's tunic tears, but he doesn't give orders. You would think he would order her to repair his clothes, but no. The Prophet takes it, takes a needle and starts repairing it straight away. The Prophet repairs it!

His wife sees him stitching and says "Oh messenger of Allah, why are you repairing that yourself? Why don't you instruct me to do it? Are you angry?"

"No."

"Well, why don't you?"

"I thought you might be busy. Aren't you busy?"

"No."

"Okay."

What happens the next day? Before he puts it on, she inspects the tunic, "Don't wear it yet, messenger, let's check it first in case it's torn."

When did he give a command? When did he give instruction? Ah, the example of the day before was enough. Giving witness.

Gentlemen, is that how you behave to your wives, or never? Not really? Ladies? Never? [Audience shouts: never!] Never, because you ladies are not like the Prophet's wife, so you're just the same! [audience: laughter] The Prophet and his wife were a perfect couple, like a lid that fits its pot perfectly. We're not like that, but more like a lid clanging noisily onto its pot!

I once discussed this at my own mosque, with the congregation in Jatayu. There were women there crying with envy. The males didn't cry, they just said emh, emh, emh out of surprise, amazed at our noble Prophet.

In fact, there was one old man who spoke to me, saying, "Pak Ghazali, that's right, I understand. I won't do that to my wife. I will just give an example. I won't make speeches. When I do that my wife's eyebrows raise up in anger. Her eyes bulge like they are about to jump out!"

I said, "That's right, *mang* [Uncle], it's better to give an example. If you give a lecture it ends up in fighting." That's what I said.

Perhaps he did give an example, waking up at three o'clock, early in the morning, waking up before his wife did, going out to the back to the kitchen, hauling water out of the well to fill the water reserve, but while doing so, bang! Bang! He crashes the bucket into the sides of the well to wake his wife up, clanging it back and forth. When the reserve is full he lights the stove, puts a pot on it to heat up water, and when the water boils he adds some coffee, but doesn't drink it, placing it instead on the table [so it can be seen] and covering it with a lid. He goes back to the bathroom and washes the mud from the market off the sandals, then puts them down to dry, then he washes his socks, hangs them out and straightens the chairs that are all over the place because they'd been watching TV yesterday from midday into the night. He then sweeps and mops the floor to give an example to his wife, wanting to follow the Prophet's example while waiting for the time for morning worship. When the time comes he shouts out the call to prayer, but does it slowly. He then performs his worship before the morning prayer, after which he does his morning worship, and after that recites supplications. He then straightens up the mattress, and puts the tangled sheets in order using the brush, then makes sure they are in line with the pillows, then folds the sheets tidily and places them at the end of the bed. Only then does he sit down in a chair and says "In the name of Allah!" loudly so that his wife can hear it, then opens the lid covering his glass while saying "In the name of Allah" again, [very loudly] *"IN THE NAME OF ALLAH THE MERCIFUL AND COMPASSIONATE!"* He may as well have said, "Look at me, I'm giving you a good example!" [audience: laughs] He doesn't do that. He drinks his coffee in his chair, glug, glug, glug while reading verses in praise of the Prophet.

Is his wife present? She is. What does she do? Eh, her eyes are wide open like an ant that's just given birth. She blinks in groggy surprise. She gives no reaction at all, but says to their child, "Praise be to Allah! Son, since your father has been going to Pak Ghazali's sermons, he's now learnt his proper place!" [audience: laughter]

Oh Allah! Oh Lord! A husband does the washing and ends up being told he knows his place! Oh my goodness! Without doubt, ladies, it's hard to give an example to a person with weak faith and little knowledge of their religion. It's hard. Because the example will only make its mark if you are giving an example to a person with strong faith and knowledge. They will gobble it up. But if you give an example to someone with weak faith and no knowledge, then everyone does their own thing, because scraps of ore only stick to the metal of a magnet. Its metal is magnetic, so when it goes down to the ore, the scraps stick to it. But an aluminum spoon! You could leave it in scraps for seven years, because it just won't stick. And it is hard to set an example to a person with no faith or knowledge of their religion. That's exactly the same as performing or dancing in front of a blind person. You can perform 700 dance moves in front of a blind person but you'll be doing it all for yourself.

Notes

Introduction

1. The analytical reduction of preaching performances to their points of political relevance is common in studies of Indonesian politics. Examples are Herb Feith's glossing of a sermon by M. Isa Anshary (Feith 1962, 283), Takashi Shiraishi's analysis of a 1920 address by Haji Misbach (Shiraishi 1990, 189), and a recent study of orations by Hadhrami preachers by Woodward et al. (2012).

2. Similar theorizations based on Indonesian realities have been made by Ward Keeler (1998) and Ahmad Baso (2002).

3. In a series of widely cited articles, Dale Eickelman (1992, 1998) has made claims for the transformative effects of media expansion and mass education in a number of Middle East countries.

4. Few preachers have successfully captured the national imagination through contemporary forms in the manner of Aa Gym. Another is the Javanese preacher and performer Emha Ainun Nadjib (b. 1953) (see Daniels 2009, 132–55).

5. The demographic statistics given here are derived from Suryadinata et al. (2003) and Badan Pusat Statistik (2008) as well as the website of the Indonesian Central Body for Statistics (BPS) (http://bps.go.id/).

6. Strictly speaking, the most densely populated province is the urban metropolis of Jakarta, which has provincial status. Jakarta is exceptional in that it consists of a single conurbation and can be distinguished from all other Indonesian provinces on that ground.

7. Other reasons may be cited to explain the broad acceptance of Islamic textual learning in West Java. First, West Javanese Islamic elites held a share of political and economic power during the colonial period. Under the so-called Preanger system (1674–1870), religious functionaries at village level held privileges for collecting duties and administering irrigation (Ensering 1987, 270–73). They developed as an economically self-supporting group able to devolve their landholdings (agricultural lands and religious infrastructure including mosques and educational institutions) by testamentary succession, thereby attaining a durable base in West Javanese society not only as religious mediators but also as economic and political actors. This overlap between West Java's Muslim leadership and its landowning class has informed analysis of important events in twentieth-century the region. Movements of resistance against the colonial government and the early Indonesian republic have been interpreted as religiously inspired uprisings against colonial and nationalist domination and as responses to threats to the economic position of a landowning class in which Islamic leaders were a major presence (Dijk 1981, 371–73; Ensering 1987; Formichi 2012; Jackson 1980; Kahin 1970, 327–28). Second, Christian missionaries made little inroads in West Java, having been forbidden by Indies government regulations from carrying out missionary work until 1865. After that they encountered serious resistance from Sundanese Muslim communities (Coolsma [1895]).

8. The science of preaching is known to Muslims in Indonesia and the Muslim world by the Arabic term *'ilm al-khatabah* (see generally, Gaffney 1994; Halldén 2005; and chap. 4 of this book).

9. According to Islamic ritual prescription, sermons must be delivered on three occasions: the Friday prayer, the festival concluding the fasting month ('Id al-Fitr), and the festival of the sacrifice ('Id al-Adha) (see Wensinck 2016).

10. A notable example of Islamically based opposition to women occupying public roles occurred during the lead-up to the 2004 Indonesian election, from which Megawati Sukarnoputri emerged triumphant as the first female president of Indonesia. Senior clerics of the Nahdlatul Ulama organization published a fatwa stating that it was prohibited for a Muslim nation to choose a woman as leader (Mulia 2005, 273–314).

11. In making this statement, Amrullah was responding to a prior fatwa produced out of a public deliberation involving his own father (see Hadler 2008, 163–68).

12. Talented children have been in demand as preachers ever since a national reality television program entitled *Dai Cilik* (Little preachers) became a hit in the 1990s. In that program, a panel of judges evaluated preaching performances by children as young as four years of age.

13. Key reference works on the Islamic modernist/reformist movement include Hodgson (1974); Moaddel (2005); and Voll (1982). Studies of the most important movements of maritime Southeast Asia include Benda (1958); Nakamura (2012); Noer (1973); and Roff (1967). The definitive study of the Bandung-based movement, PERSIS, is Federspiel (2001).

14. After his arrival in Bandung in 1927, Natsir became A. Hassan's pupil and went on to have an astonishing career as statesman and figurehead for Indonesians aspiring to Islamic political representation. He was a member of Indonesia's first parliament as a representative of the Masyumi Party, and became the republic's first prime minister (on Natsir generally, see Federspiel 2001; Kahin 2012; Luth 1999; Rosidi 1990. For Hassan's life and career, see Federspiel 2001 and Rosidi 1990). Alienated by Sukarno's attempts to construct a broadly inclusive national consensus and disappointed by the President's abandonment of constitutional reform, Natsir was marginalized in the national political scene. His audience in West Java was large, and some of his sermons have been published in Sundanese translation (Hidayat 1996).

15. This brief history of Bandung is based on Voskuil (1996).

16. Hefner (2000, 104–6) has described the support given by the "urban poor and lumpen middle-class" to conservative modernists such as Natsir.

17. The fatwa were published in four anthologies between 1931 and 1934. Since 1968, PERSIS has republished these anthologies in a single volume (Hassan 2000).

18. Accounts of the novel meanings of *dakwah* emerging at this time in Indonesia include those of Hefner (2000) and Gade (2004).

19. Although high profile preachers do not generally respond to critiques of preaching with counterarguments that assert its value, they respond publicly to defamations of their character. The national preaching star Zainuddin M.Z. (1952–2011) responded to critics of his hugely popular style by pointing to the size of his audiences and noting critically the small audiences reached by more serious preachers (*Tempo* 1992, 16). Unlike other preachers, he claimed his preaching touched (*menyentuh*) his audiences (*Tempo* 1990; Zainuddin 1997, 103–27). He also responded to public criticism about the great financial rewards he was thought to have received after his ascent to celebrity status in the 1980s. Zainuddin M.Z. pointed out that he was not the active agent behind the extraordinary trajectory of his career. He did not initiate the national tours, for example; they were initiated and planned by independent agents in the provinces, and only a small part of the money raised from his tours reached his pocket. Similarly, his defence argued, the mosques and religious institutions in which he preached made large sums from his orations, which they reinvested in religious infrastructure, something that gave him great satisfaction (*Tempo* 1990, 77–78; Zainuddin 1997, 173–77). Preachers' philanthropy is another defence against charges of financial opportunism. Successful preachers, including Tuti Alawi, Zainuddin M.Z. and Kyai Haji Al-Jauhari, have financed the construction and ongoing support of religious schools and mosques, providing a defence against accusations that they receive improper material benefits from an activity that should, in the judgement of some, be free of worldly considerations.

20. For an account of the overlaps and distinctions between these two concepts in Islamic contexts, see Eisenstadt (2002) and Salvatore and LeVine (2005).

21. As chapter 3 in this book indicates, the group represented by Shiddiq Amien can be considered from some aspects as a counterpublic group. Unlike most of the group's preachers, Shiddiq Amien found acceptance more widely than that group alone and, as such, he is included in this analysis as a preacher who succeeded before heterogeneous Bandung audiences.

22. Studies of Islamic preaching's role in constituting Islamic counterpublics in Indonesia include Baidhawy (2010); Howell (2008); and Woodward et al. (2012).

23. My understanding of verbal performance is informed by Bauman (1977); Briggs (1988); Bauman and Briggs (1990); Goffman (1981); and Hymes (1975).

24. Webb Keane's analysis of clashes between semiotic ideologies arising from Christian missionary activity on the Indonesian island of Sumba reveals the link between modernist views of language and subjectivity, on the one hand, and reformist theologies, on the other. The link lies in their shared idealisation of expressive subjects free from semiotic forms and the social relationships they index. But this imagines something impossible: that religious undertakings can proceed in disembodied forms: "The work of purification cannot fully succeed" (Keane 2007, 222).

1. Preaching Diversity in Bandung

1. Indonesian Muslims interpret these formal rules in many different ways. Ahmad Muhajir (2010) discusses diversity in the conduct of the Friday sermon. The differences can be traced also in the preaching manuals commonly found in Indonesia's Islamic bookshops which set out the formal requirements to be followed by the orator and give sample sermons for specific occasions and feast days. In villages without a suitably trained person to act as *khatib*, these printed texts are read verbatim during the sermon. A representative manual is that of Aboebakar (1953).

2. The most comprehensive study of a West Javanese *ajengan* is Horikoshi (1976).

3. An early analysis of the emergence of this class and its differences from other classes of Islamic experts can be read in Latif (1972, 34–36).

4. The transition whereby performance skill has come to be accepted as a basis for preaching competency is interpreted by some as a sign of moral decline in contemporary Indonesia. Jalaluddin Rakhmat (1997) and Solichul Hadi (2006), for example, interpret it as a sign of the waning influence of religion in society.

5. Representative sources on Indonesia's *dakwah* period include Achmad (1983); Ali et al. (1971); Frederick (1982); Hefner (2000); Meuleman (2011); and Natsir ([1996] 2000).

6. At this time heavy restrictions were placed on preachers who were pushing oppositional political agendas. Permits were required for all events, and certain West Javanese *muballigh* were frequently imprisoned for preaching at events held without permits. In an article in the Bandung newspaper *Pikiran Rakyat*, Mursalin Dahlan wrote of his experience in the "Kadugede incident." After giving a speech at an Islamic school in Kuningan, West Java, Dahlan and the event's organizing committee were arrested by security forces. The committee members were released after ten days. Dahlan was imprisoned for 105 days without trial or charges being laid (*Pikiran Rakyat*, April 2, 2011). Donald Porter (2002) has described the processes of co-option and exclusion enacted against preachers by the New Order state.

7. The two Sundanese orators to benefit most from radio broadcasts were Mohammad Arief Soleh, also known as Ki Balap (d. ?), and A. F. Ghazali (d. 2001). Ki Balap's sermons, delivered in Sundanese genres such as storytelling (*ngadongeng*) and frequently adapting the melodies of praise genres (*salawat*), were popular with audiences in the

1970s. His performances were broadcast in programs containing messages supporting government development programs. Recordings of A. F. Ghazali's multivocal sermons, originally circulated as cassettes, continue to circulate today in West Java in MP3 format.

2. The Unique Voice . . . and Its Travails

1. One experienced preacher explained that when he employed humor, he wanted to see slack bodies become temporarily energized, and, as he did so, he straightened his back and jerked his body into a vertical, erect position, imitating someone whose muscles have suddenly reacted to external stimulation. In his performances, this preacher's uses of humor created a ripple effect through his audience as listeners' bodies, which had shown overt signs of relaxation, reacted with movements of the kind he had demonstrated.

2. The literature on generic variation and intertextuality in spoken discourse is broad. Among key sources that have shaped this and the following chapters are Babcock (1977); Bauman and Briggs (1990); Besnier (1990, 1992); Briggs (1988); Briggs and Bauman (1992); and Keeler (1998).

3. *Tim sukses* performers do not consider themselves to be under any obligation to support the candidate's policies and do not see that their participation in the team should be interpreted as support for such policies. Gita, a popular *dangdut* singer from West Java and frequent participant in campaign teams across Indonesia, told the *Pikiran Rakyat* newspaper, "The thing is, I have a professional duty to sing and entertain audiences [when performing for a campaign]. So, I am not trying to support any candidate whosoever" (*Pikiran Rakyat*, September 12, 2007). See also Zainuddin M.Z.'s explanation of his support for multiple parties (1997, 224–35) and Jennifer Lindsay's (2005) analysis of campaign teams generally.

4. To receive these grants, organizing committees are required to submit a proposal to a subsection of the Kesejahteraan Rakyat (Public Welfare) department of the Bandung municipal government. The grants are not large, typically between 1.25 and 2 million Indonesian rupiah (equivalent to about $96 to $154 US in 2010 rates).

5. The narrative of Adam and Hawa, as it is found in the Qur'an, is brief and simple, and lacks many of the features appearing in Al-Jauhari's retelling.

6. In the orations of both Al-Jauhari and Shiddiq Amien (see chapter 3), reported speech and narration cluster together in passages in which Arabic textual materials are spoken and translated. Without the multivocality created by these strategies, the preacher risks losing audience attention during passages of Qur'anic translation.

7. For the role of parodic stylizations in manipulating audience's perceptions, see Besnier (1992, 174–75).

8. In a feature on the expansion of dakwah competencies published by *Tempo* magazine, Ibing denied that he should be considered as a *muballigh* and was open about his oratory's orientation toward comedy: "I have and never will aspire for my dakwah to achieve its objective. If people only hear five minutes from one hour, that doesn't matter" (*Tempo* 1992, 23).

9. This example occurs in the same performance as the one transcribed and translated in appendix A but appears after the excerpt reproduced there.

10. As noted earlier, the money paid to preachers is not sourced from the community alone. Committees raise the funds from various sources. The money involved in preaching events does not flow solely for the benefit of the preacher, for events are opportunities for committees to raise significant revenue from listeners.

11. An interjection in appendix A, segment 17, caused Al-Jauhari some surprise. The interjector appeared to endorse, perhaps with ironic intent, Al-Jauhari's surprising frankness about the financial dimensions of his preaching.

12. Al-Jauhari regards the school as a core component of his vocation as Islamic leader. It does, however, place a significant financial burden on him. During my visits there, I was able to observe the serious financial commitment he has undertaken, especially for the ongoing payment of staff salaries and the costs of developing and maintaining infrastructure.

3. Preaching "without Performing"

1. In this context, *salafi* refers to the idealization of the companions of Muhammad and two subsequent generations as Islamic paragons. These three generations are referred to as the *salaf al-salih* (pious ancestors) and are considered practitioners of a pure Islam unadulterated by subsequent innovations.

2. A notable example of PERSIS support for a context-independent Islamic position occurred in about 1937 when PERSIS ideologue Ahmad Hassan published a fatwa stating it was prohibited in Islam to establish or join with a nationalist political movement. G. F. Pijper (1977, 124–25) described this as "a remarkable standpoint in a time when Indonesia was burning with nationalism."

3. Although the authority with which Amien speaks about women's freedoms and Islamic practice is widely accepted in West Java, not all Indonesian Muslims agree that male preachers have authority to dictate women's conduct regarding their sexuality and reproductive issues. Muslim feminists in Indonesia encourage Muslim women to exercise sovereignty over these things (see, for example, Mulia 2005). Judging by his attempts to ameliorate the harshness of the norms under discussion in the sample sermon, Amien was clearly aware of the potential for women to respond negatively to them.

4. Although his mediation of hadith required him to break up the source text in the process of translation, Shiddiq Amien was very careful to preserve the integrity of the written form of the hadith in his orations. In other words, if the Indonesian translations and commentary were edited out of the examples in this chapter, the remaining Arabic texts would almost perfectly correspond to the forms in which the hadith circulate in written compilations. This correspondence can be observed by comparing the first example in the chapter with this written version of the relevant hadith, excerpted from a collection circulating widely in West Java: "Siti Aisyah said, 'We went out with no intention other than to do pilgrimage. When we arrived at Sarif, I was menstruating. The Messenger of Allah came in while I was crying. The Prophet asked, "What is with you? Are you giving birth?" I said, "Yes." The Prophet said, "This menstruation is something

that Allah has decreed for all daughters of Adam. Go ahead! Do whatever the pilgrims do except you may not circumambulate the House of Allah." ' " (Buchary n.d., 203).

5. This does not mean the self-shaping project forms the sole attraction for listeners attending the Sunday Study. For example, many listeners arrive by bus from communities outside Bandung. The experiences of traveling to and visiting this iconic location in the center of the city are without doubt part of the attraction for these listeners.

6. The question-and-answer phase of the Sunday session is not without humor. Some questions reveal significant misunderstanding or misplaced anxiety on the part of the questioner and sometimes the orator and audience treat them with respectful levity.

7. The answers given in the respective sources are as follows. Regarding Jihad in Lebanon and Palestine: the fact that victims of aggression are Shia Muslims does not affect the obligation on Indonesian Muslims to support Jihad for their sake. Regarding new Islamic movements: those who affiliate with movements that reject Islamic doctrine are nonbelievers. Regarding multilevel marketing: some marketing structures are prohibited in Islam, such as those in which the terms of remuneration are too favorable for the "upline" members, and which deprive the "downline" members of an equitable return. Regarding the vaccination: it is permissible in circumstances of necessity.

8. This collection of fatwa illustrates PERSIS's authors' preference for framing messages in simple, unelaborated discursive structures with minimal interpretation or explanatory exegesis. Hassan preferred the highly economical and focused structure of the question and answer (*soal jawab*), deploying a clear but bland style of Malay. Commenting on Hassan's Malay, Mohammad Roem said that he "did not seek beauty, but clarity, order, and directness" (quoted in Luth 1999, 38). A recent guidebook for PERSIS preachers (Zakaria 2005) contains no guidance or information about communication technique or strategies but is an arrangement of materials from the Qur'an and hadith under thematic headings with no commentary.

9. There is irony in the PERSIS preference for vernaculars. PERSIS has a reputation for being opposed to influences from Indonesian cultures on Islamic practice. Friends from PERSIS would often defend the organization's reputation to me, pointing to its publications in Sundanese, some of which have been widely received as significant Sundanese works. The thirty-volume Qur'anic translation of Moh. E. Hasim is especially valued (see Zimmer 2000). PERSIS justifies this positive evaluation of Sundanese on the grounds that it assists in the clear communication of meaning. This justification understands language as something that "permits the exchange of information and the achievement of mutual comprehension" (Bauman and Briggs 2003, 302), and in that sense, it isolates linguistic code from context in the same manner as the ideology of Ahmad Hassan, described earlier. The irony arises when those vernacular publications are valued highly for meanings other than their conveyance of clear meaning, such as for their value for the preservation of Sundanese culture and values.

10. Hassan's caricature of *mawlid*-reading has significances that harmonize with the disposition toward oratory to be analyzed in chapter 5. Hassan suggests that its participants lack control and are carried away by emotion. *Mawlid*-reading, it would seem, is a disorderly spectacle. This impression of emotional excess and abandon is replicated in progressive caricatures of Indonesia's conventional oratorical practices.

11. Natsir's illustrations of the life of the *muballigh* contain considerable pathos: "When he is facing his followers in the school, he is happy, and he radiates his happiness to those around him, . . . However! At noon, when the students at his school have gone home, he returns to his own home apprehensively; perhaps there will not be any smoke coming from the kitchen. Every time he climbs down from the speaker's dais, his feet smart as he walks home; he remembers his sick child, and has no medicine. . . . But these are his own personal secrets, and he briefly bites his lips, and swallows those recollections that flash into his thoughts . . . and tomorrow he will face his students once again in the place where he soothes people's hearts, submerging himself in his duties' (Natsir [1996] 2000, 269).

12. The Qur'anic source cited by Natsir is Al-Shura 23, which Pickthall (1930) interprets as, "This is it which Allah announceth to His bondmen who believe and do his good works. Say (O Muhammad, unto mankind): I ask of you no fee therefore, save loving kindness among kinsfolk [*al-mawaddah fi al-qurba*]."

4. The Languages of Preaching in the Islamic Public Sphere

1. In developing my argument about these distinctions, I have relied primarily on Baso (2002); Bauman and Briggs (2003); Hirschkind (2006); Keeler (1998); Salvatore (1998); and Warner (2002).

2. Writings about oratory from the pre-Independence period sometimes touch on the question of language selection. One of the themes encountered in these writings is the modernist emphasis on intelligibility, discussed in chapter 3. This statement from one of Indonesia's twentieth century modernists, Haji Abdul Malik Karim Amrullah (1908–81) is illustrative: "Our goals [as *muballigh*] will be better realised if we read the Friday sermon in the language understood by the broader population, namely, in the language used in the place concerned. In the Bugis lands, use Bugis. In Makassar, use Makassarese, and in Java, use Javanese" (Amrullah 1937, 41). When he wrote these thoughts, the national standard had not found the broad acceptance it enjoys today. Today sermons in Indonesian are widely understood.

3. A useful historical account of the Sundanese language is that of J. Noorduyn and A. Teeuw (2006). Mikihiro Moriyama (2012) explores recent changes in government policy toward Sundanese. Useful accounts of Indonesian are found in Anderson (1966); Maier (1993); Errington (1998, chap. 4); Robson (2002); and Sneddon (2003).

4. This has not always been the case. In the decades leading up to and immediately following Independence, Sundanese elites expressed anxiety about the future of the Sundanese nation (Ekadjati 2004, 2006).

5. This relatively unproblematic distinction between the regional language and national standard is not encountered everywhere in Indonesia. The majority of Sundanese express a striking sense of belonging in relation to the Republic. In Indonesian regions where the sense of inclusion in the Republic is weak or antagonistic, interlanguage processes are influenced by inequality, political repression, inequitable natural resource exploitation and ethnic marginalization.

6. In elaborating the character of Sundanese as "*basa rasa*," preachers often referred to the extraordinary popularity of the cassette recordings of the oratory of the preacher A. F. Ghazali, who died in 2000 (Ghazali 2008). Although Ghazali hardly registers in the written accounts of Sundanese Islamic society, cassette (and now MP3) sales of his Sundanese-language sermons appear to have not diminished significantly and are frequently broadcast on radio. Several contemporary Sundanese preachers have based their careers on mimicking his style and on verbatim repetition of his work.

7. Intelligibility is generally not the value that determines language selection, although it may do so in certain situations. Older members of contemporary Sundanese communities, for example, sometimes face difficulties in interpreting preaching in Indonesian, especially if variants of Indonesian marked as youth styles are prominent. If enough of them are in an audience, a preacher might be compelled to use Sundanese. Likewise, a preacher will at times have no option other than to use Indonesian because of the high presence of non-Sundanese listeners, as is sometimes the case in civil contexts in the province's major cities. Yet I attended a number of Sundanese language sermons where it seemed to me that the high presence of non-Sundanese might have dissuaded the preacher from using that language. I suggest two reasons for the preference for Sundanese in these situations: first, non-Sundanese residents of West Java often develop high-level competency in Sundanese in a short period; second, the value of Sundanese as an affective vehicle often outweighs the loss of intelligibility for a small segment of the audience (a point that reflects the argument of this chapter). For an analysis of situated communication between Javanese and their non-Javanese neighbors, see Goebel 2008.

8. By indexical meanings, I refer to context-dependent meanings that arise through relationships of contiguity or connection (Ochs 1996, 410–11; Keane 1997, 18–20). The indexical meanings of Indonesian are not those allocated by convention to its words and syntax but those that arise from the language's capacity to, in certain situations, suggest or point out dimensions of the situation at hand. In this case, that dimension is Indonesians' shared commitment to transformation, which is indexed by Indonesian, not Sundanese.

9. I am here indebted to the theoretical model of "enregisterment" proposed by Agha. Enregisterment is constituted by sociohistorical processes through which speakers come to "evaluate specific behavioural signs [such as the languages of preaching] as appropriate to particular scenarios of social-interpersonal conduct" (Agha 2007, 81–82; see also Goebel 2008).

10. Keeler identifies status as the key value cited in audience evaluations of the languages in oratory while in my analysis I nominate an aspiration for transformation as the value indexed by the national standard. The two concepts are not far apart. As pointed out earlier, transformation is a commitment that motivates some to undertake active projects, while for others it is merely an obligation to which deference must be shown. Both positions reflect the imperative for Indonesians to acquire and protect status through adequate deference to the national aspiration for transformation. The caricatures described in the introduction above convey this similarity; they depict low-status, passive subjects in forms that emphasize their incompatibility with national standards.

11. Norms of public display in Indonesian cultures play a role here also. Keeler notes that men approved of the restrained, less expressive preaching style because it is "indicative of self-possession and control, an attribute of people who are in possession of power and deserve to exercise authority" (Keeler 1998, 174).

12. Another motivation for Amien's switching, which also signals a more informal, less prepared relationship with his audience, emerged when he strained to recall a word or searched in his notes to find his position. In these fleeting moments of disorder, he switched to Sundanese to say things like "What is the word?" and "Where were we?" For examples, see appendix B, segments 15 and 25.

13. The success team performances were not his only contribution to the political party. The party's heterogeneous membership and hierarchy are attracted to his preaching style, and he is routinely invited to preach and lead prayer at hierarchy meetings.

5. The Listening Audience Laughs and Cries, the Writing Public Thinks

1. The Islamic universities fall under the responsibility of Indonesia's Ministry of Religious Affairs and were initially known as State Institutes for Islamic Religion (IAIN). The first of these were opened in Yogyakarta and Jakarta in 1960 (Noer 1978, 35). The government has moved to integrate Indonesia's IAINs more fully into the broader tertiary education system, and in 2005 IAIN Sunan Gunung Djati was legally given the status of university and renamed the Sunan Gunung Djati State Islamic University (UIN) (Natsir 2008). As not all IAINs have become UINs, the tertiary Islamic education system under the Ministry of Religion is here referred to as the UIN/IAIN system.

2. These themes emerge in Muhtadi (2004, 43–48, 259–64 and 2008, 113–26).

3. Agus Ahmad Safei's biography of Hidayat mentions the multiple intelligence concept of Howard Gardner, as well as Georgi Lozanov's accelerated learning concept (Safei 2008, 158–59). Hidayat is not the only education specialist in Bandung to be influenced by these ideas. The two concepts just mentioned are adapted, for example, in the Muthahhari "High School Plus," founded by one of Bandung's leading Islamic intellectuals, Jalaluddin Rakhmat. Schools like this one promise to produce the same subjects proposed in Hidayat's initiative: independent, capable, and innovative Muslims who will not be held back by the forces that the school's founders believe have prevented Indonesia from developing its national potential.

4. Hidayat's writings contain detailed accounts of the superiority of writing over speech as a *dakwah* media: it offers a means of self-evaluation and of reflecting on one's environment, self, and activities, thus enabling a process of arriving at the truth; the fixed messages found in books are preserved over time, unlike oratory, which is ephemeral; books allow the expression of more complex ideas than oral discourse does; and writing is a *dakwah* medium more suitable than oratory for the rhythms and lifestyles of modern Indonesian society, in which people are prevented by work commitments from attending preaching events held according to cyclical and routine schedules (Muhtadi 2012b, 93–95).

5. Writings on religious friction within West Java include Crouch (2010, 2014); Kahmad (2013); Muhtadi (2012a); Mudzakkir (2008); and Riyadi (2012).

6. The other two provinces are the Jakarta Special Region and East Java. The significance of this ranking declines when one considers that the rankings are calculated by raw numbers of incidents and ignore demographic relativities. The Jakarta Special Region, for example, being the nation's capital, is the ideal location for actions designed to attract public attention. West Java and East Java are notable for their very large populations and the high population density of their urban centres. Nevertheless, the image of West Java's Islamic public sphere has not improved at the time of writing. In 2013 West Java's governor began supporting an action campaign against the Province's tiny Shiite minority, using provincial assets (mosques, Dakwah Centre) to prosecute its campaign. This has caused consternation among some public commentators. Writing in the newspaper *Kompas*, Abdillah Toha accused the governor of "inflaming [intra-Islamic conflict in Indonesia] by creating such a provocation" (*Kompas*, February 17, 2016).

6. A Feminized Domain

1. Hidayat and Mulia occupy similar roles within Indonesian society. Both are professors in tertiary educational or research institutions (he at Bandung's State Islamic University, she at the Indonesian Academy of Sciences); both act as advisers to government (she on gender issues, he on education and social cohesion); both are prominent public commentators.

2. For spectatorship, see the discussions of Jackie Stacey (1994, 19–48) and Michele Aaron (2007). Despite its semantic reference to the sense of sight, I have preferred the term *spectatorship* over *audition*, which may be considered to be the equivalent concept for the sense of hearing. The main reason for this choice is that scholarly investigation of spectatorship, understood here as the project of understanding the viewing subject in her social situation, is well-developed in the literature on audiences (for the distinction between this understanding and spectatorship as the study of textually determined ideological subjects, see Stacey 1994, 190–248; Aaron 2007). By contrast, the work on audition is mostly oriented to what Michael Bull and Les Back (2003, 1) refer to as "the epistemological status of hearing" (e.g., Hirschkind 2006; Erlmann 2004). The social focus of this chapter distances it from that literature, bringing it into the orbit of audience studies, a field in which the sensorium is not a central object of inquiry.

3. As Anna Gade (2004, 132–36) has shown, the distinction between pedagogy and genres of skillful speaking is not watertight. Even in explicitly pedagogical settings, the audience evaluates the performer to some degree on his or her skill as a communicator independent of the referential content.

4. The text preached by Al-Jauhari (see appendix A) contains many examples of women's responses to Al-Jauhari's requests for affirmation.

5. My Sundanese research assistant, a male, described the style as *gé* (from the English "gay").

6. This view reflects widely held beliefs about the innate differences between men and women in Southeast Asian Muslim societies (Peletz 1996).

7. A reality that emerged clearly in the research was the rapid, recent growth in the infrastructure for Islamic practice in Bandung. People old enough to remember the

decades following Indonesian independence in 1945 recalled there were few mosques and few Qur'anic teachers. In contemporary Bandung, most people reside in neighborhoods with several mosques in walking distance.

8. RW is the initialism of *rukun warga*, the second-lowest level in the hierarchy of administrative divisions into which Indonesian communities are divided.

9. The obligation has its authoritative textual reference in the oft-quoted hadith, *ballighu 'anni walaw ayatan* (Arabic, Pass on [what you obtain] from me, be it even one verse). For a representative discussion of the obligation aimed at a women's audience, see Alawiyah (1997, 23–26).

10. Similar to Ward Keeler's (1990) observations of Javanese social hierarchies, women in West Java have more freedom than men to speak and act in ways that reveal unrestrained emotion but lose potency and status as a result. Women who desire to advance in career and status typically avoid unrestrained speech and actions.

11. I do not claim this as a general reality to be observed in all Bandung oratorical and pedagogical situations. West Java includes Islamic movements in which men and women hold literal interpretation of textual norms concerning women to be a nonnegotiable principle, even when these interpretations appear to limit women's liberty and opportunity (see, for example, Nisa 2013). This book's primary focus on heterogeneous audiences puts those environments outside its reach. The preachers to whom I refer in this chapter have appeal and relevance that is broadly acknowledged by Bandung audiences of diverse backgrounds, and these audiences include many listeners who reject literal interpretations of women's Islamic obligation.

12. A Qur'anic verse commonly cited as the foundation of this norm is Al-Nisa' 34, translated by Marmaduke Pickthall (1930) as follows: "Men are in charge of women, because Allah hath made the one of them to excel the other, and because they spend of their property (for the support of the women). So good women are the obedient, guarding in secret that which Allah hath guarded." A widely cited feminist analysis of this text is Hassan (1999); the key Indonesian critical readings include those of Nasaruddin Umar (1999) and Siti Musdah Mulia (2005, 291–313).

13. Ghazali's cassettes are recordings of live performances, most of them recorded at large community-based events. The example is from the cassette entitled *Tugas risalah* (The task of the messenger) (Ghazali n.d. [1990?]). My English translation can be read in full in Ghazali (2008, 91–113).

14. This style of moralizing is nicely described in a statement about the 1990s preaching superstar Zainuddin M.Z. quoted by Anna Gade (2004, 134): "Zainuddin MZ touches people rather than offends them, welcomes rather than ridicules them, embraces them rather than punches them; his examples pinch but they do not hurt."

7. Public Contest and the Pragmatics of Performance

1. Among these were the dailies *Pikiran Rakyat*, *Tribun*, and *Kompas* (West Java supplement); magazines of activist groups and organizations, including *Bina Da'wah*, *Risalah*, and *Percikan Iman*; commercially oriented tabloids such as *Tabloid Al-Hikmah*;

and mosque bulletins such as *Lembar Kajian Syakhshiyyah Islamiyyah, Pajagalan Bulletin Jum'at*, and *Uswah: Buletin Dakwah & Informasi Pusdai Jabar*.

2. This does not mean that publication occurs without there being some prior relationship between the preacher and the publisher. In most cases, publisher and preacher have common interests and know each other from previous shared experiences.

3. I do not mean here that all his orations are the same. Specific contexts require messages weighted toward different topics. His orations at the pilgrimage training, for example, are distinguished by their focus on practical issues connected with the pilgrimage. Notwithstanding these variations, my general description of his style is applicable to all sermons he delivers before heterogeneous audiences.

4. In discussing with me the pragmatic editing of messages, some Bandung preachers cited a textual-normative justification of the selective expression of ideology. One informed me that selective expression was, in fact, proper conduct for a *muballigh*. Preachers are encouraged to make calculations about their audiences and allow these calculations to determine their performances. This is supported by the hadith "Address people in accordance with the level of their faculties," and the oft-cited Qur'anic verse of Al-Nahl 125, "Call unto the way of thy Lord with wisdom and fair exhortation, and reason with them in the better way." In this verse, "with wisdom" is interpreted as an encouragement for the preacher to conform to the predispositions of his or her audience. Representative treatments of the norms are found in Natsir ([1996] 2000, 159–228) and Omar (1967, 74–108).

5. Some of Bandung's Islamic constituencies are punishing in their reproach of inconsistent preachers, especially where they can be criticized for deserting a cause. A well-known West Javanese example was the case of the celebrated preacher E. Z. Muttaqien. On his release from prison in 1966, he chose to accommodate the political realities of the Suharto regime, thereby becoming a first-call workplace preacher, and was criticized by former colleagues dedicated to an oppositional position toward the New Order government (see Rosidi 2008, 845; Shoury 2009).

6. The most recent overture was from Indonesia's Islamist party, the PKS (Partai Keadilan Sejahtera, or Prosperous Justice Party), which attempted in 2008 to persuade Nur Wahid to publicly endorse their candidates. Popular opinion has it that PKS followers were disappointed when Nur Wahid refused to agree to this request.

7. Zainuddin M.Z. moved between parties throughout his career. After supporting the PPP early in his career, he was a founding member of the PPP splinter group Partai Bintang Reformasi (Star of Reform Party), which he supported until 2007 when he, along with several other artists, rejoined the PPP.

8. DDII's role in Indonesia's Saudi-sponsored education and proselytizing network is discussed by Anthony Bubalo and Greg Fealy (2005, 59–60) and Noorhaidi Hasan (2006, 39–43).

9. The DDII's publication output has attracted negative assessments from Western scholars, particularly in relation to the DDII journal *Media Dakwah*. William Liddle (1996, 328) named the journal as "among the most extreme or militant scripturalist organs tolerated by the government." Robert Hefner (2000, 113) described it as "adamantly anti-humanist. Disdainful of speculative philosophy, it emphasizes the uncompromising

superiority of Islam and the threats posed to Muslims in a world dominated by darkly anti-Islamic powers." For an engrossing study of *Media Dakwah* against the backgrounds of Indonesian modernism and ethnic violence in West Java, see Siegel (2001).

10. Anshary's book makes many criticisms of traditionalist Muslims, which should be read in the context of NU's withdrawal from the Masyumi party (Millie 2012). E. Z. Muttaqien's book (1968) warns against the threat of communism. Both men were key Masyumi actors and were imprisoned together in Madiun in 1962 after the political tide turned against Masyumi (Noer 1987, 415).

11. These include *Menjawab soal-soal Islam kontemporer* (Rakhmat 1998), *Rekayasa Sosial* (Rakhmat 1999), and *The Road to Allah* (Rakhmat 2007).

12. Like many orators whose spoken words are transformed into print, Rakhmat is open about the passive role he takes in the production of these books, graciously acknowledging those whose work enabled the publication. In the foreword of *Rekayasa Sosial* (Rakhmat 1999), he even apologizes to the transcribers and editors for having taken so long to check the transcriptions.

13. One result of the editing process is that contrasting impressions of preachers are conveyed through written and oratorical expressions. In the writings appearing in the name of the preacher Atian Ali Da'i, for example, the activist organizations behind the publications amplify the public-contest content of his orations and remove all affective strategies. These articles give the impression that Atian is a berating ideologue, even though Atian is a masterful preacher of warmth and compelling sincerity (Millie 2009).

14. DDII is not the only activist group speaking through *Dakwah Is Not Just Oratory*. As noted, since 1980 Wahid has been a senior office bearer in the Bandung branch of MUI, the government-supported but largely independent national council of religious scholars formed by the Suharto government in 1975 (Ichwan 2005). In recent years, MUI has attracted widespread attention for its controversial fatwa on Ahmadiyah and New Islamic movements (Gillespie 2007), which are cited as authoritative references in *Dakwah Is Not Just Oratory* (Faridl 2008, 35, 196). Nur Wahid's book can be read, at one level, as a Sundanese socialization of those fatwas.

15. At the time of the furor over Al-Qiyadah Al-Islamiyah, public actors and government bodies were busy in responding to a perception of threat from new Islamic movements. As reported by the *Pikiran Rakyat* newspaper, Bandung's municipal government and the Indonesia Ulama Council opened a telephone line for people to report activities by groups they suspected of being misguided groups (*Pikiran Rakyat*, November 7, 2007), and religious teachers were invited to attend government offices for briefings and instruction about the existence of such groups (*Pikiran Rakyat*, November 22, 2007).

16. For an analysis of these polemics over a longer period, see Hefner (2000) and Bowen (2003).

8. Standing Up for Listening

1. Key sources on the dichotomy include Boland (1971); Bush (2009); Fealy (1998); and Noer (1973).

2. My work here deals with mediation through oratory, but arguments similar to the one I make here can be applied to mediations occurring in ritual (see Bowen 1993, 1997).

3. Accounts of the formation of NU are found in Fealy (1998, 17–47); Noer (1973); and Marijan (1992, 1–29).

4. The legal school widely adhered to in Indonesia is the Shafi'i school (see, generally, Feener 2007; Hooker 1984).

5. Since 1926, NU has reoriented its position in relation to the legal schools. For example, it has accommodated suggestions for a more contextual, dynamic approach to the formulation of *fiqh*, an accommodation that necessarily challenges the monolithic authority of the legal schools (Bush 2009). Nevertheless, the contemporary organization is still dominated to a significant degree by an elite class deriving authority from their mediation of the legal literature.

6. For a statement of the Muhammadiyah position, see Nasri, Nashir, and Sudjarwo (2009, 61). A similar position is adopted by PERSIS (see Feener 2007, 33).

7. This embodied authority reveals itself also in the codes of etiquette and deference to be displayed toward NU leaders. Students at NU-oriented Islamic schools sometimes show deference by dropping their glance when in the company of such leaders, or even by turning their bodies to face the wall when one passes.

8. Throughout history, NU has not placed great importance on the fixation in writing of its basic motivations and principles. When the noted NU ideologue Achmad Shiddiq wrote a summary of the organization's beliefs and purposes in 1979, he expressed the belief that no such statement was available in writing. Furthermore, his explanation for this absence was that the beliefs and purposes had "enjoyed a central position in the NU's oral tradition" (Barton 1996, 112).

9. As Robin Bush has pointed out, the organization's political self-interest was in part the motivation for these changes (Bush 2009, 65–110).

10. I have collated these terms from the accounts of Rumadi (2008, 201–31) and A. Suaedy (2004).

Conclusion

1. Representative works include Baso (2002); Eickelman (1992); Eickelman and Anderson (2003); Hirschkind (2006); Hoexter, Eisenstadt, and Levtzion (2002); Meyer and Moors (2006); Schulz (2011); Salvatore (1998, 2007); Salvatore and LeVine (2005).

2. It is not the case that Indonesian Islamic actors belong to either the sphere of the media market *or* of face to face interaction. The Bandung preacher Aa Gym, for example, maintained his physical presence in face to face preaching routines while having a higher profile than any other Muslim in the national media, and benefited from synergies between the two contexts (Watson 2005). The point here is that academic constructions of Islamic publicness are determined by the successful appropriation by Muslim actors of forms acceptable to national culture markets.

3. In situations where listeners concur in their dispositions about observance, group prayers and performances are welcome. In preaching events involving heterogeneous

audiences, I noticed that short supplications (*doa*) offered for the interests of listeners and their families were generally accepted but that preachers did not attempt to involve listeners in lengthier structures.

4. The concept of "preaching etiquette" (Arabic, *adab al-da'wah*) is a manifestation of this public recognition (Hirschkind 2006, 132–33).

5. As the discussion in chapter 3 indicates, Natsir expressed this view eloquently but framed it as a critique of Indonesian Islamic society rather than as a necessary entailment of a successful public Islamic project.

6. This is not the only cause of humor in this excerpt. Audience members' laughter after the word *pain* is partly brought on by the "wife's" use of the coarse second pronoun *sia* (you) to address her husband. In idealizations of matrimonial conduct, the wife would use a more respectful pronoun or term of address.

7. Not all the affective material produced by preachers disappears. Some is recycled in the genre of publication describable as "religious humor." Books of this genre contain jokes spoken by Islamic leaders. A recent example is Anwar (2015).

Appendix A. Wedding Sermon by Al-Jauhari

1. I acknowledge the contribution of Ahmad Bukhori Muslim to the preparation of this appendix. The assistance of Agus Ahmad Safei is also gratefully acknowledged.

Appendix B. Sunday Study Sermon by Shiddiq Amien

1. I acknowledge the valuable contributions of Ahmad Bukhori Muslim and Atep Kurnia to this transcription and transliteration.

Appendix C. Translation of Excerpt of Sermon by A. F. Ghazali

1. *Ruku'* is the plural of *rak'at*, the series of movements performed in the ritual worship (*salat*).

2. Ghazali is referring to the classification of behaviors in Islamic law. *Sunnat* means behavior that is beneficial but not obligatory, while *wajib* refers to obligatory behaviors.

WORKS CITED

Aaron, Michele. 2007. *Spectatorship: The Power of Looking On*. London: Wallflower.

Abaza, Mona. 2004. "Markets of Faith: Jakartan Da'wa and Islamic Gentrification." *Archipel* 67:173–202.

Abbas, Rafid. 2013. *Ijtihad Persatuan Islam: Tela'ah Atas Produk Ijthad PERSIS Tahun 1996–2009*. Yogyakarta, Indonesia: Pustaka Pelajar/STAIN Jember.

Abdulrahim, Muhammad Imaduddin. 2002. *Islam: Sistem Nilai Terpadu*. Jakarta: Gema Insani.

Abdurrahman, Emsoe. 2008. *Tiga Menguak Takdir Sukses: Mutiara Pengalaman Yusuf Mansur, Jefri Al-Buchori, dan Ahmad Al-Habsyi*. Bandung: Madani Prima.

Aboebakar. 1953. *Technik Chutbah: Tuntunan Untuk Mengarang Chutbah Djum'ah*. Jakarta: Kementerian Agama.

Achmad, Amrullah. 1983. "Dakwah Islam dan Perubahan Sosial." In *Dakwah Islam dan Perubahan Sosial: Seminar Nasional dan Diskusi Pusat Latihan, Penelitian dan Pengembangan Masyarakat (PLP2M)*, edited by Amrullah Achmad, 2–24. Yogyakarta, Indonesia: Prima Duta.

Agha, Asif. 2007. *Language and Social Relations*. Cambridge: Cambridge University Press.

Alawiyah, Tutty. 1997. *Strategi Dakwah di Lingkungan Majelis Taklim*. Bandung: Mizan.

Ali, Hasan, Z. Mudzakkir Djaelani, Chatibul Umam, R. H. A. Suminto, and Djabal Noor, eds. 1971. *Islam, Alim, Ulama dan Pembangunan*. Djakarta: Pusat Da'wah Islam Indonesia.

Amien, S. 2009. *Al-Quran dan Kejadian Manusia (Bag. 2): Pengajian Ahad, 3 Mei 2009* (DVD). Bandung: JIHAD/Pengajian Ahad Viaduct.

Amrullah, H. A. M. Karim. 1937. *Pedoman Moeballigh Islam*. Medan: Pedoman Masjarakat.

Anderson, Ben. 1966. "The Languages of Indonesian Politics." *Indonesia* 1:89–116.

Ang, Ien. 1985. *Watching Dallas: Soap Opera and the Melodramatic Imagination*. London: Routledge.

Anitasari, Dini, Fatimah Hasan, Lely Nurohmah, and Sri Wiyanti Eddyono. 2010. "The Role of Religious Public Spaces in Transforming Private Issues into Community Issues." Research Report written by SCN-CREST and RAHIMA for the Women's Empowerment in Muslim Contexts.

Anshary, M. Isa. (1967) 1995. *Mudjahid Da'wah: Pembimbing Muballigh Islam*. Bandung: CV Diponegoro.

Antoun, Richard T. 1989. *Muslim Preacher in the Modern World: A Jordanian Case Study in Comparative Perspective*. Princeton, N.J.: Princeton University Press.

Anwar, Gus Chalis. 2015. *Humor Para Kyai: Menabur Tawa Menuai Berkah*. Yogyakarta, Indonesia: Araska.

Aripudin, Acep, and Syukriadi Sambas. 2007. *Dakwah Damai: Pengantar Dakwah Antarbudaya*. Bandung: Remaja Rosdakarya.

Asy'ari, M. Hasyim. 2005. *Sang Kiai: Fatwa KH. M. Asy'ari Seputar Islam dan Masyarakat*. Yogyakarta, Indonesia: Qirtas.

Atkinson, Jane Monnig. 1983. "Religions in Dialogue: The Construction of an Indonesian Minority Religion." *American Ethnologist* 10, no. 4: 684–96.

Babcock, Barbara A. 1977. "The Story in the Story: Metanarration in Folk Narrative." In *Verbal Art as Performance*, by Richard Bauman, 61–80. Rowley, Mass.: Newbury House.

Badan Pusat Statistik Provinsi Jawa Barat. 2008. *Jawa Barat Dalam Angka: Jawa Barat in Figures 2008*. Bandung: Bidang Integrasi, Pengolahan dan Diseminasi Statistik.

Baidhawy, Zakiyuddin. 2010. "The Problem of Multiculturalism: Radicalism Mainstreaming through Religious Preaching in Surakarta." *Journal of Indonesian Islam* 4, no. 2: 268–86.

Barthes, Roland. 1979. *The Eiffel Tower and Other Mythologies*. Translated by Richard Howard. New York: Hill and Wang.

Barton, Greg. 1996. "Islam, Pancasila and the Middle Path of Tawassuth: The Thought of Achmad Shiddiq." In *Nahdlatul Ulama, Traditional Islam and Modernity in Indonesia*, edited by Greg Barton and Greg Fealy, 110–38. Clayton, Australia: Monash Asia Institute.

Baso, Ahmad. 2002. *Plesetan Lokalitas: Politik Pribumisasi Islam*. Jakarta Selatan: Desantara.

Bauman, Richard. 1977. *Verbal Art as Performance*. Rowley, Mass.: Newbury House.

———. 1986. *Story, Performance, and Event*. Cambridge: Cambridge University Press.

Bauman, Richard, and Charles L. Briggs. 1990. "Poetics and Performance as Critical Perspectives on Language and Social Life." *Annual Review of Anthropology* 19:59–88.

———. 2003. *Voices of Modernity: Language Ideologies and the Politics of Inequality.* Cambridge: Cambridge University Press.

Bayat, Asef. 2007. *Making Islam Democratic: Social Movements and the Post-Islamist Turn.* Stanford, Calif.: Stanford University Press.

Beck, Herman L. 2005. "The Rupture between the Muhammadiyah and the Ahmadiyya." *Bijdragen tot de Taal-, Land- en Volkenkunde* 161, nos. 2–3: 210–46.

Benda, Harry J. 1958. *The Crescent and the Rising Sun: Indonesian Islam under the Japanese Occupation, 1942–1945.* The Hague: W. van Hoeve.

Berkey, Jonathan. 2001. *Popular Preaching and Religious Authority in the Medieval Islamic Near East.* Seattle: University of Washington Press.

Besnier, Niko. 1990. "Language and Affect." *Annual Review of Anthropology* 19:419–51.

———. 1992. "Reported Speech and Affect on Nukulaelae Atoll." in *Responsibility and Evidence in Oral Discourse,* edited by Jane T. Hill and Judith T. Irvine, 161–81. Cambridge: Cambridge University Press.

Boland, B. J. 1971. *The Struggle of Islam in Modern Indonesia.* The Hague: Nijhoff.

Bowen, John R. 1993. *Muslims through Discourse: Religion and Ritual in Gayo Society.* Princeton, N.J.: Princeton University Press.

———. 1997. "Modern Intentions: Shaping Islamic Subjectivities in an Indonesian Muslim Society." In *Islam in an Era of Nation-States: Politics and Religious Renewal in Muslim Southeast Asia,* edited by Robert W. Hefner and Patricia Horvavtich, 157–81. Honolulu: University of Hawaii Press.

———. 2003 *Islam, Law, and Equality in Indonesia: An Anthropology of Public Reasoning.* Cambridge: Cambridge University Press.

Brenner, Suzanne. 1996. "Reconstructing Self and Society: Javanese Women and the Veil." *American Ethnologist* 23, no. 4: 673–97.

Briggs, Charles L. 1988. *Competence in Performance: The Creativity of Tradition in Mexicano Verbal Art.* Philadelphia: University of Pennsylvania Press.

Briggs, Charles L., and Richard Bauman. 1992. "Genre, Intertextuality, and Social Power." *Journal of Linguistic Anthropology* 2, no. 2: 131–72.

Brody, Leslie. 2000. "The Socialization of Gender Differences in Emotional Expression: Display Rules, Infant Temperament, and Differentiation." In *Gender and Emotion: Social Psychological Perspectives,* edited by Agneta Fischer, 24–47. Cambridge: Cambridge University Press.

Bubalo, Anthony, and Greg Fealy. 2005. *Joining the Caravan? The Middle East, Islamism and Indonesia.* Alexandria, NSW: Lowy Institute.

Buchary, ed. n.d. *Al-Djaami' ush-Shahieh: Muchtasar Hadits Shahieh Buchary.* Parts 1 and 2. Translated into Sundanese by Mhd. Ramli. Bandung: Panerangan Islam.

Bull, Michael, and Les Back, eds. 2003. *The Auditory Culture Reader.* Oxford: Berg.

Bush, Robin. 2009. *Nahdlatul Ulama and the Struggle for Power within Islam and Politics in Indonesia.* Singapore: Institute of Southeast Asian Studies.

Butsch, Richard. 2008. *The Citizen Audience: Crowds, Publics, and Individuals.* New York: Routledge.

Cook, Michael. 2000. *Commanding Right and Forbidding Wrong in Islamic Thought.* Cambridge: Cambridge University Press.

Coolsma, S. [1895]. *Ismaïl en Moerti: De Eerstelingen uit de Soendaneezen.* Rotterdam: J. M. Bredée's N.V. Boekhandel.

Crapanzano, Vincent. 2000. *Serving the Word: Literalism in America from the Pulpit to the Bench.* New York: New Press.

Crouch, Melissa. 2009. *Indonesia, Militant Islam and Ahmadiyah: Origins and Implications.* Melbourne: University of Melbourne, Centre for Islamic Law and Society.

———. 2010. "Implementing the Regulation on Places of Worship in Indonesia: New Problems, Local Politics and Court Action." *Asian Studies Review* 34:403–19.

———. 2014. *Law and Religion in Indonesia: Conflict and the Courts in West Java.* Oxon, U.K.: Routledge.

Cupumanik. 2009. "Asep Truna: Dalang Da'i." *Cupumanik* 76/VII/4:59.

Daniels, Timothy. 2010. *Islamic Spectrum in Java.* Surrey: Ashgate.

Dedeh, Mamah. 2009. *Menuju Keluarga Sakinah: Curhat ke Mamah Dedeh: Solusi-Solusi Berdasarkan Al Qur'an dan Hadits untuk Mencapai Kehidupan Bahagia dalam Pernikahan.* Jakarta: Gramedia.

Dewan Da'wah Islamiyah Indonesia (DII). 2001. *Khittah Da'wah: Dewan Dakwah Islamiyah Indonesia.* Jakarta: Dewan Dakwah Islamiyah Indonesia.

Dijk, C. van. 1981. *Rebellion under the Banner of Islam: The Darul Islam in Indonesia.* The Hague: Nijhoff [KITLV Verhandelingen 94].

Doorn-Harder, Pieternella van. 2006. *Women Shaping Islam: Indonesian Women Reading the Qur'an.* Urbana: University of Illinois Press.

Eickelman, Dale F. 1992. "Mass Higher Education and the Religious Imagination in Contemporary Arab Societies." *American Ethnologist* 19, no. 4: 643–55.

———. 1998. "Inside the Islamic Reformation." *Wilson Quarterly* 22, no. 1: 80–89.

Eickelman, Dale F., and Jon W. Anderson, eds. 2003. *New Media in the Muslim World: The Emerging Public Sphere.* 2nd ed. Bloomington: Indiana University Press.

Eisenstadt, Shmuel N. 2002. "Concluding Remarks: Public Sphere, Civil Society, and Political Dynamics in Islamic Societies." In *The Public Sphere in Muslim Societies,* edited by Miriam Hoexter, Shmuel N. Eisenstadt, and Nehemia Levtzion, 139–61. Albany: State University of New York Press.

Ekadjati, Edi S. 2004. *Kebangkitan Kembali Orang Sunda: Kasus Paguyuban Pasundan, 1913–1918.* Bandung: Pusat Studi Sunda/ Kiblat.

———. 2006. *Nu Maranggung dina Sajarah Sunda.* Bandung: Pusat Studi Sunda.

Ensering E. 1987. "De Traditionele en Hedendaagse Rol van Lokale Religieuze Leiders in de Preanger, West-Java." *Bijdragen tot de Taal-, Land- en Volkenkunde* 143, nos. 2–3: 267–92.

Erlmann, Veit, ed. 2004. *Hearing Cultures: Essays on Sound, Listening, and Modernity.* Oxford: Berg.

Errington, James Joseph. 1998. *Shifting Languages: Interaction and Identity in Javanese Indonesia.* Cambridge: Cambridge University Press.

———. 2000. "Indonesian's Authority." In *Regimes of Language: Ideologies, Politics and Identities,* edited by Paul V. Kroskrity, 205–28. Santa Fe: School of American Research.

Fakultas Dakwah IAIN. 1975. *Sewindu Fakultas Dakwah*. Fakultas Dakwah IAIN Jami'ah ar-Raniry: Darussalam Banda Aceh.

Faridl, Miftah. 2008. *Da'wah lain Saukur Ceramah: Tarékah Ngabénténgkeun Islam dina Haté Umat*. Bina Da'wah: Bandung.

Fealy, Greg. 1998. "Ulama and Politics in Indonesia: A History of Nahdlatul Ulama, 1952–1967." PhD diss., Monash University.

———. 2005. "Islamisation and Politics in Southeast Asia: The Contrasting Cases of Malaysia and Indonesia." In *Islam in World Politics*, edited by Nelly Lahoud and Anthony J. Johns, 152–69. Oxon, U.K.: Routledge.

———. 2008. "Consuming Islam: Commodified Religion and Aspirational Pietism in Contemporary Indonesia." In *Expressing Islam: Religious Life and Politics in Indonesia*, edited by Greg Fealy and Sally White, 80–94. Singapore: ISEAS.

Federspiel, Howard M. 2001. *Islam and Ideology in the Emerging Indonesian State: The Persatuan Islam (PERSIS), 1923 to 1957*. Leiden, the Netherlands: Brill.

Feener, R. Michael. 2007. *Muslim Legal Thought in Modern Indonesia*. Cambridge: Cambridge University Press.

Feith, Herbert. 1962. *The Decline of Constitutional Democracy in Indonesia*. Ithaca, N.Y.: Cornell University Press.

Formichi, Chiara. 2012. *Islam and the Making of the Nation: Kartosuwiryo and Political Islam in 20th-century Indonesia*. Leiden, the Netherlands: KITLV.

Foulcher, Keith. 2000. "*Sumpah Pemuda:* The Making and Meaning of a Symbol of Indonesian Nationhood." *Asian Studies Review* 24, no. 3: 377–410.

Frederick, W. 1982. "Rhoma Irama and the *Dangdut* Style." *Indonesia* 34:103–32.

Frisk, Sylva. 2009. *Submitting to God: Women and Islam in Urban Malaysia*. Denmark: NIAS Press.

Gade, Anna M. 2004. *Perfection Makes Practice: Learning, Emotion, and the Recited Qur'an in Indonesia*. Honolulu: University of Hawai'i Press.

Gaffney, Patrick. 1994. *The Prophet's Pulpit: Islamic Preaching in Contemporary Egypt*. Berkeley: University of California Press.

Geertz, Clifford. 1960. "The Javanese *Kijaji*: The Changing Role of a Cultural Broker." *Comparative Studies in Society and History* 2, no. 2: 228–49.

Ghazali, A. F. n.d. [1990?] *Tugas Risalah*. Audio cassette tape. Bandung: Gita Record/MTR Records.

———. 2008. *The People's Religion: The Sermons of A. F. Ghazali*. Selected, transcribed, and translated by Julian Millie. Bandung: Cupumanik.

Gillespie, Piers. 2007. "Current Issues in Indonesian Islam: Analysing the 2005 Council of Indonesian Ulama Fatwa no. 7: Opposing Pluralism, Liberalism and Secularism." *Journal of Islamic Studies* 18, no. 2: 202–40.

Goebel, Zane. 2008. "Language, Class, and Ethnicity in Indonesia." *Bijdragen tot de Taal-, Land- en Volkenkunde* 164, no. 1: 69–101.

Goffman, Erving. 1981. *Forms of Talk*. Philadelphia: University of Pennsylvania Press.

Guillot, Claude. 1990. *The Sultanate of Banten*. With Hasan M. Ambary and Jacques Dumarcay. Jakarta: Gramedia.

Habermas, Jürgen. 1989. *Structural Transformation of the Public Sphere: An Inquiry into a Category of Bourgeois Society*. Cambridge, Mass.: MIT Press.

Hadad, Toriq. 1998. *Amarah Tasikmalaya: Konflik di Basis Islam*. Jakarta: Institut Studi Arus Informasi.

Hadi, Solichul. 2006. *Da'i Selebritis*. Penerbit Harmonie.

Hadler, Jeffrey. 2008. *Muslims and Matriarchs: Cultural Resilience in Indonesia through Jihad and Colonialism*. Ithaca, N.Y.: Cornell University Press.

Halldén, Philip. 2005. "What Is Arabic Rhetoric? Rethinking the History of Muslim Oratory Art and Homiletics." *International Journal of Middle East Studies* 37:19–38.

Harjono, Anwar. (1996) 2000. Introduction to *Fiqhud Da'wah: Jejak Risalah dan Dasar-dasar Da'wah*, by Mohammad Natsir, xii. Jakarta: Media Da'wah.

Hartley, John. 1992. *Tele-ology: Studies in Television*. London: Routledge.

——. 2002 *Communication, Cultural and Media Studies: The Key Concepts*. 3rd ed. London: Routledge.

Hasan, Noorhaidi. 2006. *Laskar Jihad: Islam, Militancy, and the Quest for Identity in Post–New Order Indonesia*. Ithaca, N.Y.: Cornell Southeast Asia Program Publications.

Hassan, A. 2000 *Soal-Jawab Tentang Berbagai Masalah Agama 1-2-3*. Bandung: Diponegoro.

Hassan, Riffat. 1999. "Feminism in Islam." In *Feminism and World Religions*, edited by Arvind Sharma and Katherine K. Young, 248–78. Albany: State University of New York.

Hefner, Robert. 1987. "Islamizing Java? Religion and Politics in Rural East Java." *Journal of Asian Studies* 46, no. 3: 533–54.

——. 1998. "Secularization and Citizenship in Muslim Indonesia." In *Religion, Modernity, and Postmodernity*, edited by David Martin, Paul Heelas, and Paul Morris, 147–68. Oxford: Blackwell.

——. 2000. *Civil Islam: Muslims and Democratization in Indonesia*. Princeton, N.J.: Princeton University Press.

Heryanto, Ariel. 1995. *Language of Development and Development of Language: The Case of Indonesia*. Canberra: Department of Linguistics/ANU.

Hidayat, Yaya, ed. 1996. *Khutbah-Khutbah Jum'ah*. Bandung: Al-Huda.

Highlight. 200–?. *Highlight; Dompet Dhuafa Bandung*. Bandung: Dompet Dhafa.

Hikam, M. 1994. "Khittah dan Penguatan Civil Society di Indonesia: Sebuah Kajian Historis dan Struktural atas NU sejak 1984." In *Gus Dur dan Masyarakat Sipil*, edited by Ellyasa K. H. Dharwis, 133–64. Yogyakarta, Indonesia: LKIS.

——. 1996. *Demokrasi dan Civil Society*. Jakarta: LP3ES.

Hirschkind, Charles. 2006. *The Ethical Soundscape: Cassette Sermons and Islamic Counterpublics*. New York: Columbia University Press.

Hodgson, Marshall G. S. 1974. *The Venture of Islam: Conscience and History in a World Civilization*. Chicago: University of Chicago Press.

Hoesterey, James B. 2008. "Marketing Morality: The Rise, Fall and Rebranding of Aa Gym." In *Expressing Islam: Religious Life and Politics in Indonesia*, edited by Greg Fealy and Sally White, 95–112. Singapore: ISEAS.

——. 2012. "Prophetic Cosmopolitanism: Islam, Pop Psychology, and Civic Virtue in Indonesia." *City & Society* 24, no. 1: 38–61.

Hoexter, Miriam, Shmuel N. Eisenstadt, and Nehemia Levtzion, eds. 2002. *The Public Sphere in Muslim Societies*. Albany: State University of New York Press.

Hooker, M. B. 1984. *Islamic Law in Southeast Asia*. Singapore: Oxford University Press.

Horikoshi, Hiroko. 1976. "A Traditional Leader in a Time of Change: The Kijaji and Ulama in West Java." PhD diss., University of Illinois at Urbana-Champaign.

Hosen, Nadirsyah. 2002. "Revelation in a Modern State: Muhammadiyah and Islamic Legal Reasoning in Indonesia." *Australian Journal of Asian Law* 4, no. 3: 232–58.

———. 2004. "Nahdlatul Ulama and Collective *Ijtihad*." *New Zealand Journal of Asian Studies* 6, no. 1: 5–26.

Howell, Julia Day. 2008. "Modulations of Active Piety: Professors and Televangelists as Promoters of Indonesian '*Sufisme*'." In *Expressing Islam: Religious Life and Politics in Indonesia*, edited by Greg Fealy and Sally White, 40–62. Singapore: ISEAS.

Husin, Asna. 1998. "DDII: Philosophical and Sociological Aspects of Da'wah: A Study of Dewan Dakwah Islamiyah Indonesia." PhD diss., Columbia University.

Hymes, Dell. 1975. "Breakthrough into Performance." In *Folklore: Performance and Communication*, edited by D. Ben-Amos and K. S. Goldstein, 11–74. The Hague: Mouton.

Ichwan, Nur Moch. 2005. "'*Ulamā*, State and Politics: Majelis Ulama Indonesia after Suharto." *Islamic Law and Society* 12, no. 1: 45–72.

Jackson, Karl. 1980. *Traditional Authority, Islam, and Rebellion: A Study of Indonesian Political Behavior*. Berkeley: University of California Press.

Jaiz, Hartono Ahmad. 2005. *Ada Pemurtadan di IAIN*. Jakarta: Al-Kautsar.

Junaedi, Jujun. 2008. *Tausiyah K. H. Jujun Junaedi dina raraga Maulid Nabi Muhammad SAW sareng resepsi walimatul Titi Martini, S.Tp ka Yuda Anwari, S.Sos, pelaksanaan: Minggu, 8 April 2007, di lingk. Pasar Inpres-Sumedang*. Unauthorized DVD retailed in Bandung.

Kahin, Audrey R. 2012. *Islam, Nationalism and Democracy: A Political Biography of Mohammad Natsir*. Singapore: National University of Singapore Press.

Kahin, G. McTurnan. 1970. *Nationalism and Revolution in Indonesia*. 2nd ed. Ithaca, N.Y.: Cornell University Press.

Kahmad, Dadang. 2013. *Multikulturalisme, Islam dan Media: Respons Ormas Islam dan Peran Bulletin Jumat Menyebarluaskan Gagasan Multikulturalisme*. Bandung: Pustaka Djati.

Kaptein, Nico. 1993. "The *Berdiri Mawlid* Issue among Indonesian Muslims." *Bijdragen tot de Taal-, Land en Volkenkunde* 149, no. 1: 124–53.

Keane, Webb. 1997. *Signs of Recognition: Powers and Hazards of Representation in an Indonesian Society*. Berkeley: University of California Press.

———. 2007. *Christian Moderns: Freedom and Fetish in the Mission Encounter*. Berkeley: University of California Press.

Keeler, Ward. 1990. "Speaking of Gender in Java." In *Power and Difference: Gender in Island Southeast Asia*, edited by Jane Monnig Atkinson and Shelley Errington, 127–52. Stanford, Calif.: Stanford University Press.

———. 1998. "Style and Authority in Javanese Muslim Sermons." *Australian Journal of Anthropology* 9, no. 2: 163–78.

Kern, R. A. 1898. *Geschiedenis der Preanger Regentschappen: Kort Overzicht*. Bandung: De Vries en Fabricius.

Kipp, Rita Smith, and Susan Rodgers. 1987. "Introduction: Indonesian Religions and Their Transformations." In *Indonesian Religions in Transition*, edited by Rita Smith Kipp and Susan Rodgers, 14–25. Tucson: University of Arizona Press.

Kitley, Philip. 2008. "Playboy Indonesia and the Media: Commerce and the Islamic Public Sphere on Trial in Indonesia." *South East Asia Research* 16, no. 1: 85–116.

Laffan, Michael Francis. 2004. *Islamic Nationhood and Colonial Indonesia: The Umma Below the Winds*. London: RoutledgeCurzon.

Latif, Nasaruddin. 1972. *Teori & Praktek Da'wah Islamijah (Penerangan Agama)*. Djakarta: Dara.

Latif, Yudi. 2000. "Menuju Transformasi Dakwah Islam." In *Dakwah Kontemporer: Pola Alternatif Dakwah Melalui Televisi*, edited by Asep S. Muhtadi and Sri Handajani, 3–18. Bandung: Pusdai Press.

Legge, John. 2003. *Sukarno: A Political Biography*. 3rd ed. Singapore: Archipelago Press.

Lichter, Ida. 2009. *Muslim Women Reformers: Inspiring Voices against Oppression*. Amherst, N.Y.: Prometheus.

Liddle, William. 1996. "Media Dakwah Scripturalism: One Form of Islamic Political Thought and Action in New Order Indonesia." In *Toward a New Paradigm: Recent Developments in Indonesian Islamic Thought*, edited by Mark Woodward, 323–57. Tempe: Centre for Southeast Asian Studies, Arizona State University.

Lindsay, Jennifer. 2005. *Performing in the 2004 Indonesian Elections*. Singapore: Asia Research Institute / National University of Singapore.

Livingstone, Sonia. 2005. "On the Relations between Audiences and Publics." In *Audiences and Publics: When Cultural Engagement Matters for the Public Sphere*, edited by Sonia Livingstone, 17–41. Bristol, U.K.: Intellect.

Lukmana, Iwa. 2005. "Sundanese Speech Levels." In *Islam dalam Kesenian Sunda dan Kajian Lainnya Mengenai Budaya Sunda*, edited by Ajip Rosidi, 65–84. Bandung: Pusat Studi Sunda.

Luth, Thohir. 1999. *M. Natsir: Dakwah dan Pemikirannya*. Jakarta: Gema Insani.

Mahmood, Saba. 2005. *Politics of Piety: The Islamic Revival and the Feminist Subject*. Princeton, N.J.: Princeton University Press.

Maier, H. M. J. 1993. "From Heteroglossia to Polyglossia: The Creation of Malay and Dutch in the Indies." *Indonesia* 56:37–65.

Madjid, Nurcholish. 1987. *Islam, Kemodernan dan Keindonesiaan*. Bandung: Mizan.

Marcoes, Lies M. 1988. "The Muballighah as a Mediator in Religion: A Case Study in Bogor and Sukabumi." Paper delivered at the Royal Institute of Linguistics and Anthropology International Workshop on Indonesian Studies no. 3: "Women as Mediators in Indonesia." Leiden, the Netherlands, September 26–30.

Marijan, Kacung. 1992. *Quo Vadis NU? Setelah Kembali ke Khittah 1926*. Jakarta: Erlangga.

Meuleman, Johan. 2011. "*Dakwah*, Competition for Authority, and Development." *Bijdragen tot de Taal-, Land- en Volkenkunde* 167, nos. 2–3: 236–69.

Meyer, Birgit, and Annelies Moors. 2006. Introduction to *Religion, Media and the Public Sphere*, edited by Birgit Meyer and Annelies Moors, 1–25. Bloomington: Indiana University Press.

Millie, Julian. 2008. "Non-Specialists in the *Pesantren*: The Social Construction of Islamic Knowledge." *Review of Indonesian and Malaysian Affairs* 42, no. 1: 107–24.

——. 2009. "Regional Preaching Scenes and Islamism: A Bandung Case Study." In *Radicalisation Crossing Borders: New Directions in Islamist and Jihadist Political, Intellectual and Theological Thought and Practice*, edited by Sayed Khatab, Muhammad Bakashmar, and Ela Ogru, 150–68. Caulfield, Australia: Global Terrorism Research Centre.

——. 2010. "Rendra the Muslim." *Inside Indonesia*. July 2. http://www.insideindonesia.org/rendra-the-muslim-2.

——. 2012. "Preaching over Borders: Constructing Publics for Islamic Oratory in Indonesia." In *Flows of Faith: Religious Reach and Community in Asia and the Pacific*, edited by Lenore Manderson, Wendy Smith, and Matt Tomlinson, 87–103. Dordrecht, the Netherlands: Springer.

Millie, Julian, and Agus Ahmad Safei. 2010. "Religious Bandung." *Inside Indonesia*. May 23. http://www.insideindonesia.org/religious-bandung.

——. 2016. "Religious Bandung II: The Champion Arrives." *Inside Indonesia*. May 22. http://www.insideindonesia.org/religious-bandung-ii-the-champion-arrives.

Moaddel, Mansoor. 2005. *Islamic Modernism, Nationalism, and Fundamentalism: Episode and Discourse*. Chicago: University of Chicago Press.

Moriyama, Mikihiro. 2012. "Regional Languages and Decentralisation in Post-New Order Indonesia: The Case of Sundanese." In *Words in Motion: Language and Discourse in Post-New Order Indonesia*, edited by Keith Foulcher, Mikihiro Moriyama, and Manneke Budiman, 82–100. Tokyo: Research Institute for Languages and Cultures of Asia and Africa, Tokyo University of Foreign Studies.

Mudzakkir, Amin. 2008. "Politik Muslim dan Ahmadiyah di Indonesia Pasca Soeharto: Kasus Cianjur dan Tasikmalaya." Paper presented at Seminar International Kesembilan: Politik Identitas: Agama, Etnisitas, dan Ruang/Space dalam Dinamika Politik Lokal di Indonesia dari Asia Tenggara, di Percik Village, Salatiga.

Muhajir, Ahmad. 2010. "Praying Across Borders." *Inside Indonesia*. April 22. http://www.insideindonesia.org/praying-across-borders.

Muhtadi, Asep Saepul. 2004. *Komunikasi Politik Nahdlatul Ulama: Pergulatan Pemikiran Politik Radikal dan Akomodatif*. Jakarta: LP3ES.

——. 2008. *Komunikasi Politik Indonesia: Dinamika Islam Politik Pasca-Orde Baru*. Bandung: Remaja Rosdakarya.

——. 2009a. "Mencari Landasan Ilmiah Ilmu Dakwah." In *Dimensi Ilmu Dakwah: Tinjauan Dakwah dari Aspek Ontologi, Epistemologi, Aksiologi, hingga Paradigma Pengembangan Profesionalisme*, edited by Aep Kusnawan, Asep S. Muhtadi, Agus Ahmad Syafe'i, Syukriadi Sambas, and Enjang AS, 33–41. Bandung: Widya Padjadjaran.

——. 2009b. "Pengembangan Lembaga Fakultas Dakwah." In *Dimensi Ilmu Dakwah: Tinjauan Dakwah dari Aspek Ontologi, Epistemologi, Aksiologi, hingga Paradigma Pengembangan Profesionalisme*, edited by Aep Kusnawan, Asep S. Muhtadi, Agus Ahmad Syafe'i, Syukriadi Sambas, and Enjang AS, 137–46. Bandung: Widya Padjadjaran.

——. 2012a. "Violence in a Climate of Freedom." *Inside Indonesia*. February 10. http://www.insideindonesia.org/violence-in-a-climate-of-freedom.

——. 2012b. *Komunikasi Dakwah: Teori, Pendekatan, dan Aplikasi.* Bandung: Simbiosa Rekatama Media.

Muhtadi, Asep S., and Agus Ahmad Safei. 2003. *Metode Penelitian Dakwah.* Bandung: Pustaka Setia.

——. 2006. "Catatan Awal Editor." In *Pemberdayaan Ekonomi Berbasis Umat,* edited by Asep Saepul Muhtadi and Agus Ahmad Safei, 6–19. Bandung: Pemerintah Provinsi Jawa Barat.

——. 2007. "Catatan Editor." In *Transformasi Sosial Berbasis Kearifan Lokal dalam Konteks Masyarakat Jawa Barat yang Multikultural,* edited by Asep Saepul Muhtadi and Agus Ahmad Safei, vi–ix. Bandung: Pemerintah Propinsi Jawa Barat.

——, eds. 2008. *Kesalehan Multikultural: Menelusuri Nilai-Nilai al-Quran dalam Praksis Budaya Lokal.* Bandung: Pemerintah Propinsi Jawa Barat.

——. 2009. *Meniti Jalan Tauhid: Menulusuri Jejak Dakwah dan Pemikiran Prof. Dr. H. Miftah Faridl.* Bandung: Ad-Da'wah.

Muhtadi, Asep Saepul, Dindin Solahudin, Ahmad Sarbini, and Agus Ahmad Safei. 2007. *Pedoman Pengembangan Dakwah Berbasis Budaya Lokal.* Bandung: Pemerintah Provinsi Jawa Barat.

Mulia, Siti Musdah. 2005. *Muslimah Reformis: Perempuan Pembaru Keagamaan.* Bandung: Mizan.

Mulkhan, Abdul Munir. 2005. *Islam Sejati: Kiai Ahmad Dahlan dan Petani Muhammadiyah.* Jakarta: Serambi.

Muttaqien, E. Z. 1968. *Sikap Muslim: Diungkapkan dalam Berbagai Chutbah.* Bandung: CV. Diponegoro.

Muzadi, Abdul Muchith. 2002. "Menata NU dengan Lisan dan Teladan." *Gerbang: Jurnal Studi Agama dan Demokrasi* 5, no. 12: 29–137.

Muzakki, Akh. 2007. "Accusations of Blasphemy: Are Recent Fatwa Evidence that Moderate Islam Is a Myth?" *Inside Indonesia.* July 15. http://www.insideindonesia.org/accusations-of-blasphemy.

——. 2008. "Islam as a Symbolic Commodity: Transmitting and Consuming Islam through Public Sermons in Indonesia." In *Religious Commodifications in Asia: Marketing Goods,* edited by Pattana Kitiarsa, 205–19. Oxon, U.K.: Routledge.

Naipaul, V. S. 1981. *Among the Believers: An Islamic Journey.* London: Andre Deutsch.

Nakamura, Mitsuo. 2012. *The Crescent Arises over the Banyan Tree: A Study of the Muhammadiyah Movement in a Central Javanese town c.1910–2010.* 2nd ed. Singapore: ISEAS.

Nasri, Imron, Hader Nashir, and Didik Sudjarwo, eds. 2009. *Manhaj Gerakan Muhammadiyah: Ideologi, Khittah, dan Langkah.* Yogyakarta, Indonesia: Suara Muhammadiyah.

Natsir, Muhammad. (1996) 2000. *Fiqhud Da'wah: Jejak Risalah dan Dasar-dasar Da'wah.* Jakarta: Media da'wah.

Natsir, Nanat Fatah. 2008. "Risalah Utama." In *Transformasi IAIN Menjadi UIN: Menuju Research University,* edited by Nanat Fatah Natsir, Ahmad Tafsir, and Darun Setiady, 1–71. Bandung: Gunung Djati Press.

Nisa, Eva F. 2013. "The Internet Subculture of Indonesian Face-Veiled Women." *International Journal of Cultural Studies* 16, no. 3: 241–55.

Noer, Deliar. 1973. *The Modernist Muslim Movement in Indonesia 1900–1942*. Oxford: Kuala Lumpur.

——. 1978. *Administration of Islam in Indonesia*. Ithaca, N.Y.: Cornell Modern Indonesia Project.

——. 1987. *Partai Islam di Pentas Nasional*. Jakarta: Pustaka Utama Grafiti.

Noorduyn, J., and A. Teeuw, eds. and trans. 2006. *Three Old Sundanese Poems*. Leiden, the Netherlands: KITLV.

Ochs, Elinor. 1996. "Linguistic Resources for Socializing Humanity." In *Rethinking Linguistic Relativity*, edited by John J. Gumperz and Stephen Levison, 407–37. Cambridge: Cambridge University Press.

Omar, Toha Jahja. 1967. *Ilmu Da'wah*. Djakarta: Wijaya.

Ong, Aihwa. 1999. "Muslim Feminism: Citizenship in the Shelter of Corporatist Islam." *Citizenship Studies* 3, no. 3: 355–71.

Ouellette, Laurie. 1999. "TV Viewing as Good Citizenship? Political Rationality, Enlightened Democracy and PBS." *Cultural Studies* 13, no. 1: 62–90.

Peletz, Michael G. 1996. *Reason and Passion: Representations of Gender in a Malay Society*. Berkeley: University of California Press.

Pickthall, Marmaduke, trans. 1930. *The Koran*. London: W. H. Allen.

Pijper, G. F. 1934. *Fragmenta Islamica: Studiën over het Islamisme in Nederlandsch-Indië*. Leiden, the Netherlands: Brill.

——. 1977. *Studiën over de Geschiedenis van de Islam in Indonesia 1900–1950*. Leiden, the Netherlands: Brill.

Porter, Donald. 2002. *Managing Politics and Islam in Indonesia*. London: RoutledgeCurzon.

Pusat Da'wah Islam. 1972. *Forum Da'wah*. Djakarta: Pusat Da'wah Islam Indonesia.

Rahardjo, M. Dawam. 1993. *Intelektual Inteligensia dan Perilaku Politik Bangsa: Risalah Cendekiawan Muslim*. Bandung: Mizan.

Rakhmani, Inaya. 2013. "Regime and Representation: Islam in Indonesian Television, 1962 to 1998." *Review of Indonesian and Malaysian Affairs* 47, no. 1: 61–88.

Rakhmat, Jalaluddin. 1997. *Catatan Kang Jalal: Visi Media, Politik, dan Pendidikan* Bandung: Remaja Rosdakarya.

——. 1998. *Menjawab soal-soal Islam kontemporer*. Bandung: Mizan.

——. 1999. *Rekayasa Sosial: Reformasi, Revolusi atau Manusia Besar?* Bandung: Remaja Rosdakarya.

——. 2007. *The Road to Allah: Tahap-Tahap Perjalanan Ruhani Menuju Tuhan*. Bandung: Mizan.

Reid, Anthony. 1979. *The Blood of the People: Revolution and the End of Traditional Rule in Northern Sumatra*. Kuala Lumpur: Oxford University Press.

Risalah. 2006. "Kontroversi Fatwa Jihad." *Risalah* 44, no. 6: 14–17.

Risalah. 2007. "Menangkal Aliran Sesat." *Risalah* 45, no. 9: 14–15.

Risalah. 2009. "Keputusan Sidang Dewan Hisbah." *Risalah* 47, no. 6: 14–38.

Riyadi, Hendar. 2012. "The Islamic Worldview behind Cikeusik." *Inside Indonesia*. February 10. http://www.insideindonesia.org/the-islamic-world-view-behind-cikeusik.

Robson, Stuart. 2002. *From Malay to Indonesian: The Genesis of a National Language*. Clayton, Australia: Monash Asia Institute.

Roff, William R. 1967. *The Origins of Malay Nationalism*. Singapore: University of Malaya Press.

Rosidi, Ajip. 1983. *Pembinaan Minat Baca, Bahasa dan Sastera*. Surabaya: Bina Ilmu.

———. 1990. *M. Natsir: Sebuah Biografi*. Jakarta: Girimukti Pasaka.

———. 2004. *Masa Depan Budaya Daerah: Pikiran dan Pandangan Ajip Rosidi*. Jakarta: Pustaka Jaya.

———. 2008. *Hidup Tanpa Ijazah: Yang Terekam dalam Kenangan*. Jakarta: Pustaka Jaya.

Rosyad, Rifki. 2006. *A Quest for True Islam: A Study of the Islamic Resurgence Movement Among the Youth in Bandung, Indonesia*. Canberra: ANU E Press.

Rudnyckyj, Daromir. 2010. *Spiritual Economies: Islam, Globalization, and the Afterlife of Development*. Ithaca, N.Y.: Cornell University Press.

Rumadi. 2008. *Post Tradisionalisme Islam: Wacana Intelektualisme dalam Komunitas NU*. Cirebon, Indonesia: Fahmina Institute.

Saefuddin, Encang. 2014. *Fiqhud Dakwah: KH. Drs Shiddiq Amien, MBA*. Bandung: Mujahid Press.

Safei, Agus Ahmad. 2002. *Hijrah Menuju Cahaya*. Bandung: Pustaka Setia.

———. 2008. *Kucari Jalan Terba[l]ik: Simfoni Diri Dr. Asep Saeful Muhtadi*. Bandung: Insan Komunika.

Salvatore, Armando. 1998. "Staging Virtue: The Disembodiment of Self-Correctness and the Making of Islam as Public Norm." In *Islam—Motor or Challenge of Modernity* [Yearbook of the Sociology of Islam 1], edited by Georg Stauth, 87–120. Hamburg: Lit Verlag.

———. 2001. "Mustafa Mahmud: A Paradigm of Public Entrepreneurship?" In *Muslim Traditions and Modern Techniques of Power* [Yearbook of the Sociology of Islam 3], edited by Armando Salvatore, 211–24. Münster: Lit Verlag.

———. 2007. *The Public Sphere: Liberal Modernity, Catholicism, Islam*. New York: Palgrave Macmillan.

Salvatore, Armando, and Mark LeVine. 2005. "Introduction: Restructuring the Public Sphere in Muslim Majority Societies." In *Religion, Social Practice, and Contested Hegemonies: Reconstructing the Public Sphere in Muslim Majority Societies*, edited by Armando Salvatore and Mark Le Vine, 1–27. New York: Palgrave MacMillan.

Sambas, Syukriadi. 2006. "Pohon Ilmu Dakwah Islam: Reformulasi Disiplin dan Subdisiplin Bidang Ilmu Dakwah." In *Pandangan Keilmuan UIN: Wahyu Memandu Ilmu*, edited by Nanat Fatah Natsir, Ahmad Tafsir, and Darun Setiady, 383–400. Bandung: Gunung Djati Press.

———. 2009. "Wilayah Kajian Ilmu Dakwah." In *Dimensi Ilmu Dakwah: Tinjauan Dakwah dari Aspek Ontologi, Epistemologi, Aksiologi, hingga Paradigma Pengembangan Profesionalisme*, edited by Aep Kusnawan, Asep S. Muhtadi, Agus Ahmad Syafe'i, Syukriadi Sambas, and Enjang AS, 105–21. Bandung: Widya Padjadjaran.

Santi, Budie. 2005. *Perempuan Bertutur: Sebuah Wacana Keadilan Gender dalam Radio Jurnal Perempuan: Skrip Radio Jurnal Perempuan*. Jakarta: Yayasan Jurnal Perempuan / The Ford Foundation.

Schlesinger, Philip. 2000. "The Nation and Communicative Space." In *Media Power, Professionals, and Policies*, edited by Howard Tumber, 99–155. Abingdon, Oxon: Routledge.

Schulz, Dorothea Elisabeth. 2011. *Muslims and New Media in West Africa: Pathways to God*. Indianapolis: Indiana University Press.

Shields, S. A. 1987. "Women, Men, and the Dilemma of Emotion." *Sex and Gender: Review of Personality and Social Psychology* 7:229–50.

Shiraishi, Takashi. 1990. *An Age in Motion: Popular Radicalism in Java, 1912–1926*. Ithaca, N.Y.: Cornell University Press.

Shoury, Lukman. 2009. "Di Antara Pro dan Kontra." In *Ajengan Dalam Kenangan: Kumpulan Kesan Mengenai Sosok dan Kiprah Dr. (H.C.) K.H. E.Z. Muttaqien*, edited by Septiawan Santana K., Agus Halimi, Rena Yulia, and Yenni Yunianti, 111–17. Bandung: Lembaga Studi Islam UNISBA.

Siegel, James T. 2001. "*Kiblat* and the Mediatic Jew." In *Religion and the Media*, edited by Hent de Vries and Samuel Weber, 271–303. Stanford, Calif.: Stanford University Press.

Smith-Hefner, Nancy J. 2007. "Youth Language, Gaul Sociability, and the New Indonesian Middle Class." *Journal of Linguistic Anthropology* 17, no. 2: 184–203.

Sneddon, James. 2003. *The Indonesian Language: Its History and Role in Modern Society*. Sydney, Australia: University of New South Wales Press.

Snouck Hurgronje, C. 1970. *Mekka in the Latter Part of the 19th Century: Daily Life, Customs and Learning: The Muslims of the Archipelago*. Translated by J. H. Monahan. Leiden, the Netherlands: Brill.

Soemardjan, Selo. 1964. *Gerakan 10 Mei 1963 di Sukabumi*. Bandung: Eresco.

Soerjo, Tirto Adhi. 2008. *Karya-Karya Lengkap Tirto Adhi Soerjo*. Edited by Iswara N. Raditya and Muhidin M. Dahlan. Jakarta: I. Boekoe.

Solahudin, Dindin. 2008. *The Workshop for Morality: The Islamic Creativity of Pesantren Daarut Tauhid in Bandung, West Java*. Canberra: ANU E Press.

Spanjaard, Helena. 1990. "Bandung, the Laboratory of the West?" In *Modern Indonesian Art: Three Generations of Tradition and Change 1945–1990*, edited by Joseph Fischer, 54–77. Berkeley: Festival of Indonesia.

Stacey, Jackie. 1994. *Star Gazing: Hollywood Cinema and Female Spectatorship*. London: Routledge.

Starrett, Gregory. 1998. *Putting Islam to Work: Education, Politics, and Religious Transformation in Egypt*. Berkeley: University of California Press.

Steenbrink, Karel. 2005. "A Catholic Sadrach: The Contested Conversion of Madrais Adherents in West-Java between 1960–2000." In *Een Vakkracht in het Koninkrijk: Kerk- en Zendingshistorische Opstellen Aangeboden aan dr. Th. van den End ter Gelegenheid van zijn Vijfenzestigste Verjaardag*, edited by Chr. G. F. de Jong, 286–307. Heerenveen: Groen.

Suaedy, A. 2004. "Muslim Progresif dan Praktik Politik Demokratisasi di Era Indonesia Pasca Suharto." *Tashwirul Afkar* 16:6–25.

Sullivan, Norma. 1994. *Masters and Managers: A Study of Gender Relations in Urban Java*. St. Leonards, NSW: Allen and Unwin.

Supratman, Achdiat, ed. 2008. *Membangun Motivasi Kerja Pegawai Penanaman Nilai-Nilai Spiritual*. Bandung: Biro Kepegawaian Setda Propinsi Jawa Barat.

Suryadinata, Leo, Evi Nurvidya Arifin, and Aris Ananta. 2003. *Indonesia's Population: Ethnicity and Religion in a Changing Political Landscape*. Singapore: Institute of Southeast Asian Studies.

Swartz, Merlin. 1999. *Arabic Rhetoric and the Art of the Homily in Medieval Islam*. Cambridge: Cambridge University Press.

Tempo. 1978. "Islam Naik, Pelahan-pelahan." *Tempo* 41, no. 8: 44–49.

———. 1990. "Laporan Utama: Saya Ustad, Bukan Artis." *Tempo* 20, no. 9: 74–83.

———. 1992. "Laporan Utama: Sampaikan Quran Walau Seayat." *Tempo* 22, no. 6: 13–24.

———. 2011. "Laporan Utama: Tragedi Ahmadiyah." *Tempo* 3951:26–37.

Thompson, John B. 1995. *The Media and Modernity: A Social Theory of the Media*. Stanford, Calif.: Stanford University Press.

UIN Sunan Gunung Djati (SGD). 2006. *Profil Universitas Islam Negeri Sunan Gunung Djati Bandung*. Bandung: UNI Sunan Gunung Djati.

———. 2007. *Panduan Akademik: Fakultas Dawkah dan Komunikasi*. Bandung: UIN Sunan Gunung Djati.

Umar, Nasaruddin. 1999. "Kodrat Perempuan dalam Perspektif Al-Quran." In *Memposisikan Kodrat: Perempuan dan Perubahan dalam Perspektif Islam*, edited by Lily Zakiyah Munir, 91–109. Bandung: Mizan.

Voll, John O. 1982. *Islam, Continuity and Change in the Modern World*. Boulder, Colo.: Westview Press; Essex, U.K.: Longman.

Voskuil, R.P.G.A. 1996. *Bandoeng: Beeld van een Stad*. Amsterdam: Asia Maior.

Wahid Institute. 2009. *Annual Report on Religious Freedom and Religious Life in Indonesia*. Jakarta: Wahid Institute.

Walikota et al. 2009. *Bandung Agamis: Landasan, Pendekatan, Indikasi, dan Program Aksi*. Bandung: Sekretariat Daerah Kota Bandung.

Warner, Michael. 2002. "Publics and Counterpublics." *Public Culture* 14, no. 1: 49–90.

Watson, C. W. 2005. "A Popular Indonesian Preacher: The significance of AA Gymnastiar." *Journal of the Royal Anthropological Institute* 11:773–92.

Wensinck, A. J. 2016. "Khuṭba." *Encyclopaedia of Islam*. 2nd ed. Edited by P. Bearman, Th. Bianquis, C. E. Bosworth, E. van Donzel, and W. P. Heinrichs. Brill Online: http://referenceworks.brillonline.com.ezproxy.lib.monash.edu.au/entries/encyclopaedia-of-islam-2/khutba-SIM_4352.

Williams, Michael C. 1990. *Communism, Religion and Revolt in Banten*. Athens: Ohio University Press.

Woodward, Mark, Inayah Rohmaniyah, Ali Amin, Samsul Ma'arif, Diana Murtaugh Coleman, and Muhammad Sani Umar. 2012. "Ordering What Is Right, Forbidding What Is Wrong: Two Faces of Hadhrami Dakwah in Contemporary Indonesia." *Review of Indonesian and Malaysian Affairs* 46, no. 2: 105–46.

Woolard, Kathryn A. 1998. "Introduction: Language as a Field of Inquiry." In *Language Ideologies: Practice and Theory*, edited by Bambi B. Schieffelin, Kathryn A. Woolard, and Paul V. Kroskrity, 3–50. New York: Oxford University Press.

Yayasan Darma Bakti. 2009. *Yayasan Darma Bakti Jawa Barat: Pusdai, Bale Asri, Masjid Atta'awun*. Bandung: Yayasan Darma Bakti.

Zada, Khamami, and A. Fawaid Sjadzili, eds. 2010. *Nahdlatul Ulama: Dinamika Ideologi dan Politik Kenegaraan*. Jakarta: Kompas.

Zainuddin. 1997. *Dakwah & Politik: "Da'i Berjuta Umat."* Bandung: Mizan.

Zakaria, A. 2005. *Materi Da'wah untuk Da'i dan Muballigh*. Bandung: Risalah Press.

Zimmer, Benjamin G. 2000. "*Al-'Arabiyyah* and *Basa Sunda*: Ideologies of Translation and Interpretation among the Muslims of West Java." *Studia Islamika* 7, no. 3: 31–65.

Index

JML

CPSIA information can be obtained
at www.ICGtesting.com
Printed in the USA
BVOW09s1045050817
491014BV00001B/27/P